John O'Farrell is the author of two best-selling books, *Things Can Only Get Better*, a memoir, and *The Best a Man Can Get*, a novel. His name has flashed past the end of such productions as *Spitting Image, Have I Got News for You* and the film *Chicken Run*. His column appears in the *Guardian* every Saturday.

Global Village Idiot

John O'Farrell

BLACK SWAN

GLOBAL VILLAGE IDIOT
A BLACK SWAN BOOK : 0 552 99964 4

Originally published in Great Britain by Doubleday,
a division of Transworld Publishers

PRINTING HISTORY
Doubleday edition published 2001
Black Swan edition published 2002

3 5 7 9 10 8 6 4 2

Set in 11/12¼pt Melior by
Kestrel Data, Exeter, Devon.

Black Swan Books are published by Transworld Publishers,
61–63 Uxbridge Road, London W5 5SA,
a division of The Random House Group Ltd,
in Australia by Random House Australia (Pty) Ltd,
20 Alfred Street, Milsons Point, Sydney, NSW 2061, Australia,
in New Zealand by Random House New Zealand Ltd,
18 Poland Road, Glenfield, Auckland 10, New Zealand
and in South Africa by Random House (Pty) Ltd,
Endulini, 5a Jubilee Road, Parktown 2193, South Africa.

Printed and bound in Great Britain by
Clays Ltd, St Ives plc.

Contents

Author's note

My apologies are offered for any factual inaccuracies
discovered subsequent to publication, but all details
have been thoroughly researched by spending five
minutes on the Internet and then giving up. For
example, to check the story of nurses giving sex
education in schools, I called up the search engine and
entered the words 'nurses' and 'sex'. And then I was
thrown out of the British Library.

In an anthology such as this there is always a
problem of topicality and context, but where events
have moved on I have inserted a footnote to remind
the reader of the situation when the column first
appeared. So it is explained that this man called 'Peter
Mandelson' to whom I refer was in fact quite
a well-known Labour politician at the time. More
importantly, every effort has been made to remove any
references which might subsequently seem inappropriate or vaguely offensive. And if you're reading
this, Queen Mother, may I wish you the speediest of
recoveries, Ma'am.

Introduction

There is not enough humour in politics. Zany election candidates don't count, as they are not really politicians; no one would ever seriously consider their wacky policies such as raising the school leaving age to forty-three or privatizing air traffic control. But it's hard to think of many real politicians with a well-honed sense of irony, unless you count Mrs Thatcher telling the Argentines that their ships would be safe outside the exclusion zone and then sinking the *Belgrano* anyway. If politicians didn't take themselves so seriously then maybe we wouldn't be so inclined to laugh at them, so this collection is in part a plea for more political jokes – and not just the sort that populate the shadow cabinet. There are, of course, some politicians who do attempt gags from time to time and occasionally I've been asked to supply one-liners for Labour MPs. I gave one to Tony Blair soon after he was elected: 'Let's spend a billion quid building a giant theme park on a rubbish tip in Greenwich.' Unfortunately he didn't realize I was joking.

These comment pieces extend over two centuries – or twenty-four months, depending on how you look at it.

After a quick résumé of Labour's first two years, they cover the period from William Hague's shock victory in the thrilling Euro-elections of June 1999 to his tragic defeat in the general election two years later. Collectively I hope they make up some sort of *fin-de-siècle* political diary, although frankly this is probably stretching it a bit. 'A load of jokes about some stuff that was in the news' is probably more accurate. The big issues that people were talking about, the dramas and excitement that caught our imagination – none of these is included because I'm not a TV reviewer. But it was undeniably an incredible period to have lived through. Who could forget where they were when they heard the news that proportional representation would be used for the new regional assemblies? Or that memorable day when Paddy Ashdown resigned as leader of the Liberal Democrats? Yes; S Club 7 were in the charts, England's football team drew 0–0 with Finland and Alistair Darling was Chief Secretary to the Treasury; it was a great time to be in your late thirties. All right, we may not have been able to prevent all power being centralized in the hands of a few multinationals or to avert impending ecological catastrophe but at least we now know that there are two 'n's in 'millennium'.

The turn of the century did have its occasional disappointments, of course. The new Millennium Bridge was closed after engineers decided it couldn't take the weight of all those people rushing away from the Dome. General Pinochet was sent back to Chile for refusing to be Labour's candidate for Mayor of London. (In any case Jack Straw said he wasn't tough enough on law and order.) And New Labour developed this middle-class Islington image that so infuriated Tony Blair it made him want to slam down his glass of Chianti and storm off back to the villa in Tuscany.

And I was offered the chance to write about it all in the newspapers. Back then I naively imagined that publications such as the *Independent* and the

12

Guardian must be the journals that were studied by our political leaders, just as, in the United States, if you wanted to keep up with what the Clinton administration was reading you subscribed to *Readers' Wives' True Confessions*. In fact if Downing Street is anything like the other streets in Britain's inner cities, the only paper they get delivered on a regular basis would be the local freesheet. So the main issues they read about are 'Mobile Phone Mugger Strikes Again', followed by an advertising feature on local tandoori restaurants. Because I was mostly writing in the *Grauniad* I took it as a given that most readers would be on the left and that we'd all prefer to be under a Labour government rather than a Tory one, so any sniping is very much in the spirit of the 'critical friend'. OK, maybe one of those friends who still owe you money and fail to turn up to anything you invite them to, and who slag you off behind your back, but a friend none the less.

It has sometimes been tricky laughing at the antics of a Labour government while I remained a party member. A large number of these pieces were written after I had been selected as a parliamentary candidate and the level of interference from the control freaks at Millbank was quite appalling. Not once did they ring up and say, 'Why are you criticizing the government?' On no occasion did they try to twist my arm, bend my ear, bribe, bully or coerce me and frankly it is just not good enough. Actually, come to think of it, there was one communication from Labour HQ. I wrote something about the party treasurer, imagining that he must be hanging his head in shame, and I got an e-mail explaining that 'he' was in fact a 'she'. 'Aha!' I declared. 'Now we see it! The spin doctors are trying to control what I write now, are they? Don't like the way I present the facts, eh?' Next they'll be expecting me to take the trouble to check.

A writer who consistently toed an official party line would make for pretty boring reading, so I promise that at no time do I use the phrases 'No return to Tory boom and bust', 'For the many not the few', 'A lot done; a lot to do' or the more seasoned 'Maggie, Maggie, Maggie! Out! Out! Out!' In fact most of the pieces in this collection are not about British party politics at all, but cover all manner of subjects from asteroids to advertising. There is nothing about my battle with bulimia or my hectic schedule trying to balance childcare with occasional appearances on UK Living and very few references to my work for charity, probably because I don't do any. Despite the sensitivity of some of the subjects, I refute accusations of writing cheap gags since the *Guardian* pays quite reasonably these days. These are withering attacks on the chaos that is capitalism, and if I can make a few extra bob repackaging them and flogging them all over again in book form then so much the better. *Things Can Only Get Better* was an account of Labour's eighteen miserable years in opposition. If you haven't read that book yet I won't spoil it for you by telling you who wins at the end. I suppose this collection is a sort of jumbled sequel, a political 'What Happened Next?' Most of the articles are about three pages long – the idea being that you can sit down and read one piece a day, or possibly two, depending on whether you had All Bran or boiled eggs for breakfast. And then I hope you will look back and think, yes, I remember the unique flavour of those years; I remember the first time I heard an Abba tribute band or watched a 1980s theme night on Channel 4. Maybe one day they'll make a retrospective about all those retrospectives. But in the meantime here is one interpretation of the events and issues that shaped the turn of the century: a time of famines, wars, terrorism, floods, cloning, sieges and earthquakes. And that was just in *Brookside* . . .

J.O'F.
June 2001

Things can only get bitter

The first twenty-four months in the life of a Labour government

29 April 1999

It was five o'clock in the morning on 2 May 1997.
Tony Blair stepped up to the podium outside the Royal
Festival Hall and uttered those famous words that sent
a shiver down the spine of the British establishment.
'Right!' he said. 'Forget all that stuff we said before
the election about business and Tory spending plans –
we are going to squeeze the rich for every penny
they've got . . .' The crowd gasped as they realized
what a brilliant electoral trick he had just pulled
off. '. . . We've won a huge majority and now we are
going to nationalize the banks, bring in free public
transport, abolish private education and get rid of
nuclear weapons. We're going to repossess County
Hall, pull out of NATO, cancel third world debt and
put Mrs Thatcher on trial for anything we can think
of,' and then he and Cherie raised their fists and led
the crowd in a chorus of 'The Red Flag'.

Well, that's how I remember it but then I was very,
very drunk. He could have read out the nutrition guide
from the side of a cornflakes box – I still would have

15

cheered like it was the greatest day in the history of the labour movement. I suppose against all the evidence of Tony Blair's middle-class moderation there had still been one little bit of me that was hoping he might be a secret radical socialist – a red under the sofa-bed. There are others on the left that hate him for this apparent treachery. They seem to be shocked that the Tony Blair they voted for has turned out to be a moderate social democrat of the centre left. But of course there has been no betrayal. The point about Tony Blair is that he is the first Labour leader *not* to have moved to the right once he has taken office. He was always like that.

Labour hit the ground running. Within forty-eight hours, Gordon Brown handed over control of interest rates to the Bank of England. The British public gasped at the audacity of this move and then said to one another, 'What does that mean exactly?' Since then the Chancellor has greatly reduced youth unemployment under the New Deal, put up income support payments for children under eleven by £8 a week, introduced a minimum wage and increased pensioners' winter fuel allowance fivefold (from £20 to £100). The government have also introduced free eye tests for pensioners (although the leaflet announcing this will obviously be in very, very small writing). These moves have all been refreshingly redistributive. The last budget in particular was far more radical than most Labour supporters would have dared to hope for, but the interesting thing is that you won't hear the government proudly reasserting its socialist credentials. On the contrary, if they do something vaguely left wing they will blush and stutter and try to pretend that they are raising child benefit again because that is what is best for business. They are on a long-term mission to retain the trust of all those former Conservative supporters without whose votes Tony Blair cannot stay at Number 10. When Jack Straw announced that Pinochet would face extradition to Spain he didn't punch the air and boast that 'Pinochet might have tea with Thatcher but under a Labour government fascist dictators are arrested!'* Instead he looked all sombre and responsible and claimed that this was a purely legal matter, not a political one. Suddenly Glenda Jackson looked like the second-best actor on the government benches.

They have also been particularly modest about the battle to amend the Sexual Offences Act. For a party that seeks the support of the Mondeo drivers of middle England, politically speaking there is little to be gained from lowering the age of homosexual consent. So, sadly, you won't see Tony Blair wearing a pink triangle and blowing a whistle on the Gay Pride march. But he is persevering with it as a policy because he believes it is right and important, even when the excuse of persistent opposition from the House of Lords could have made it so easy to abandon.

There are of course some momentous achievements that do not have to be played down. The Good Friday agreement was brought about thanks to the personal determination of certain key players and although for me John Hume is the real hero of the peace process, Tony Blair and Mo Mowlam should also take a good deal of credit. The new spirit of reconciliation means I am supposed to be nice about those scary men in the bowler hats as well, so – er – well done for getting all those lumps out of Homepride flour.

Another great achievement has been the establishment of Scottish and Welsh Parliaments. Realizing that the Scots had no desire to be dictated to by a Westminster cabinet dominated by Englishmen like Gordon Brown, Robin Cook, Donald Dewar and

*Rather disappointingly General Pinochet was eventually sent home. After the former dictator had spent several months living on a private estate by Wentworth golf course, with neighbours such as Bruce Forsyth and Russ Abbot, it was decided that he had suffered enough.

George Robertson, this government have become the first in memory to surrender willingly some of their own power and influence. Labour is introducing proportional representation, which should help the opposition make some electoral inroads into Scotland and Wales where they failed to win a single seat two years ago. And with the way that William Hague is performing at the moment, he could well double his tally of MPs there.

There are of course some policies of which few Labour supporters can feel so proud. The introduction of tuition fees for university students was defended on the grounds that it is mainly middle-class kids who receive higher education and that children from poorer backgrounds will still get their fees paid. But I can't help feeling that the net result will still be that fewer working-class children get to university, and that is not something a Labour government should have presided over. Maybe they were hoping that the students could raise the extra money by extending rag week by a few days; that the wages of university professors could be paid by students being sponsored to sit in bathtubs of jelly dressed in their pyjamas.

This week of course sees the end of the government's two-year bizarre adherence to the Conservatives' spending plans. I keep watching the news in the hope of seeing Gordon Brown being handed a huge cheque and shouting, 'Now I'm going to Spend! Spend! Spend!'

It was wonderfully far-sighted of the previous government to put some money aside for the bombing of Serbia, because it obviously would have been impossible unless John Major had budgeted for it in advance. I suppose few people would have expected Tony Blair to be the one NATO leader to break rank with the United States. However, when Iraq was bombed back in January we were the only other country involved. It seems that Britain has become to America what Monica Lewinsky was to Bill Clinton.

When the US wants instant military gratification, we're just a phone call away, no questions asked. And one day we will wake up heartbroken when we tearfully realize they don't really care about us at all.

Like every government, this cabinet has also brought us a sprinkling of scandals. Robin Cook showed us not only that power made men attractive but also that he must be very powerful indeed. While Gordon Brown was raising five billion from the windfall tax, Lord Irvine was spending three-quarters of it on the new wallpaper for his private apartments. Peter Mandelson felt compelled to resign after it was revealed that he had taken out one of those attractive interest-free mortgages from the Geoffrey Robinson Building Society. Ron Davies had a knife put to his throat, was robbed of his wallet and his mobile phone and threw away an entire political career without ever stopping to consider what his actions might do to house prices in the Clapham Common area where I live.

But none of these embarrassments has dented New Labour's popularity. This government has had a longer honeymoon than many people have marriages. This is not just because the Tories are so deeply unimpressive. If people did not actively approve of this administration then the Liberals' poll rating would have dramatically increased to fill the gap. Labour continues to stand at around the 50 per cent mark because two years on they still come across as sincere, fresh and competent. And although some may think that the only substance this government has is hidden at the top of Jack Straw's house, on the news there is a constant stream of little stories that jolt us into remembering that the avarice and bigotry that ruled this country for eighteen years are over. Of course we all wish they were more aggressive in their assault on poverty and inequality, but we knew what we were getting when we all put our cross next to the Labour candidate on 1 May 1997 and, two years on, the programme we voted for is being delivered. This makes Tony Blair a unique prime minister – so far he is doing what he promised he'd do in the way he said he would. And while many on the left can't forgive him for that, the British people find it the most refreshing thing to happen in politics for a generation. Whether they'll continue to forgive him for ironing his jeans is quite another matter . . .

At this halfway stage it would be foolish of me to attempt to predict that Labour will be re-elected, especially if this article were ever to be reprinted in some collection or other. Were my political forecasts to be proved correct, people would only think I'd added this bit in after the event. Nevertheless I'm prepared to stick my neck out and guess that Labour will win the next general election with another large majority. And maybe John Prescott will punch a voter about nine or ten days into the campaign and Hague will resign the day after his defeat. Oh, and there will be a foot and mouth epidemic and confusing ballot papers in Florida will delay the result of the American presidential election and England will beat Germany 5–1 in Munich with goals from Steven Gerrard, Emile Heskey, and a hat trick from young Michael Owen.

Fifty-seven channels and there's nothing on

3 May 1999

I saw a newspaper headline recently that proclaimed 'THE DIGITAL DECEPTION – most viewers won't notice the difference, says TV watchdog'. If only this were true. The depressing thing is that when we do all have 200 television channels we really will notice the difference. There won't be anything to watch.

Why do the people who bring us all this extra 'choice' presume that *more* is necessarily *better*? Are they suggesting that there is so much great TV on the existing terrestrial channels that there just isn't room for it all? 'Coming up on ITV2 – all the out-takes from *Central Heating Engineers from Hell* that we couldn't show on ITV1 because there just wasn't time.' You can only spread money and talent so thinly and having 200 channels will be like the National Gallery having 200 pictures of that tennis player scratching her bum. New technology is a wonderful thing, but just because we *can* do something doesn't mean we *should* do something. We have the ability to travel to the moon but realized pretty quickly that if we want to go to a lifeless desert we can go to Maidenhead town centre on a Saturday night.

Apparently one of the great advantages of digital TV is that it is interactive. At last – I can choose from which camera I watch a televised football game. Obviously that is infinitely preferable to having a professional sports director do that for me. Then we are told that the quality of the sound and picture is superior on digital TV. Isn't that rather missing the point? Fantastic! A clearer sound on *The Jerry Springer Show*. Wouldn't it be better if we *couldn't* hear what that obese woman from West Virginia was shouting at her husband's mistress/sister? It's not the quality of the reception on my TV set which depresses me late at night when I am too tired to get off the sofa and I flick through all the dozens of free channels that the cable delivers to my TV set. If there is no football (the only reason I caved in and got cable in the first place) and there is nothing I fancy on UK Gold or Paramount, I will flick through the fifty or so remaining channels until my head aches and frustration eventually drives me upstairs to bed. It's like tasting your way through two dozen different pot noodles in search of a satisfying meal. The Bravo Channel originally featured old black and white films which were the perfect late night viewing. That obviously can't have made them any money because a glance at the TV listings tells me that this week's highlights include such artistic triumphs as *Scary Sex, Erotic Confessions* and *Can You Keep It Up for a Week?* This is the dismal fate of so many channels that are struggling to hold on to even the tiniest audience share (and incidentally the denouement of *Erotic Confessions* was all over the place). L!ve TV was launched with bold claims about how it would change the face of television but the channel soon descended into a desperate tabloid jamboree of topless darts, strip masterbrain and weather forecasts presented by a trampolining dwarf.

Another brilliantly pointless channel is BBC News 24. John Birt has cut the budgets of the shows we actually watch to pay for the self-indulgent white elephant of round-the-clock news. So if it's 4 a.m. and you want to know how the election campaign for the Scottish Parliament is going you just switch to channel 49 and they will keep you bang up to date on all the developments since 3 a.m. The Scottish Secretary will be sitting there in his pyjamas being grilled by someone not as good as Jeremy Paxman.

'Minister, will the government's strategy be changing in response to the fact that the Scottish electorate appear to have gone to bed?'

'Er, no – this is perfectly normal at this stage in the campaign – there's nothing to say. Why did you wake me up?'

'Hang on, we have to interrupt you there, Minister, because we have some breaking news: Prime Minister Tony Blair has just rolled over in his sleep and mumbled, "I wish those Serbian demonstrators in Whitehall would shut up!" More on that and other stories at 5 a.m.'

Other new channels on the way include Climate Classics, featuring those golden weather reports from the 1960s and '70s, and the Home Shoplifting Channel, where you see something you like on the Shopping Channel and then they go round and nick it for you. Not one of these channels is honest enough to call itself the Rubbish Channel – because that is what you get when you try and make TV programmes for nothing. Yet more and more new low-budget television stations keep appearing. Eventually the remote control will be larger than the TV set, it will have two hundred buttons and the only one we'll need will be the button that says 'Off'.

Don't mention the euro!

24 May 1999

This week saw the launch of the Pro-European Conservative Party by a couple of Tory politicians who are so anonymous that they ought to be in the shadow cabinet. They feel so strongly about the issue of Europe that they are even prepared to damage Conservative chances at the ballot box. William Hague can hardly complain about this, as it is exactly the same formula that saw the rest of the Tory Party choose him as leader rather than the more voter-friendly Kenneth Clarke. But now Europe is the one issue that Hague wishes he could sweep under the carpet. So what sort of contest should happen to come along next to test his accident-prone leadership? The elections to the European Parliament. Hurrah! It's as if Labour in 1981 had been forced to campaign in a Trident or Polaris Phone Vote.

For the next few weeks, Tory candidates will attempt to get elected to the European Parliament without ever getting into a discussion about Europe. It's the political equivalent of 'Don't mention the war!' Indeed the Second World War is what still shapes the

Little England mentality of most Conservatives half a century later, though it's not just a jealous mistrust of the Germans that shapes the sceptics' antipathy for the euro. The division in the party goes far deeper than that. The house of the Conservative Party has two supporting walls. One is capitalism and the other is patriotism. And now these European builders have come in and shaken their heads and told them that one of these walls is going to have to give way. Business demands that we let go of the pound – but the Tories' narrow brand of patriotism demands that we must have our own currency with the Queen's head on it. And the reason the Tories' house is going to come crashing down is because they, of all people, refuse to grasp that as sure as their little plastic Union Jacks are Made in China, capitalism is going to win hands down.

Because deep down people don't really care whether they have pounds in their pockets, or dollars, euros or Club Med bar-beads. What they care about is *how many of them they have to spend*. And if they can get cheaper lager by clubbing together and hiring a mini-bus to go to Boulogne for the day, then patriotism and the British economy doesn't enter their heads (although not much of anything enters their heads by the time they have drunk all the lager). Worrying about the status of the pound is for people who have too many pounds to worry about anything else.

The Conservatives want the sort of control that the global economy will no longer allow them. Similarly they are against tax and legislative harmonization because they say that countries should retain more control over their own affairs. But this is a party that was against the establishment of Scottish and Welsh Parliaments. Do they believe that countries should have more control over their own affairs or not? Of course what they are really against is having any more control or influence taken away from the English upper middle classes, who are now the only people they represent. They have become the English National Party – William Hague plays St George while Ann Widdecombe stands around saying, 'Now who on earth could we get to play the dragon?'

For all their sound and fury, nobody else seems to mind that the euro is coming. The indifference that has greeted the prospect of Britain losing the pound has been put down to political apathy. But the fact that people no longer seem to care about national symbols like passports and currencies should be an inspiration to the left: if people aren't bothered that they are going to lose the pound, then maybe they wouldn't be that bothered to lose that woman who has her head on all the coins either. If the Tories want Europe to be more streamlined then maybe we should get rid of all these different heads of state. King Albert II of Belgium could become our Single European Monarch and we could have *his* head on the euro – it would be worth getting the Germans to propose it just to watch the Conservative Party implode even further . . .

In fact the Conservatives went on to win the Euro-election. This was the first national election to use proportional representation and also featured the lowest ever turnout. Fears that the correlation between the way votes were cast and the way seats were allocated might confuse voters did not arise. Because there were no voters.

Any readers left?

13 June 1999

This month sees the fifth birthday of *Red Pepper*, the radical red and green magazine which has defied all predictions by surviving in a market that has seen so many left-wing publications put in the back of the 2CV and driven down to the newspaper recycling depot. It competes with a handful of other socialist titles and although its circulation has recently improved, the market for radical periodicals remains woefully tiny. The socialists who launch left-wing magazines need not worry about the ethics of making millions from sales because it is not a moral dilemma with which they will ever be faced. However, it's not for want of trying. Only this week, for example, I received a carefully targeted mailshot from the *New Statesman* that said, 'Dear John O'Farrell, Subscribe now and get a free copy of *Things Can Only Get Better* by John O'Farrell.' As it happens I've already read it.

Perhaps it's a little unfair that left-wing papers should be judged solely by their performance in the capitalist market place. Indeed Hilary Wainwright from *Red Pepper* says that the magazine was created to fill a political gap rather than a gap in the market. But it seems amazing that even when thirteen and a half million people have elected a Labour government, left-leaning journals cannot break through and sell alongside more mainstream publications like *Asian Babes* and *Guns and Ammo Monthly*.

The perceived wisdom is that people do not want to read about politics. In fact, millions of highly political publications are bought every day in this country, but the ones that sell do not wear their politics on their sleeves. The *Telegraph* doesn't call itself the *Daily Capitalist* – 'Read how the bosses are making massive profits out of the workers.' *The Times* doesn't have a little by-line saying, 'Defending the interests of the establishment and maintaining the class system.' Similarly on the left you can read some fairly radical opinions hidden away in the pages of *Time Out* or the 'Footnotes' pages of *Private Eye*. But if a magazine wishes to be overtly political it seems doomed to be sold only in progressive bookshops or outside Woolworth's by people wearing donkey jackets and fingerless gloves.

Perhaps it is because being 'political' is still seen as a term of abuse by many people in this country. An ordinary Labour voter might be happy to be seen reading *Viz* or *Loaded*, but they would feel self-conscious sitting on the tube reading something which might make them appear like a deranged lefty or even worse – an intellectual. Those of us who do buy these magazines find that they contain very little to cheer us up. We buy them because we feel guilty. For many years I guiltily subscribed to the *New Internationalist* and studied its clearly laid-out charts and graphs showing how the West was hogging seven-eighths of the world's guilt and how we really ought to share more of our guilt with developing countries. Left-wing publications are the political equivalent of *Slimming Magazine*. By buying them you are not actually doing

28

anything to tackle the problem, but at least you've acknowledged that something really ought to be done.

That is an inherent problem with articles that challenge the way we live. Flicking through magazines is something we do for pleasure, yet reading about the victims of the bombing of Belgrade makes you feel terrible. There is an inherent feel-bad factor that you just don't get when you read *Elle Decoration*. This is particularly true of publications of the far left where the editorial line is to be opposed to *everything*. There are still many writers on the left who are instinctively oppositionist – railing against anything which is perceived as mainstream or popular, thereby condemning themselves and their papers to the margins. Every time I flick through the pages of *Socialist Worker* I still feel like I am being shouted at five minutes after I've bought it.

At least with magazines like *Red Pepper*, *New Internationalist*, *Tribune* and *New Statesman* you cannot always predict what the line is going to be. And considering they cannot afford to pay proper rates for their articles they still manage to attract contributions from impressively high-profile writers. Perhaps these journalists are prepared to take a pay cut because they understand that it is not just how many people are reading your stuff that matters; it's also who is reading it. By their very nature these magazines are read by people who are at the centre of decision-making. Now that there are over 400 Labour MPs in the House of Commons a well-argued piece in the *New Statesman* or *Tribune* can be far more influential than their modest circulations might at first suggest. They have a direct line to the people in power, much as the editorials of *What Caravan* did when John Major was Prime Minister.

But it is still depressing that we live in a society where there are more magazines devoted to steam trains than there are to politics. Most political debate in this country takes place within a very narrow range; we are given the impression that there is nothing to the left of Tony Blair and nothing to the right of – well, Tony Blair. That's why it is important to read and support publications which broaden the discussion – even if you think you may not agree with much of what they say. So go out and buy a copy of *Red Pepper* or *New Statesman* or *Renewal* or *Tribune* or *New Internationalist* and at least have a look at *Socialist Worker* to see what other people have got to say. Because it's healthy to have our presumptions challenged, it's interesting to read about issues that are not given prominence in the mainstream press and it is vital that the voice of the radical left continues to be heard. And anyway you've got to hide your copy of *Hello!* in something.

Putting out the writs

19 September 1999

On a German satire show last week, a rubber puppet of Gerhard Schröder stripped off and made sexual advances towards a passing waitress. The only reason I know about this is because Schröder is now threatening to sue the show, thereby broadcasting this image to a far wider audience than the satirists could ever have hoped to reach.

Once a politician adds fuel to the flames, they are bound to be embarrassed further; whether it's Jeffrey Archer's spotty back or Bill Clinton's distinctive birthmark. Michael Portillo thought that he could control and direct the story about his one homosexual experience. He hadn't bargained on dozens of men with handlebar moustaches and leather cycling helmets running out of the woods on Clapham Common saying, 'Michael, you forgot to mention me!'

In all the years I wrote for *Spitting Image* we were never threatened with legal action by a politician because, unlike Schröder, British MPs are generally too sensible to risk giving greater ammunition and publicity to their critics. Kenneth Baker is clearly not really a slug; this could have been proved by any court in the land simply by pouring salt on top of him. Nothing illustrates the folly of a politician going to court over a joke better than last year's case involving Rupert Allason. When I was working on *Have I Got News for You* we wrote a frankly rather weak joke about Allason which included the phrase 'conniving little shit'. He decided to sue Hat Trick Productions because we called him 'conniving'. Presumably he did not contest the assertion that he was a little shit. We thought a man with Rupert Allason's connections ought to be able to pull in some pretty impressive character witnesses. So who did he persuade to take the stand to defend his good name? His mum. Rupert's mum was on Rupert's side. And we thought a man with Rupert Allason's money would be able to afford the very best representation. So who did the modest Mr Allason think would do the best job? Rupert Allason, of course. He was sadly mistaken. One of the first rules of the courtroom is never ask a question to which you do not already know the answer. Allason sought to prove what sort of cad the producer was by asking if he ever did any work for charity. Colin Swash looked rather bemused but, being the thoroughly decent chap he is, obligingly reeled off a rather impressive list of sponsored walks and Saturday mornings given over to shaking tins in the High Street. It was then put to Allason that suing people was a bit of a hobby of his – that he issued writs hoping people would settle out of court and he would make a bit of money. Allason denied this. Cue the video of Rupert Allason's appearance on *Clive Anderson Talks Back* (another Hat Trick show). Rupert boasts, 'Suing people is a bit of a hobby of mine . . .' His case collapsed and Allason slunk away, having had it confirmed by a court of law that he was a conniving little shit, while Colin Swash signed a copy of the *Have I Got News for You* book for each member of the jury.

The threat to our freedom of speech (of which the right to be rude about our politicians is a vital part) does not come so much from the law courts or directly from MPs, but from a far more insidious source: those friends of the politicians who inhabit the higher echelons of the broadcasting organizations. For example, last year John Birt ruled that no reference might be made to the sexuality of Peter Mandelson. Mandelson may have been embarrassed to have everyone learn that he is gay, but he must have been mortified for us all to learn that he is a friend of John Birt. It made for a memorable edition of *Have I Got News for You*, but needless to say that specific show was left out when the series was recently repeated. John Birt does not interfere because of any great principle about the right to privacy. He interferes to protect his mates. Earlier this year I appeared on *The News Quiz* and made a fairly run-of-the-mill joke about two items in that week's news. The joke was that, given the way the law then stood, 'If an eighteen-year-old boy has an affair with a seventeen-year-old boy he's breaking the law. But if a middle-aged man has an affair with a girl in the sixth form they make him Chief Inspector of Schools.' As a result of this gag John Birt rang up Radio 4 to suggest my joke was 'defamatory', which of course translates as 'rude about my friend Chris Woodhead'. Similarly the spineless suits in the BBC management forced writer/director Guy Jenkin to cut lines from his fine satirical dramas *Lords of Misrule* and *Crossing the Floor*. One line that obviously had to go was a reference to David Mellor having sex with women other than his wife.

In all the above cases the jokes had been cleared by BBC lawyers but the management were more concerned about offending figures in the establishment than they were about defending the rights of programme makers. And in this way an atmosphere is created where producers often censor themselves rather than risk crossing the management. Politicians in Britain don't need to rely on judges, they have friends who are self-appointed judges inside the BBC. So the German Chancellor should take a leaf out of our book and forget the use of the law courts – the modern way to neuter satire is to befriend the heads of the television network. Schröder should just take them out to a nice restaurant somewhere. Or maybe he just can't trust himself not to strip off and leap on the waitresses . . .

Schröder subsequently won another libel case which has actually made it illegal to suggest that he dyes his hair. Typical redhead.

Ninety-two lords a-leaping

4 November 1999

In New Labour's New Britain we presume that the people who pass and amend the laws by which we live our lives have to meet certain criteria by which they justify their position. And it has to be said that for most of us, the achievement of having once been married to Princess Margaret is not in itself quite enough. If every ex-spouse of the royal family was in the House of Lords, then on recent form that wouldn't leave much room for anyone else.

The fact that Snowdon (who failed to turn up to any debates in the last two full sessions of Parliament) will be part of the modernized House of Lords is symbolic that the reform of the Lords does not go far enough. It is of course a great step forward that Labour is abolishing the hereditary principle. Lord Callaghan thinks this is a good idea, and so does the Leader of the House of Lords, his daughter Baroness Jay. But of the ninety-two hereditary peers remaining in the Upper House, a large majority are Conservatives. This has been seen as a price worth paying to get stage one of the legislation through Parliament. But leaks from Lord Wakeham's proposals for the future of the Lords suggest that only one-fifth of the new House of Lords will be directly elected, with the rest being appointed by an 'independent' commission. This is a bold leap forward from the seventeenth century to the eighteenth century.

The House of Lords needs to be made more relevant. It has been suggested that one way to do this might be to fill it with people with whom the British people feel some affinity. But somehow I can't quite picture the idea of Lord Chris Tarrant sitting in the Speaker's chair asking frontbenchers who face a tricky question if they'd like to phone a friend. Another suggestion has been that the chamber should be wholly elected. This sounds fine in theory but given the recent turnout in the European elections I can't imagine people on Britain's council estates being enthused as they listened to the distorted voice of the canvasser on their entryphone urging them to go out and vote for Viscount Sir Rupert de Billiers-Farquarson-Twistleton-Stewart of Roxborough and the Glen. Anyway by the time the returning officer had read out all the names of the Lords who were standing for election it would be time for the next general election.

We need a second chamber that does what it does now, namely revise and delay, and act as a check and balance against the increasingly docile and compliant House of Commons. But it cannot do that effectively if it is packed with appointees of the Prime Minister of the day or alternatively with the descendants of the bastard offspring of the King of four hundred years ago. The House of Lords must be democratic. Indeed, the fact that part of our legislature is not elected means that we are in breach of the European Convention on Human Rights, but for some reason there has been less outcry about this than about the loss of *One Man and His Dog* to satellite television.

At the last general election Labour got 43 per cent of

the vote, the Conservatives got 30 per cent and the Liberals 17 per cent. This should be how the political composition of the House of Lords is made up. Each party should have an allocation to fill according to the size of its popular vote at the general election, with crossbenchers making up the arithmetic. How those parties choose to fill their red benches would be up to them. They could be elected by party members or they could be appointed by the party leader. Yes, there would be patronage and favours, but crucially not all from the one person or one committee. It would be 'proportional patronage'; instead of the Lords having a permanent Tory majority, the Lords would reflect the way that the British people voted as a whole.

There would still be a place for former MPs. Because whisper it not, but parliamentary experience is actually quite useful for a house whose primary function is to amend and oversee the legislation coming through from the Commons. And if they wanted, the Tories could still have the appropriately named Baroness Strange who does such a marvellous job with the flowers. Say what you like about the democratically elected second chambers of other Western democracies but none of them has a member who can arrange flowers like Baroness Strange. The scheme would make the house democratic without losing its most effective members. I told this plan to a friend of mine and he said he had read somewhere that Billy Bragg had been proposing exactly the same idea. So the proportionally allocated second chamber now has the backing of a singer/songwriter from Essex and an occasional TV gag writer. Sadly, that's not really enough to get it talked about in the places that count. If only one of us had once been married to Princess Margaret. Then we'd have the right to propose it in Parliament.

Ken Livingstone, I presume

11 November 1999

The City of London recently embarked upon the ancient ceremony of choosing a new ceremonial figure-head. Every Michaelmas the liverymen in Common Hall choose two aldermen who have served in the office of sheriff and then one of these emerges as the new Lord Mayor of London. Bizarre and antiquated maybe; but it sounds more democratic than the system Labour are using.

The day Labour decided that the restoration of a London-wide authority should centre around the election of an individual mayor, it became inevitable that personalities would count for more than policies. There's no business like showbusiness except 1990s politics. Jeffrey Archer's victory over Stephen Norris was based on a simple personality difference. Archer had one; Norris didn't. Tory members knew who Archer was because Archer is such a spectacular self-publicist – which is of course the reason he wants to be mayor in the first place.

The Liberals had a problem because they had only one MP who'd been on *Have I Got News for You* a lot and on that basis they'd already given him leadership of the party. So now they are lumbered with a candidate who is not even a household name in her own house. She desperately needs to get her name about more, but I won't spoil the fun by saying it here.

And now Labour are also in trouble because the candidate that they want to get the nomination has not been on telly nearly as much as the one that they don't. The outsider, Glenda Jackson, used to be on telly a lot but then she did terrible damage to her political chances by deciding to concentrate on politics. In keeping with the showbiz theme, next week's selection panel is threatening to turn into a political version of *Blind Date*. The three Labour hopefuls will sit on stools behind a screen while Tony asks each of them completely unscripted questions. 'Contestant number one – people say I like to get my own way. Would you cuddle up to me or rub me up the wrong way?' Then the screen will disappear and Tony will do his best to look surprised and delighted with his choice as he throws his arms around the bearded Yorkshireman who used to be his health secretary.

Opponents of the government claim that Ken Livingstone is popular among Labour members because they are fed up with the control freaks in Millbank and they wish to register a protest. But if the anti-Millbank candidate was John Cryer or another low-profile leftwinger the Labour Party wouldn't have this problem. Ken is popular because he has consistently maintained a very high profile whether through appearances on chat shows or advertising Red Leicester cheese. I once co-wrote a radio show called *A Look Back at the Future* set in the twenty-first century, in which Livingstone was Labour Prime Minister. We couldn't decide which impressionist did the best Ken Livingstone, until we realized that no one played that part better than Red Ken himself. He came along, did an uncanny Ken Livingstone and the audience clapped and cheered.

Because no one plays the part of martyr victim better than Red Ken. We loved him for it when the baddy was Mrs Thatcher and now the baddies are those bossy apparatchiks at Millbank he's revived his greatest role and it's playing all over London now. But the trouble is that this is the role Ken will play if he gets to be mayor. He will continue to be poor picked-on Ken; because like all showbiz personalities he'll always give the audience the lines for which they grew to love him. Which is fine if you want entertainment but not if you want the best leadership London could have.

Ken originally became leader of the GLC on a vote of GLC councillors (or by storming County Hall with guns supplied by the IRA, depending on which tabloid you were reading). It was a masterly political fix, but for today's Livingstone to complain about stitch-ups is like General Pinochet protesting about being detained unfairly. And now Tony Blair is haunted by the spectre of Red Ken running London again. He believes that it threatens to undermine all the work he has done dragging Labour out of the self-indulgent 1980s. But for me the scarier prospect is of Labour losing competence as a political machine and returning to the useless farce of the 1980s. I cannot believe that Millbank are trying to fix it for Frank Dobson, because these people do not normally make such a hash of political fixing. The well-oiled machine of the 1997 general election campaign seems like a million miles from the identical letters that went out from various London MPs saying why they were supporting Frank Dobson. I'm just relieved there wasn't a photocopied letter to Brent East members from Ken Livingstone saying why he'd be supporting Frank.

Labour should allow Ken Livingstone to compete for the nomination. It's one thing to exclude by-election candidates whom no one knows or cares about, but with the exception of actors who leave *Coronation Street* to go to Hollywood you can't just make famous people disappear. Livingstone's opponents within the Labour Party should openly and honestly explain why they believe he'd make a bad mayor of London. Then hopefully we could have a proper debate about what each candidate stands for instead of the bickering about the process that we have had so far. The only alternative to this route is to make the former health secretary a bigger showbiz star than Ken or Glenda. And for me, the image of Frank Dobson snogging Geri Halliwell on the front of the *Sun* is more than the Labour Party could cope with right now.

Labour did eventually allow Livingstone to compete for the nomination although some argued that the method of selection was designed to benefit Tony Blair's preferred choice, just because question one of the selection process was 'Who can name the most teachers at Frank's old school?'

Don't ban fox-hunting – it's far too unpopular

18 November 1999

Opponents of fox-hunting say that it belongs to another century but I for one am glad that fox-hunters have failed to move with the times. Urban foxes have thankfully not given rise to urban fox-hunting. It's bad enough having a fox in my back garden, I don't want a load of foxhounds and stallions leaping over from next door and galloping all over my begonias. But what right do I have to object? Us city folk just don't understand the ways of the country, do we?

It appears that the pro-hunters were given a lifeline last year with the announcement of an inquiry headed by Lord Burns into the effects of a ban on rural life. It has promised to be neutral, although it is hard to imagine that any foxes will be consulted. 'Hello, Mr Fox, my name is Janice. I am currently doing a survey on hunting. You may be aware that it is currently the custom to chase you and members of your family across the countryside for two hours before you are ripped apart by a pack of dogs. Do you think ending this practice would: a) improve your quality of life;

b) deny you the fun of the chase; or c) make no difference?' According to the Countryside Alliance, most foxes would shrug and answer, 'Er -"b", I s'pose.'

Poor Lord Burns will have to talk to all those dreadful people who appear on the television to protest that they are not just a bunch of toffs, which they do in an accent so posh you think you are watching a hilarious parody. 'We care about life in the countryside,' they say. Well, until Sunday evening anyway, when they load up the Range Rover and head back to Kensington for the week. One of them recently claimed that there were plenty of commoners on their marches, which was a bit of a giveaway because the word 'commoner' is only ever used by the sort of rich country folk whose names, like their shotguns, are always double-barrelled.

This is partly why fox-hunting is so deeply unpopular. There is only one thing the English hate more than people being cruel to animals, and that is snobby rich people being cruel to animals. So why has the government apparently been dragging its feet on this issue? One moment it appears that the fox-hunters face imminent abolition, then the government won't make time for a Private Members' Bill; then the PM gets them in his sights again, then there is going to be an inquiry. It's almost as if they have been deliberately stringing it out for as long as possible. *Don't the fox-hunters recognize these tactics?* Can't they see that Labour is enjoying the thrill of the chase, that they are having political sport with country sports? The RSPCA would like hunting killed off quickly and humanely, but that takes all the fun out of it. The pro-hunters are going to be hounded all the way up to the election. 'Tally-ho!' shouts Tony Blair as he sets off in his red jacket and riding hat, galloping after the fox-hunters and followed by packs of voters all baying for blood.

Because fox-hunting is that most precious of political issues, one that unites his party, is popular in

43

the country, will not be expensive to enact and forces the leader of the opposition into an embarrassing and untenable position. There can be few sights that gladden hearts in Downing Street as much as that of William Hague in his 'look-at-me-I'm-from-Yorkshire' tweed cap leading a march for the rights of posh people to be cruel to animals. Public opinion overwhelmingly demanded that fox-hunting be abolished immediately. And that is why it wasn't.

So we can expect more marches to come. More fox-hunters coming through our cities terrifying all the poor foxes who moved into town to get away from them. Obviously it's frustrating that hunting still goes on but there is something you can do until Labour finally deliver their promise. The next time there is a pro-hunting march through your city just grab one of the protesters, drag him down an alleyway and nick his watch and his wallet. And when he protests, just say to him, 'You country folk! You just don't understand the ways of the city, do you?'

Lies, damned lies and Jeffrey Archer's life story

22 November 1999

Shares in comedy writers will plummet today but Jeffrey Archer used his inside information and sold all his on Friday. First the Tories closed the steelworks. Then they closed the coal mines. Yesterday British satirists were mourning their closure of the last great comedy gold mine in Britain. Jeffrey Archer is quitting politics. Angry scenes were witnessed in Soho as gag writers declared an all-out strike in protest. Custard pies were hurled from picket lines. Police hit back with rubber truncheons. Now pensioners may face the festive season without jokes in their Christmas crackers. The army will have to be called in to write the gags for Rory Bremner. It is, quite literally, a very serious situation.

Jeffrey Archer's candidacy for Mayor of London had promised to keep us entertained all the way up to May. At the offices of *Have I Got News for You* researchers had built up a huge collection of wonderful snippets which were to be detonated at intervals over the next five months. They say every politician has a skeleton in his closet. Archer has a walk-in wardrobe of them. The Conservative Party were clearly dreading the campaign and I sense that this weekend's conversation between William Hague and Lord Archer went something like this:

'Anyway, William, I don't think this is a resigning issue.'

'OK, Jeffrey – I accept your resignation.'

'No, I was saying, I think we can ride this one out.'

'So will you announce your resignation or shall I?'

What is incredible is that the Tories ever thought that Archer was fit to run the capital city. This man was their number one choice. Would you trust Jeffrey Archer with your PIN number? There are lies, damned lies and Jeffrey Archer's life story. Archer is now in the impossible position that no one will believe anything he says ever again.

'So, Jeffrey – were you the mystery second gunman in the Kennedy assassination?'

'No!'

'Oh – he obviously was then.'

Over the years, the Archer mix of naff showmanship and casual disregard for the truth has provided meat for hungry satirists in an age when our politicians have become disappointingly sanitized. When I worked on *Spitting Image*, his little puppet could be brought into any sagging sketch to tell a few out-rageous lies and then just disappear again. Ian Hislop and Nick Newman once wrote a splendid *Mastermind* sketch in which Jeffrey Archer answered questions on the life of Jeffrey Archer. He got every answer wrong, so Magnus Magnusson put him straight on all the porkie pies that Archer had told about himself down the years. Soon afterwards Archer was foolhardy enough to come on *Clive Anderson Talks Back*. 'There's no beginning to your talents,' said Clive famously as he probed the great storyteller about his duplicitous past. After the show we were treated to the sight of the real Archer, ranting and raving out in the studio car park, threatening to sue if the programme was broadcast. With this memory I am comforted that at least this spectacular downfall could not have happened to a more horrible man. Don't take my word for it; go into any branch of Waterstone's and ask the booksellers there if Jeffrey Archer has ever been in to sign. Ask whether he behaved with politeness and humility or whether he was an arrogant bully.

This is the sort of politician that British satirists want. The Americans have a philanderer as a president; the Russians have a drunkard. What do we get? A church-goer with a new baby on the way. So we must turn to the Conservatives to step in and rescue the British comedy industry. Immediate steps should be taken to make Jonathan Aitken the Tory candidate for Mayor of London with Neil Hamilton as his deputy. Otherwise British entertainment may never recover from this double whammy. First they take away our favourite target. And now, worst of all, Jeffrey Archer suddenly has time to write another novel. Haven't we suffered enough?

Give thanks we don't have Thanksgiving

25 November 1999

Today is Thanksgiving Day in the United States. The Pilgrim Fathers were so grateful that their first harvest had been safely gathered in, they decided to have a special holiday in which everyone could give thanks to God by getting into their cars and sitting in a traffic jam. Given current trends it is quite likely that Thanksgiving Day will be celebrated in this country within the next twenty years. It falls conveniently midway between Hallowe'en and Christmas and would fill a yawning gap in the shops' promotional timetable that currently has Christmas stretching right back to early autumn. American consumerism has always been one step ahead. Instead of spending eight weeks gearing their customers up to buy one turkey, they slot in an extra festival at the end of November so everyone has to buy another one four weeks beforehand. It cannot be long before British shops try this scam on us.

Ten years ago Hallowe'en was not a commercial event in this country, and then 'trick or treating' was imported from the United States. Now we are subjected to the horrific sight of plastic goblin masks at the terrifying price of £2.50 each and are forced to buy variety packs of fun-size chocolate bars (£3.99) to give to calling children if we do not want our front doors sprayed with spooky spider's web spray (small cans £1.99 each). If there is a week in the calendar when there is nothing obvious to flog us, the shops will make something up. Father's Day was invented by an American greetings card company and there was actually a genuine attempt by the same people to launch a 'Secretary's Day', when employers could express their thanks to their overworked assistants. This one never really took off, presumably because the bosses kept sending their secretaries out to buy the cards they were going to give them. Giving presents on birthdays is a twentieth-century development. It seems that the cynical capitalists will never miss an opportunity to flog you something – a point that I make in my book *Things Can Only Get Better*, an excellent Christmas gift at only £6.99.

Since most of the significant days in our calendar were originally Christian festivals it is no wonder that these are the dates that the new religion of consumerism has seized for itself. The resurrection of Christ is celebrated by buying lots and lots of over-packaged chocolate eggs, obviously. The martyrdom of St Valentine is remembered by the doubling of flower prices. The church has no right to complain about the way their holy days have been hijacked by the new religion of shopping, because latching on to the festivals of existing religions was exactly how Christianity got itself established. 'Yuletide is just becoming too Christian these days,' said the pagans, bemoaning how the winter sacrifice at Stonehenge was being spoilt by a class of five-year-olds singing 'Little Donkey'. Many of the ways we once celebrated the birth of Christ pre-date his arrival. In pre-Roman Britain it was traditional during the winter festival that elderly relatives would come and stay for far too long, turn up the heating and nick all the brazils from the bowl of nuts on the sideboard. We no longer acknowledge the shortest day of the year, perhaps because now it feels like the longest when you are watching *The Great Escape* for the twentieth bloody time.

So just as the Winter Solstice gave way to a celebration of the birth of Christ, the new religion of shopping has made the whole of December its holy month. The modern cathedrals of Bluewater and Lakeside Thurrock are packed with worshippers. 'Lo! I bring news of great joy to all mankind. Dixons are doing Pokémon Blue Nintendos at £24.99.' The spending frenzy builds to a fervent climax by Christmas Eve as panic sets in because for one day of the year the shops are going to close. But fear not, the sales start at 9 a.m. on Boxing Day – and then millions of people go shopping all over again. The fundamentalists get into their sleeping bags and camp outside the department stores so they can be first to hear the joyful ringing of the tills. They sleep on the streets alongside all the people who have been bankrupted by the whole crazy money-go-round.

And that is the problem with the rampant consumerism which has become the hollow substitute for any spiritual depth in our lives. Just like the church before it, consumerism promises a happiness it cannot deliver. Heaven was in the next life, not this one. The eternal fulfilment promised by the ownership of a Sega Dreamcast is out of reach for most people. But still we are presented with more and more things we feel we must buy and more shopping festivals in our calendar on which we should buy them.

Today in the holy land of consumerism, everyone will over-indulge on roast turkey and pumpkin pie. We should just be grateful that for the time being we are spared that one particular burden on our overstretched family budgets. So let's give thanks that we don't have

Thanksgiving. Great idea, say the shops, we could have a special day when we do this. How about the last Thursday in November? Shops are open to midnight.

Allow me to demonstrate

2 December 1999

Angry mobs, baton charges and burning police vehicles are not what you normally expect to see at Euston station on a Monday evening. 'That's strange,' I said to myself when I saw the pictures on the news. 'That's not how people usually react to the cancellation of the 18.08 to Milton Keynes.' I had been completely unaware that there was such a strong groundswell of feeling against the World Trade Organization. But now I actually feel rather ashamed that I'm not doing anything about the destruction of the planet or the increasing poverty in the third world. I did do one bit of campaigning last year, lobbying my local councillors on an issue close to my heart. It was successful too, and our street got road humps soon afterwards. But somehow the overthrow of global capitalism just seems like a slightly bigger fish.

Some commentators have suggested that this week's violence erupted out of an increasing sense of powerlessness in citizens of the undemocratic global economy. There may be some truth in this, but seeing the bloke next to you get his head smashed open by a police truncheon must also be a factor. I have been on enough marches and protests to know how violence erupts. There is a symphonic narrative to a demonstration. It begins quietly – a gentle stroll with a few light diversions along the way, such as the vision of the statue of a nineteenth-century statesman holding a placard saying, 'I'm gay and I'm proud. Abolish Clause 28.' Eventually the symphony enters its second movement as the chanting begins. It is led by someone with a cheap megaphone, so distorted that you cannot tell what it is you are shouting about. He might well be screaming, 'The opposite of In is . . .' and you all reply, 'Out! Out! Out!'

Then the march reaches its destination and its climax. A tense stand-off begins in which a bunch of young blokes in jeans and T-shirts wait around to find out what will happen if they shout insults at a line of policemen in full riot gear. The police may well be on the receiving end of the odd improvised light missile, but sticks of plywood broken off the SWP banners are unlikely to pierce a line of reinforced riot shields. But that is all the provocation needed before the order comes down: 'Send in the Overreaction Squad!' These are officers who have had months of training at Hendon Police College in how to completely overreact to perfectly containable situations. Those who do not act with extreme and unnecessary violence are told they don't make the grade. If they respond to this news by tipping up the desk and punching their senior officer in the face then they are back in again.

When the police charge a crowd of demonstrators anyone is fair game. This is the moment when a jolly day out turns into a scene of ugly and upsetting violence. On one demo I remember seeing an old hippie who would clearly never hurt anyone being felled by the truncheon of a policeman in full riot gear. One moment he is telling everyone to cool it, the next he has blood pouring down his face and he's crying from shock and frustration and you don't feel like cooling it at all, you feel an enormous anger that makes you want to hit back at the idiots who could do such a thing to a harmless bloke who just went on a march because he wanted to make the world a better place. With one stupid piece of indiscriminate violence the police manage to turn us all into an angry spitting mob.

As a general rule the genuinely ugly violence on demonstrations is started by the police. According to that well-known anarchist Glenys Kinnock, the awful scenes witnessed in Seattle this week were no exception. A few years back there was an attempt by some German police officers to discover who really started the trouble and they infiltrated a demo disguised as protesters. They got their answer when they were set upon by several uniformed policemen and beaten senseless. Of course there are always a handful of demonstrators who go looking for violence, but that doesn't mean that anyone has to give it to them.

In this era of reconciliation I am surprised that Tony Blair has not made any effort to bring the police and eco-warriors closer together. Truncheons should not be made from tropical hardwoods but from trees grown in sustainable forests. More effort should be made to recruit officers with big metal studs through their eyelids. For their part, eco-warriors should spend a month working out in the police gym and then be kitted out with a macho black padded uniform and riot shield with extra-long baton. The temptation to whack someone in a clown costume doing circus acts must be quite strong.

But for now it seems depressingly inevitable that these protests will end in violence. On Monday night the situation forced Railtrack to close Euston station as pitched battles were fought between police and rioters, vehicles were set alight and the mob wreaked havoc in their protests against global capitalism and world poverty. And then at last the silent majority found that they too had something to be angry about.

'Honestly,' they tutted to themselves, 'what excuse will Railtrack come up with next?'

Neil before the judge

9 December 1999

Over the past few weeks hundreds of thousands of pounds have been spent in the High Court in yet another attempt to solve the impossible riddle of 1990s Tory politics. Question: 'Are you a liar?' Answer: 'No!' Neil Hamilton says that if it hadn't been for Fayed he would be a significant politician and would now be on the Tory front bench, which strikes me as something of a contradiction in terms. Given the political views held by Hamilton and the employment practices of Mohammed Al Fayed, this trial is the legal equivalent of the Iran/Iraq war; I feel like I want both sides to lose. But it is undeniably a case that has everything: great characters, glamour and drama. So surely the greatest injustice has been done to us, the British public. Why is this libel trial not on our tellies?

It is now over a decade since the eyes had it and television was brought into Parliament. The traditionalists had argued that this would change everything but they've been proved wrong and it's reassuring that the level of debate in the Commons is just as appalling as it always was. The same would be true of the televising of courtrooms. The O. J. Simpson trial showed that you can get just as big a miscarriage of justice *with* TV cameras as we in Britain have always managed without them.

The principle was established centuries ago, but now the public gallery should be expanded to include our living rooms. Millions of people would then have the opportunity to see for themselves the youthful impartiality of British judges and the broad cross-section of the British class system represented by the legal profession. I just can't imagine why they don't want to let the cameras in.

Maybe the objectors are worried that television would open the door to advertising. That when the prosecuting counsel described the unspeakable abomination that the burglar left in the middle of the carpet, the judge would interrupt and sing, 'Well do the Shake and Vac and put the freshness back.' Or perhaps they think that witnesses would seek to make a quick buck by a crafty piece of product placement. But I certainly can't imagine any of the witnesses in the Neil Hamilton libel trial taking a couple of thousand pounds to promote something they didn't believe in.

There is of course the problem that judges have quite a high enough opinion of themselves as it is without becoming TV celebrities. That showbiz status would have them saying to their agents, 'Do you think they can tell it's a wig?' They would develop their own gimmicks and catchphrases. 'Don't forget your toothbrush!' has a different ring to it when you are sending someone straight off to prison for twenty years. Of course twenty years might not be long enough. The studio audience might not like the bloke and shout, 'Higher! Higher!'

The best moments could then appear on a brand new panel game, *A Question of Court*. I can already picture a TV executive thinking that he has had a stroke of genius in suggesting Clive Anderson as host.

Clive Anderson would show the clip of Jeffrey Archer in the dock swearing that he was telling the truth and then ask the panel, 'What happened next?'

Of course in reality the same restrictions would apply to courtroom archives as currently apply to parliamentary footage. Those of us in the light entertainment industry have always found it very frustrating that we are not allowed to use any footage from Parliament on comedy programmes. Neither are we allowed to put our words into MPs' mouths. That's Alastair Campbell's job, obviously. But if even one solitary camera had been placed in the courtroom, imagine what we could have enjoyed. When a man like Jonathan Aitken is sent to prison you want to see the expression on his face. We could look back at the original footage of the Archer trial and actually see the witnesses lying under oath. And we really could enjoy the drama of Court 13 this week.

But there is another argument which is more powerful than any question of justice or democracy. The main reason that we must have TV cameras at the Old Bailey is so that we don't have to look at any more of those crappy crayon drawings. Defendants always look like dead Russian leaders who have had too much make-up put on for the lying-in-state. Judges have the same distorted bone structure normally seen only in those pictures they sell in Paris of rosy-cheeked children weeing into the river Seine. If contempt of court is a criminal offence, why don't they ever prosecute the bloke in the corner with the pastel crayons and the artist's sketch pad? Why can't these people just stick to sketching dishonestly flattering portraits of American tourists in Leicester Square?

If it were for this reason only we should force the law courts to join the twentieth century in the few weeks they have left. Of course the trouble is that Sky TV would get Hamilton v Fayed while the poor old

BBC would be left with contested parking tickets at Swindon Magistrates. The BBC will have to take Sky to court over the deal. Rupert Murdoch v Greg Dyke at the High Court. They could have a whole channel devoted to that one.

From here to paternity

16 December 1999

This week new paternity rights became law, entitling parents to thirteen weeks' leave after their children are born. Because the leave is unpaid there is a risk that only the very rich will be able to afford to deposit the newborn baby with a Croatian teenager while they have a month's skiing followed by two months in the Maldives. But clearly it is a big step in the right direction. Now men cannot be sacked for taking time off work to be with their newborn babies. 'Damn!' they'll all be thinking. 'Now I'll have to come up with another excuse.'

The rights came into effect yesterday – with the bizarre consequence that parents of any baby born before midnight on Tuesday were not eligible. In labour wards up and down the land you could hear midwives shouting, 'Don't push!' or 'OK, the baby's head is out . . . Now could you just hang on like that for another forty-seven minutes?' In the case of twins born either side of midnight I suppose the parents get the statutory thirteen weeks' leave, but to stay within the spirit of the law they should make an effort not to bond with the older one.

The legislation is part of the government's very laudable plan to get fathers more involved with the care of their newborn children. But the question on everyone's lips at Westminster is, will the man who made this legislation possible take advantage of it himself? Of course the Prime Minister will be there at the birth of his fourth child, encouraging Cherie to 'meet the challenge of the new millennium'. But then what? Will he just go back to work? Most men like to make out that their job is really important, and as Prime Minister, Tony Blair does possibly have a case. But he would be contradicting all the government's messages about parenting if he did not at least take some time off work. And it's not as if his deputy has much to do at the moment; I mean, all he's got is Environment, Transport and the Regions.

What will make it harder for Tony Blair is that not only does he work at home, but even if he did try and take some time off, ministers would still keep coming round to his house, stepping over the buggy in the hallway to have meetings in the cabinet room. How is Tony supposed to ignore that? With the baby in his arms he would put his ear to the door and hear all the old Labour tendencies resurfacing without him.

'So that's agreed then, we'll renationalize all the public utilities without compensation to shareholders . . .' and then Tony will tentatively put his head round the door.

'Oh hi, Tony!'

'Sorry, did I hear something about renationalization?'

'Oh, don't worry about any of that. You carry on looking after the baby. See you in thirteen weeks.'

'Right – um – nothing I can help with?'

'Tony, I think that Babygro looks like it needs changing . . .'

The other alternative is for Tony to take the baby to

work with him. Nothing could be more disarming than a party leader standing at the dispatch box with a little baby wriggling in his arms. The angry hostility of Prime Minister's Questions would evaporate overnight.

'Madam Speaker, is the Prime Minister aware that his new baby is really, really lovely and looks just like his dad?'

'Madam Speaker – this may be the case, but I think if the honourable members opposite were to look at these photos of babies that were born under the last Conservative government they will find that they looked much more like their mum.'

That's what happens when there is a baby present. It completely takes over as the focus of attention in the room. A shadow minister might deliver the most damning speech on government policy, with shocking statistics, brilliant quotes and a blistering personal attack on the Prime Minister. But while the baby is trying to grab Madam Speaker's little finger, no one is going to take the slightest notice. With a bit of training it could probably even learn to be sick every time John Redwood starts speaking.

Foreign heads of state will have to meet the Prime Minister when he is free, namely at half-past three in the morning when it's Tony's turn to get up. The weekly audiences with the Queen may lose some of their formality. 'Can you just take that dirty nappy out to the wheelie-bin please, Your Majesty. Baby's just gone and weed all over the changing mat.'

Frankly it's very hard to see the Prime Minister doing any of this. He can't just give up work, yet he cannot be seen not to set an example. There is only one foreseeable outcome. Although pregnancies are generally forty weeks long, soon we can expect an announcement that the government cannot find the time for the birth of the baby during the next parliamentary session and that the baby cannot be delivered this side of the general election. It may seem a bit hard on Cherie, but many of the homeless and the unemployed have had to learn to wait for Labour promises to be delivered. Cherie will just have to hold on as well. Women used to go into labour after nine months. New labour takes a little bit longer.

What's the story, mourning Tory?

23 December 1999

If you were to write an epic novel set inside the Conservative Party over the past twenty years, Neil Hamilton would be your central character. In the 1980s when greed was good and the Tories consistently won elections and law suits, Hamilton put out the writs and dined at the Ritz. He became a minister, and in what must have been a particularly thin year was named 'Parliamentary Wit of 1990'. Ten years on he is a ruined man, his party is in tatters but, bizarrely, neither of them really believe that they have done anything wrong.

The level of self-deception is almost heroic. Christine Hamilton is the posh equivalent of those angry mums who storm into the head teacher's office shouting, 'My Darren never done nothing! He always gets picked on by you teachers for burning down school buildings just 'cos he happened to have some firelighters and a box of matches in his pocket.' Against all the evidence Christine still believes that her husband is being picked on. Never mind that Parliament found him guilty, never mind that a jury found him corrupt, never mind that 60 per cent of voters in a safe Conservative seat voted for the anti-sleaze candidate. He's her little boy and they're all ganging up on him again.

There is an enormous arrogance that comes with this refusal to admit the error of your ways. When you consider how great Neil Hamilton's fall has been, only then do you get a sense of the level of pride that came before it. Unlike John Profumo who accepted his fate and threw his life into charitable works, today's Tories are proven to be dishonest and then just carry on lying about their innocence. The bizarre thing is that when Hamilton and Archer and Aitken look indignant and victimized they really seem to believe it – they've heard their own lies so often that they have finally become convinced by them. The looks of outrage and injustice on the Hamiltons' faces outside the High Court reminded me of the incredulous expressions of Mr and Mrs Ceausescu when they were captured and executed in Romania ten years ago this week. They really can't see what they have done wrong.

Neil Hamilton has now achieved the almost impossible task of making Mohammed Al Fayed look like the good guy. Of course as a Fulham supporter my problem with Fayed is that he is not nearly corrupt enough. All season I have been appalled by our club chairman's consistent failure to bribe referees. Week in, week out, outrageously fair decisions are made in favour of the opposing teams. Not one visiting goalie has been sent off for handball. Not one penalty has been awarded for blocking a Fulham shot on goal. But with the politicians Fayed has been more generous. It seems strange that a businessman can stand up in court furiously insisting that he has indeed bribed politicians and nobody is at all concerned whether or not this might constitute some sort of offence.

Somebody else will have to take on Al Fayed, and this duty must now fall to the royal family. This will be the first great libel trial of the next century: the Duke of Edinburgh suing the Harrods boss over allegations made about a plot to murder Diana. I'm sure His Royal Highness must know some rich people who could help fund his legal bill. Prince Philip will sit in Court 13, his plucky and ever-loyal wife Elizabeth at his side, biting back her tears and clutching her husband's arm as she recalls how hurtful the allegations against him have been. Perhaps Her Majesty may have to go into the witness box herself.

'Did you have champagne and caviar for breakfast that morning?'

'I expect so, that's what we have most days . . .'

Of course whatever the outcome of that trial, the Hamiltons will interpret it as further proof of their innocence. When you have become as detached from reality as they are, every piece of evidence serves to convince you further of the fantasy into which you have disappeared. And for Neil and Christine Hamilton's self-deception, read the collective psyche of today's Tory Party. They really believe that schools are attempting actively to promote homosexuality. They really believe that the Labour Party is full of IRA supporters and that Tony Blair is determined to surrender control of this country to the Reichstag. In the 1980s their values were the common currency, but now their homophobia and their petty jingoism are the irrelevant rantings of a bygone age. Now the Conservatives are like a lunatic fringe party. Soon we can expect to see them outside Woolworth's next to the Socialist Workers on a Saturday afternoon shouting *Daily Telegraph*! Get your *Daily Telegraph*! Britain out of Europe! Start the hospital closures!'

There has been a seismic shift away from the extremism, greed and dishonesty of the 1980s and the displaced victims of that change, like Aitken and Archer, are now scattered all around. This week in the epic story of the decline of a once-powerful political party, the last of its great symbolic villains finally became a ruined man when a jury gave their verdict on Neil Hamilton. It was the final scene of a momentous tragi-comic novel. I'm just praying Christine doesn't get a fortune for the film rights.

A nightmare vision of the new millennium

30 December 1999

Isn't it always the way? You spent a thousand years fighting wars, trying to sort out whose frontier is where, who should have independence from whom. Then just when you think you've sorted it all out, just when you have peace in Ireland and the Balkans, and dozens of new countries, just when you think all the border disputes from East Timor to Slovakia are finally sorted out, you discover that international boundaries don't count for anything any more.

John Lennon asked us to imagine that there weren't any countries. Well, 1999 was the year when we didn't have to imagine any more. Suddenly Bill Gates was more powerful than Bill Clinton, Rupert Murdoch more powerful than Tony Blair, and the chairman of the Moscow Discount Vodka Warehouse could make Boris Yeltsin do whatever he wanted.

'Sovereign' states are only one of many ways in which the world is now divided. In our trade disputes we fought America; in our military operations we took orders from America and the only time we got really cross with them was when they cheered too much for winning a golf match. In fact sporting loyalties illustrate how confusing it has all become. The said golf match was between Europe and the United States, whereas in football we got all passionate about England v Scotland. But I told my Australian neighbour that I would be hoping for an Aussie victory over France in the Rugby World Cup Final. 'Blimey!' he said. 'Don't you feel any sort of loyalty to your own hemisphere?'

But with the advent of globalization all regional allegiances are increasingly irrelevant. We might as well organize ourselves according to our star signs as to our country of birth. 'At the world trade talks today the Aries delegation stormed out claiming that the Sagittarians were being typically contrary and over-cautious, while for their part Aries were accused of being impetuous though good with their hands. This latest breakdown underlines a historic incompatibility between the two fire signs.'

It is of course more likely that our loyalties will develop in the direction of our economic interests. But to prevent this happening along the lines of class, they will try to turn us into product patriots, ready to fight to the death in the cause of the brand names that we consume or produce. The owners of Apple Macs already behave like this; a defiant persecuted minority waging a jihad against anyone who questions the superiority of their laptops. As the world divides into economic blocks this brand loyalty will be exploited just as nationalism was before it.

And so the next world war won't be between countries, it will be between Microsoft and the Disney Corporation. Computer nerds in combat anoraks will do cyber-battle with smiling Disney squaddies with Mickey Mouse ears attached to their helmets who say 'Have a nice day!' before they shoot you. The US President may try to reassert the old order by threatening to use his nuclear capability against Bill Gates, only to find that his computerized nuclear arsenal is completely dependent on a programme called 'Microsoft Bomb'. Military alliances will be made with other multinationals. News International regiments will be mobilized: 'Fix bayonets and remove bikini tops.' Coca-Cola will crush Pepsi and be named the official soft drink of the Third World War. Finally the war will end as Ronald McDonald commits suicide in an underground bunker by taking an arsenic pill inside a Strawberry McMilkshake. His death is delayed by two days as it takes him so long to finish the shake. At least there's one thing to look forward to.

Or maybe globalization will take us the other way, into a bland but peaceful monoculture. There will be nothing to fight about because we will all be living exactly the same existence, consuming a universal pick 'n' mix international lifestyle. Everyone will be drinking Australian lager in mock-Irish pubs, eating Pret A Manger sushi, listening to the same hit Latin record from the same hit Hollywood film and all purchased with one harmonized currency. Nothing reduces freedom of choice like unbridled capitalism. Obviously we will all be speaking English, but it will be an unrecognizable and naff abbreviated lower-case version as currently communicated by e-mail. Occasionally something exciting will happen, such as the discovery of an obscure Amazonian tribe who still pursue quaint ancient customs like paying for their Internet provider. But otherwise we will be safe to travel anywhere in the world in the reassuring knowledge that nothing will be any different wherever we go.

That is the grim choice between war and peace presented by globalization. John Lennon wanted us to imagine there were no countries. Somehow I get the feeling he never quite thought it through . . .

Tonight we're gonna party like it's 1999

(a political review of the year)

31 December 1999

There are some pieces of news that you will never forget where you were when you heard them. I was in a pub back on the night of 16 July this year and a stranger said to me, 'Have you heard? John F. Kennedy has been killed.' And I thought, 'Blimey, mate, you're a bit behind with the news.'* This year's contender for the Kennedy Award was not the election of his name-sake to the Liberal Democrat leadership, nor even the riveting ups and downs of the single European currency, but the sudden and unexpected resignation of Jeffrey Archer. It was the political equivalent of seeing that bloke who whizzed past you in the bus lane being pulled over by the police. Archer's fall was symptomatic of the pattern of politics throughout the year. Every time we started to get a bit fed up with the government, along came the Tories to remind us

---

*The former president's son, also called John F. Kennedy, was killed in a straightforward flying accident. Or was it?

71

why everyone voted Labour in the first place. 'Stand back, Prime Minister!' Hague would shout. 'If anyone's going to be made to look foolish round here, it's going to be me.'

The mayoral race was the most dramatic example of the Conservatives' tendency to gallop to Tony Blair's rescue like the American sixth cavalry. The search for a candidate had been the biggest thorn in Labour's side all year. 'Aha!' thought the Tories. 'Here's our chance to show how competent and honourable we are in contrast. Let's have Jeffrey Archer and Stephen Norris as our two front runners, they're both squeaky clean.' Suddenly both are disqualified; Archer accused of lying under oath and Norris of lying under a brunette called Sheila. This was the year that only people with an immaculate past were permitted to stand for public office. People like Martin McGuinness.

Issues of Labour cronyism would be kept off the front pages by Neil Hamilton's libel trial. Questions of Labour Party funding would be overshadowed by Michael Ashcroft's huge donations from his Belize bank account. Every time Hague tried to turn over a new leaf, the blots soaked through. Even when the Conservatives beat Labour in the Euro-elections, more coverage was given that month to Jonathan Aitken being sent to prison. The Conservative broadsheets simply had to give it in-depth coverage. It was an issue of justice and democracy and more importantly Aitken had posh and pretty daughters who could be put on the front page every day.

Of course losing the Euro-elections is what you would normally expect from a government in mid-term, but it's the Conservatives who have been consistently way behind in the polls. This may have been the case throughout Hague's political life, but at least before the Tories had the slight compensation of being in power. William Hague has hit back with some good jokes, but none as funny as the one his party played on him when they made him leader. He has tried to appear tough, to show that he's in charge. He ordered his front-benchers to do everything they could to make sure that they became ministers after the next election, to which Shaun Woodward said, 'OK, bye-bye,' and joined the Labour Party.

There were still plenty of problems for New Labour but none of them seemed to stick to Teflon Tony: the selection of Labour's leader in Wales, the battle over French imports of British beef, the slide of the euro and, most of all, the growing unease that this government would not tolerate any form of dissent. In March Tony Blair announced that NATO planes were being sent in to bomb Serbia. There were one or two anxious faces as they nodded around the cabinet table, mainly because they'd misheard him and thought that they were agreeing to the bombing of *suburbia*. 'I know a lot of them didn't vote for us out in Bromley but it doesn't mean we have to bomb them, does it, Prime Minister?'

The Kosovo crisis was another issue on which the Tories found it hard to land a punch on the government, especially since bombing parts of mainland Europe was rapidly becoming official Conservative Party policy. Their only quibble was that the RAF weren't dropping their load over France. Although they were not offended by innocent civilians being killed by British bombers, they were outraged by the idea that in the future homosexuals would be permitted to take part in this sort of operation. Previously it had been against military law for any member of the military to be a homosexual, although this was never extended to include the Minister of Defence.

Changing the subject completely, Michael Portillo returned to the Commons in November anxious to prove that he was now a moderate liberal. He may have dabbled with Thatcherism in his youth, but it was just a phase he was going through and it was all a long time ago. The return of the leader-in-waiting rounded off a thoroughly miserable year for William Hague. He may have been an ineffective leader in 1999 but at least there was no obvious successor. It is part of the bizarre nature of this Parliament that a Labour defeat in the Chelsea by-election is interpreted as bad news for the Conservative leadership.

It leaves you wondering if it isn't all part of some great master script that was drawn up by Labour in opposition. That Alastair Campbell has planned the bad news as well as the good. The point about really professional news management is that you can't just keep saying the government are great and hope that the public will keep on buying it. You have to construct some sort of overall narrative, some highs and lows. So the papers went for John Prescott or Robin Cook or Jack Straw, but it just made Tony appear all the greater by comparison. Like Her Majesty the Queen, it is acceptable to criticize the people around her, her advisers and favourites, but you can never utter a word against the monarch in person. It was the year when everyone did their utmost to make the Prime Minister look unassailable. To have got the cabinet to work in concert to this end is pretty impressive but to have persuaded the opposition to do likewise is unprecedented.

Nothing has gone right for the Conservatives this year, but next year they promise things will be different. They are preparing a massive assault on New Labour, carefully timed to bring them a crushing victory in May's local council elections and in the contest for London mayor. The strategy is specifically calculated to damage fatally the personal popularity of the Prime Minister himself, to leave him nowhere he can turn. 'Ha!' they will say. 'Let's see how Blair answers that. There's nothing in Alastair Campbell's script that can save him now!' And Tony will emerge sombrely on to the steps of Downing Street, stride up to the microphones and say, 'It gives me great pleasure to announce that Cherie has just given birth to twins.' We'll all remember where we were when we heard that.

The end of the world is nigh – appoint a task force

6 January 2000

Sixty-five million years ago the dinosaurs were wiped out when a huge asteroid struck the Earth. When you think about it, this was an incredible bit of bad luck – that all the world's dinosaurs happened to be standing in the same place at the time. Maybe they were attending a conference on the dangers of asteroids. The triceratops that were being laughed at for insisting there was a very real danger must have felt pretty smug in the last few seconds before they all copped it.

But now the problem is apparently back again. This week the government appointed a task force to look into the dangers posed by meteorites. Research on this front has been slow to develop. No money was spent during the 1980s because President Reagan was confident that if an asteroid was going to destroy Earth, then Superman would fly up and punch it back into outer space. Now at last various countries are waking up to the danger. So who is Britain's real-life superhero who is going to save us from obliteration in the manner of Bruce Willis in *Armageddon*? Step forward Sir Crispin Tickell, chancellor of Kent University and prominent environmentalist. Pah, what chance do the asteroids have now!

The effects of falling meteorites do make for some frightening reading. A relatively small meteorite would destroy an area the size of Essex. The problem is that there is no guarantee that it would indeed be Essex. A larger rock, such as the six-mile-wide asteroid that hit the Earth at the end of the Cretaceous era, would trigger a nuclear winter, acid rain, forest fires and a series of devastating waves causing massive global floods. Still, as long as you've got your health, eh? But just imagine having to watch the astrologist on Breakfast TV giving us the predictions from his look at the stars: 'You stubborn Leos are all going to be wiped out as well, I'm afraid. You may find yourselves feeling edgy and nervous all morning and then very flat in the afternoon . . .'

It's been claimed this week that individually we have a greater chance of being killed by a falling asteroid than we do of winning the National Lottery. I must confess that I have a problem with this statistic. Every Saturday night we learn that there is one lucky jackpot winner who lives in the West Midlands. Dale Winton does not tell us, 'And this week's unfortunate victim of a falling meteorite lived in the Great Yarmouth area. And remember, if no one is killed by falling space debris then it is a rollover week and the asteroid will be twice as big on Wednesday night!' In reality the chances of a huge meteorite hitting the Earth are extremely remote and more importantly there is very little we could do if one did. You could try putting on your cycle helmet, I suppose, but against a rock several miles wide travelling at seventy thousand miles an hour this would probably offer limited pro-tection. Scientists have been talking with great confidence about how a nuclear missile could be fired at the incoming rock to send it off course but I am not convinced. If our smart bombs cannot even avoid the Chinese Embassy in Belgrade then what chance does a one-off missile have of hitting a rock travelling at twenty miles a second? It's not as if we could go back to the suppliers after the earth had been destroyed and ask for our money back.

For every issue of public safety there is a political equation that has to be applied. 'How big is the risk?' divided by 'Can we afford to do anything about it?' The risk of London flooding was considered serious enough to warrant the building of the Thames Barrier, whereas the likelihood of killer sharks swimming up the Thames was so remote that it was never worth throwing Mrs Thatcher in. In the case of asteroids, the gap between the possibility of the event and the expense of averting it has never looked wider. This is why task forces are so useful. The important thing is that something is seen to be done. The government have put their political telescopes to their eye and said, 'The chances of political fallout occurring from this issue in the future may be very small, but it's worth constructing a small taskforce shield just in case.'

The grim truth is that there are some cosmic dangers that we tiny humans are powerless to do anything about. Eventually the Earth will spin out of its orbit or the sun will burn out or some cataclysmic space event will occur that will end life on Earth. It's a shame but at least it will give you the chance to tell Marjorie in Accounts that you love her. In the meantime there are millions of avoidable deaths that occur every year through unnecessary poverty, preventable diseases or wars that should never be fought. These things are the real disasters, not the risk of some lumps of old comet falling out of space. What we have to do to save planet Earth is bring these issues to the top of our political agenda and the world leaders will be forced to step in and really save the world. Ha! And we thought the chances of being struck by a meteorite were remote . . .

Is there a spin doctor in the house?

13 January 2000

How many civil servants does it take to change a light bulb?
None, we've always had that light bulb and we don't see why we should change it now.

Suddenly we have a government that has thought about what it wanted to do before it came into office and wants to implement these policies as quickly and effectively as possible. And shock, horror: most of the people they are bringing in to help implement the Labour manifesto are actually supporters of those policies! 'This is not democratic!' the cry goes up. Now Lord Neill is promising to impose a tough new code of practice on these 'special advisers'. So would it be more democratic to have the Labour policies that the country voted for being implemented by people who would rather they were not? Would it be more democratic if Labour's manifesto was obstructed and that the status quo of the Major and Thatcher years was maintained? The people who complain about the

Aunt Sally of special advisers are in reality just resentful that the government is getting its way. They want the civil service to be as neutral as it was when it was populated entirely by Old Etonians.

Most of today's civil servants are very honourable men and women who do their best to remain politically impartial. But any organization that has spent eighteen years implementing the policies of Margaret Thatcher and John Major is going to have a fairly strange idea of what is 'neutral'. When Vlad the Impaler's regime came to an end and the Wallachian civil service found themselves working for a new king, they were shocked at his radical proposals. 'What, stop impaling people altogether?! Surely you mean gradually phase it out after hearing evidence from the Guild of Impalers . . .'

There is of course no such thing as being 'apolitical'. The ministers the civil service are working for are interweaving 'national interest' with party advantage at every turn, and it has always been so. For example, in the run-up to the last general election the Conservatives introduced a radical extension of police powers. The main purpose of this legislation was to try to split the opposition and make Labour seem soft on crime. The civil servants who worked on these proposals were being employed for wholly party political ends.

The appointment of special advisers is an acknowledgement that there is obviously a party political dimension to a minister's work and it helps cordon off that part of the job. But just to keep things in proportion, out of the hundreds, sometimes thousands of people working for each government department, the number of special advisers working for each minister is just two. The Treasury, with two ministers, has four, the same number that it had under the Conservatives. But just because they are likely to be Labour supporters does not mean they spend their whole time putting the boot into William Hague. There are quite enough Tories doing that without everyone else joining in. No, their crafty underhand plot is to make the Chancellor look good by helping the economy run as well as possible. It was one of the Treasury's special advisers, Ed Balls, who with Gordon Brown developed the policy of granting independence to the Bank of England. This was not the act of a party apparatchik seeking to gain petty short-term advantage over the opposition; it represented a sacrifice of political power for the perceived good of the economy as a whole. As a Labour Party member, my problem with this government is that they are nowhere near partisan enough in their political appointments. Liberal Democrats are placed on cabinet committees and top jobs are dished out to the likes of Chris Patten and David Mellor. This is the ugly face of pluralism, particularly in the case of David Mellor.

And the few civil servants I know seem to appreciate having someone they can talk to, who knows the minister from old and can generally predict how they are likely to react to a given proposal.

'No, I wouldn't suggest stricter penalties for possession of soft drugs to the Home Secretary right now. He's just popped out to drive his son down to Kennington police station.'

The acres of newspaper space given over to the phenomenon of spin doctors is a symptom of the government's success. Papers are struggling to attack the core policies of the government, so they attack the messengers. It is like when you lose an argument with your partner and you are reduced to saying, 'All right, I know I should have checked the car had an engine before I bought it, but you don't have to tell me in that tone of voice.' Spin doctors are a part of politics; Bernard Ingham was a spin doctor, Joe Haines was a spin doctor, the people who stitched the Bayeux tapestry were spin doctors. In fact the Saxons who were at Hastings complained to the Tapestry

Complaints Commission. 'It wasn't like that at all,' they said. 'It's a completely one-sided account and we demand the right to knit our own version of events!'

The advent of special advisers is not a big deal, and the idea that Downing Street has placed loyal supporters in every corner to spin the government line is nothing more than a paranoid fantasy.

(Note to Alastair Campbell: I put your piece in under my name like you said. I had to change the font – hope this is OK. John)

There's nowt so queer as homophobes

20 January 2000

I've just read a leaflet in which homosexuality was portrayed as normal and acceptable and that was enough for me, I've decided to suddenly become gay. One brief glance at some mildly tolerant literature has forced me to leave my wife and kids and henceforth I shall have to spend my weekends browsing around Heal's soft furnishings and watching old Judy Garland movies.

This is what happens in the minds of those who oppose the repeal of Clause 28. These people think that if you do not condemn homosexuality as an ungodly perversion every time it is mentioned, then children will automatically become gay and run around the playground going, 'Urrggghh! Bazza kissed a girl, Bazza is straight – he's a bloody hetero!' The idea that propaganda can reverse your sexuality is patently ridiculous. Every day in our society we are constantly exposed to aggressively heterosexual propaganda and it doesn't make Julian Clary decide to become a scaffolder so that he can leer at passing

83

young women. We are what we are: gay, straight or MP for Chelsea.

But yesterday saw the launch of a media campaign in Scotland to prevent Clause 28's overdue removal from the statute books. £500,000 has been donated to this cause by the Stagecoach boss, Brian Souter, and on Monday the leader of the Catholic Church in Scotland, Cardinal Thomas Winning, described homosexuality as a perversion. Gay rights campaigners angrily condemned his remarks, saying, 'Oooh, get her!'

Section 28 is one of the madder pieces of legislation to have been rushed through Parliament during the Thatcher years. It was a law which the right-wing tabloids effectively wrote by proxy after they seized upon an innocent specialized book called *Jennie lives with Eric and Martin* which apparently demonstrated everything that was wrong with loony Labour councils. The book was in fact only used in rare cases where children were being brought up by gay male couples, but according to papers like the *Daily Telegraph* hard-left Labour councils were forcing impressionable youngsters to become homosexual. School assemblies had been abandoned and in their place kids were being compelled to wear leather motorcycle caps and listen to Dusty Springfield records. The eating of quiche was made compulsory. 'School outings' took on a completely different meaning.

Soon the outcry reached fever pitch; Tory MPs were furious that ordinary schoolchildren were being exposed to homosexuality when they themselves had to spend a fortune on boarding school fees for the same privilege. And so a law was passed making it illegal for local councils to promote homosexuality as normal or 'acceptable'. Which means of course that unless schools were going to deny completely the existence of homosexuality, they were legally bound to describe it as 'unacceptable'. English teachers were obliged by law to say things like 'The set book for this term is *The Ballad of Reading Gaol* which Oscar Wilde wrote while he was in prison for being a disgusting queer and quite right too, the filthy pervert should have been flogged as well, except he probably would have enjoyed it.'

But since this regressive law was passed in the mid-1980s, something unexpected and wonderful has happened. Homosexuality has become accepted. Suddenly there are openly gay ministers, even gay Conservatives, and generally people don't care any more. A few weeks ago Michael Barrymore was on the cover of *OK!* magazine with his partner. A few years ago this would have been inconceivable. The change of atmosphere has been hastened by legal steps taken by this government in its first couple of years in office. The age of consent for gays has been lowered, gay male couples have won joint parental rights and the ban on gays in the services has been repealed. 'Gay sailors!' said the opponents. 'Whatever next? Homosexuals in MI5?'

With his political antennae as finely tuned as ever William Hague has chosen this moment to harden his party's stand on gay issues. It has been whispered that the Conservatives' resurgent homophobia is a roundabout way of attacking the next leader in waiting, but whatever its cause it is as shameful as it is politically misguided. Of course there is still too much homophobia in our society; there are still gay-bashers who feel they are given a legitimacy by the likes of Brian Souter and Cardinal Winning. But the campaign in Scotland will fail for the same reason that Clause 28 was completely misconceived. You cannot change anyone's sexuality with a book and you cannot throw £500,000 worth of leaflets at an issue and hope that it will turn back the tide of tolerance which has been coming in for years. Instead there should be a new piece of legislation – call it Section 29 – which makes it an offence to incite hatred against minorities. If these homophobic Scottish Conservatives weren't such a ridiculous minority themselves, this might not be such a bad idea. Donald Dewar must have the courage of his convictions and see through the abolition of Section 28 north of the border. And instead of trying to defuse the row, he should use his powers to punish Cardinal Winning for being such a bigot. Then at mass on Sunday the leader of the Catholic Church in Scotland will be forced to announce, 'And now we will sing Hymn number 299, "YMCA" by Village People.' Kissing the bishop's ring will never be the same again.

Why was Mother Nature a single mum?

28 January 2000

The area of IVF, frozen embryos and human fertility is a very sensitive ethical issue and not a subject for cheap jokes and smutty innuendo. But here goes anyway.

This week's announcement that frozen eggs may be released for conception has major implications for the future of family planning. Women will now be able to freeze their own eggs and keep them for later use, unless of course the freezer breaks down and they have to rush round to their next-door neighbour's with the contents of their ovaries pressed between a packet of frozen peas and some McCain oven chips. The eggs will of course come with their own 'fertilize-by' date. Three stars on the side of the packet above where it says 'Best Before Jan 2010'.

The next stage takes place in a special building where people spend all day aiming frozen sperm in the general direction of frozen eggs, which all sounds rather like an unheated student house on Dartmoor I once stayed in. Successful fertilization can take some time, but when you have five billion sperm to choose from you can't expect Mrs Egg to make her mind up right away. One of the more bizarre objections I have heard to IVF is that there is no love in the act of conception. As if the test tube should take the woman out to dinner first, go back for coffee and say, 'You're so much more than just a friend . . .'

The voices that normally oppose every development in fertility treatment have been reluctant to criticize a decision which will give the chance of motherhood to women who have become infertile through cancer treatment. But shock, horror and hold the *Daily Mail*'s front page, this ruling will also allow women to freeze eggs until they choose to have babies later in life for personal or social reasons. Josephine Quintavalle, director of Comment on Reproductive Ethics, said, 'Whenever you do that you are putting the child second to your career and the welfare of the child has to come first.'

There is an unspoken assumption that because women's fertility falls away at around the time they reach forty, they must be less suitable as potential mothers; that reduced egg production is just nature's way of making sure that babies get the best mothers. Well, on this occasion nature has got it wrong. Nature makes it easier for a woman to get pregnant when she is fourteen than when she is forty, so what does Mother Nature know? And anyway, what happened to Father Nature? Maybe she should have chosen someone who was going to stick around before she started laying down the rules for all the other mums.

It is not fair that women should have to put up with worrying about their ability to have babies as they head towards forty. If we are allowed to use contraception to plan our families, then why not developments in technology? Imagine if the history of human fertility had been the other way round. That the only way to conceive a child was to plan and time your pregnancy using cryo-technology. And then a new potion was developed called 'Martini and lemonade' which when drunk all night increased your chances of getting pregnant in the back of the van of the bloke who ran the mobile disco. We would think the new system was complete madness. Babies produced through accidents, babies produced randomly to couples who didn't want them . . . This is what happens at the moment. Thousands of babies are conceived in this country every year, none of them to perfect parents, many of them unplanned and born into families that will struggle to raise them. That's fine, most parents will rise to the challenge and give their children all the love and support that their circumstances allow. But suppose a woman wants to wait till she's found someone who'll be a really good father, or until she feels she has the financial security that a new baby needs? To say that such a mother is crossing a line of moral unacceptability is clearly bonkers.

As ever, the opposition to this comes from religious groups. A number of church leaders have expressed opposition to IVF, though half of them probably thought they were being quizzed about some terrorist organization. No doubt at some point in the Bible it clearly states, 'Thou shalt not have thy seed put in liquid nitrogen, nor shall the eggs of woman be cryogenically stored till she hath found her Mr Right through the computer dating agency, verily.' But the reason they instinctively oppose this new development is that deep down the church does not like change. They are still sulking from being proved wrong about the sun going round the earth and frankly they've been struggling to keep up ever since.

But I like to think that Jesus would have had sympathy with women who wanted to bring children into this world when they were best placed to cope with them. Why am I so confident that our lord would have been in favour of test-tube babies? The religious conservatives should stop and think about it for a moment. Who was the first ever baby to be produced through artificial insemination? Why, Jesus Christ himself of course.

There's no place like the Home Counties

3 February 2000

This week John Prescott announced he will not give the go-ahead for thousands of *Brookside*-type estates across the South East of England. Few could argue with this; who wants to live in a cul-de-sac where every week there is an armed siege or someone is burying their husband under the patio?

Apart from grabbing the headlines, the *Brookside* image neatly illustrated the type of homes that the planners want to build right across the Home Counties. They imagine that if you build a million more homes in one already overcrowded corner of England then you will solve the housing shortage, but of course in the long term you would only add to it. More people moving to the South East would demand more services, more shops, more schools; which would bring new jobs and a renewed demand for new houses until the only strip of greenery left would be that patch of grass outside Parliament where the Minister of the Environment would come to announce that the site had just been bought for development by Barratt Homes.

The planners who proposed the million new homes had hoped that they would be finished by 2016, although you could probably add on another couple of years while a million families waited for the builders to come back and remove that pile of sand from the front drive and finish the front wall like they promised. Instead of setting the diggers loose on the Cotswolds, the Department of the Environment has indicated that 60 per cent of new homes should be built on 'brownfield' sites – derelict land that was formerly used for something called 'British manufacturing industry'. There are already dozens of these new estates along the Thames estuary which all claim to be just half an hour from London (if you are travelling by Concorde, assuming that it flies directly overhead, which it does). Building a few estates out in the derelict wastelands of Essex is the planning equivalent of a loft conversion. Yes, you could squeeze in a bedroom or two but that doesn't mean you would want to sleep up there yourself.

Rents are now so high in central London that the cheapest places to live are the automated superloos. These cost ten pence for fifteen minutes, and as long as you have a plentiful supply of coins and you don't mind the door flying open suddenly every quarter of an hour then you have a compact bijou residence in a central location with WC and – well, that's about it. As for house prices in the capital – these are spiralling so fast that cardboard boxes are being snapped up for conversion into flats.

So what can be done about the housing shortage in the South? As New Labour has become the yuppie party, you would imagine that their solution to the North/South divide would be to knock it through into one, with maybe a pair of panelled doors that could be folded across in the evening when the North of England was looking a bit untidy. But the long-term solution to the problem has to be to reverse the trend in which most of the new jobs being created are in the South East. There are one or two employment opportunities in the North but generally these are for burly ex-miners, forced to dress up in Victorian costumes and guide visitors around the World of Coal Industrial Heritage Experience. We need a long-term strategy to attract proper industry to the regions and if this doesn't work then some of the institutions of London should be relocated out of the capital. The army, for example, could vacate its prime central London locations and move to Rotherham, so that when all the squaddies got drunk and trashed the town centre at least nobody would notice. The stock exchange should be moved to Eastbourne. Then every time the brokers shouted, 'Buy! Buy yen at 14.7!' all the old people would say, 'Well, I'll think about it – I may come back but there's a few other currencies I want to look at first . . .' The Houses of Parliament should be forced to move to Sellafield, and then whenever there is a safety scare we can all enjoy watching the energy minister having to stand up and say that everything is perfectly safe. Well, it will look like the energy minister; it will in fact be a cardboard cut-out with a tape recorder fixed to the back. And the royal family should be relocated to Toxteth in Liverpool. This area currently has a high proportion of single-parent families living off the state, so a few more shouldn't make any difference.

Whatever the government decides to do, it needs an overall strategy – you cannot leave urban planning to the whim of market forces. There are dozens of places – such as Mexico City, Lagos and Dacca – where the laws of supply and demand have been allowed to create endless smog-filled urban sprawls. So John Prescott is right to reject plans to build on the green belt. But the government cannot deny the supply without reducing the demand. The North/South divide is still growing and has to be tackled sooner or later. Of

course they could always try just waiting a couple of
centuries. I saw another headline recently: 'Whole
of South East to be under water in 200 years'. That
should certainly even things out a bit.

Out of their heads

10 February 2000

Among the many effects of smoking cannabis are a distorted sense of reality and an inexplicable sense of paranoia. Judging from the Conservatives' new drugs policy unveiled on Tuesday, I can only conclude that William Hague and Ann Widdecombe must have spent all of Monday night sitting up smoking Lebanese black and listening to *Dark Side Of The Moon*. Their new policy proposes mandatory jail sentences for anyone caught in possession of cannabis within four hundred yards of a school. Given the density of our cities this would make literally millions of people instantly guilty of an imprisonable offence. 'We will build more prisons if necessary,' said the shadow Home Secretary. Yes, that'll work, Ann; nobody ever became more reliant on drugs while they were in prison.

The Conservatives have started with the words 'drugs', 'children' and 'tough' and built their policy from there. We are now in the long run-up to the next general election and so we can expect the level of debate on emotive issues such as drugs to spiral inexorably downwards. This country does have a serious narcotics problem but it is not 'tough on drugs' to come up with cynical, unworkable policies or to fuel the ignorance that prevents real progress being made against heroin and the other 'class A' drugs. If William Hague is really concerned about people smoking dangerous substances perhaps he should ask Lady Thatcher why she is taking money from the tobacco giant Philip Morris. Or indeed why Kenneth Clarke is deputy chairman of BAT.

The problem with William Hague is that when he says he has never smoked cannabis I believe him. Perhaps if someone could donate some hash cakes to the Conservatives' summer fete in his constituency he might just lighten up a bit. He hopes he can increase his support by sounding tough on drugs, but because he is heading into an area where the British people are more experienced than he is, he will find his draconian stance striking a chord with only an ill-informed minority.

The trend across the rest of Europe is towards a relaxation of the laws against cannabis and in the Netherlands, where it is legally available, consumption of marijuana is actually lower than in the UK. Not only do I believe that cannabis should be legalized in this country but, in order to annoy the Conservative Party as much as possible, I think Britain should be forced to legalize it by a Euro-commissioner, preferably a gay one who has made a large donation to the Labour Party.

We will, of course, first need a cabinet working group to examine the effects of smoking cannabis; a 'joint' committee, as it were. After many hours Mo Mowlam and Clare Short will emerge from the smoke-filled room, giggle slightly and announce that they have got the munchies and are heading off to buy some Cadbury's Fruit and Nut from the all-night garage.

Of course the legalization of cannabis will take

some adjusting to. Packets of twenty will have to state clearly, 'HM government health warning – these cannabis cigarettes may cause you to smile inanely and then go on and on about how red the ketchup bottle is.' There will have to be a new drugs breathalyser test for drivers. One big blow into the white tube, and then pass it on to the person next to you for a go. Will cannabis advertising be permitted on Formula One cars? And if so, won't the drivers think, 'Hey, what's the big hurry, guys, let's just park up here and look at the shapes of the clouds for a while.'

The reason it's hard to feel panic-stricken at the thought of tobacconists selling little packets of grass next to the king-size Rizlas is that, apart from a hefty windfall for the Treasury, nothing much would change. The only major difference to our society would be that the police would then be freed up to concentrate on the real killer drugs rather than wasting their time on a law that has become the modern equivalent of prohibition.

There is a widely held misconception that although cannabis may be a 'soft' drug, it inevitably leads on to harder things. But the fact that a majority of heroin users may have had cannabis during their lives is no more significant than the fact that most meths drinkers will have once tasted beer. Cannabis is not the wonderful health-giving herb that some of its hippie proponents suggest, but neither is it addictive, dangerous or anti-social. It might make you a bit boring but if that was a crime William Hague would already be serving a life sentence.

A recent survey revealed that 49 per cent of young people have tried cannabis, and most of them will have found it to be a harmless and mildly pleasurable experience. But this week the Conservatives said to them, 'Yeah, well, heroin is just like that too!' This makes William Hague the real dope dealer; flogging the odd mind-bending line outside the school gates, touting the stimulants that give a cheap high to the blue-rinse reactionaries he normally deals with. So, kids, if you see a strange-looking man trying to sell you a drugs policy, remember: *Just Say No.**

*The Conservatives hard line on soft drugs was eventually blown apart by the discovery that over half of the shadow cabinet had smoked cannabis. Apparently it's the only way they can get through those meetings.

www.over-hyped.com

By common consent we are currently in the middle of a revolution. The Internet revolution differs slightly from the French and Russian revolutions in that rather than overthrowing the old world order in the quest for liberty and equality for all mankind, this revolution enables you to check the recipes from *Celebrity Ready, Steady, Cook* without buying the *Radio Times*. Bliss was it in that dawn to be alive.

This week, plans for a new Internet university were announced. It will be just like being at real university, except that everything will happen on your computer screen. There'll be a little traffic cone icon that you can pick up and drag back to your home page. There'll be a live chat page where you can make yourself a blobby coffee and stay up until three in the morning listening to the intellectual bloke talk about Italian Renaissance painters, never daring to ask him why he keeps mentioning characters from *Teenage Mutant Ninja Turtles*. You will have immediate access to all the research material you need and e-mail with which to return your work instantly to your tutor; but all this will do is make it harder to come up with excuses as to why you are still two weeks late with your essay.

The electronic university is the latest headline in a long list of wonderful things that a computer and modem can do for mankind. There are e-bookshops where you can buy self-help guides to help you deal with the anxiety you felt ever since you divulged your credit card number over the Internet. There are virtual jobs in virtual offices where you go virtually mad never talking to another human being from one day to the next. Suddenly the Internet is the solution to everything. The Prime Minister is lying awake at night trying to think of a way forward for the peace process in Northern Ireland. 'Have you thought about looking on the Internet?' asks Cherie. And obviously there it is, instantly available and all for the price of a local call. The way to end world poverty, the secret of eternal happiness, the cure for cancer – apparently you can find out anything from the Internet. The only problem is that when you enter the words 'cure' and 'cancer', your search engine will find four million sites, the first of which is the diary of a fifteen-year-old boy from Milwaukee whose favourite band is the Cure and whose star sign is Cancer. And for some reason you find yourself reading ten pages about his trip to summer camp in Vermont before you accept that this site isn't going to have the information you were looking for.

The usefulness of the Internet has been hyped out of all proportion. All it does is make information more easily available. The downside of this is that in doing so it creates an enormous amount of new material, most of which is just information for its own sake. Like mobile phone users on trains on the way to the office, loudly reporting that they are on a train and on their way to the office, much of what is posted on the Internet is up there because it *can* be, not because it *needs* to be. The medium is the message.

Clearly there are some specialist occupations for which the Internet is a vital resource, but since I am not a white supremacist with an interest in hardcore pornography I find that most of the sites are not really for me. Knowledge is a wonderful thing, but for the time being I can survive without the latest major league baseball statistics delivered instantly to my e-mail address.

But imagine if a new craze suddenly came over from America called 'the library'. Inside were these things called 'books' about everything – encyclopaedias, great works of literature, children's stories, manuals, history books, more reading material than you could ever hope to devour. And you could take these texts out of the library for free because these 'book' things were even more portable than a laptop; you could 'read' them on the bus, in bed at night, anywhere. We would think it was the most fantastic development in the world.

Yet today libraries are closing while funding for the Internet seems limitless. Is this because we have read all the books there are to read? No, it is simply that the Internet is new. It is so new that even the cynical British have failed to see that it is not a superhighway at all, but the information equivalent of the M25 in the rush hour. In a few years' time things will be back to normal and we will all be complaining about how our favourite site on the world wide web takes ten seconds to access when it used to take only five, and telling our spoilt children that in our day we had to get the weather off Teletext. Then at least it will be useful – it will be something new for us to moan about. But in the meantime if you are one of the 80 per cent of people in this country who are not yet online, do not let all the hype make you believe you are missing out on something wonderful.

When people talk about 'surfing' the net you can rest assured that they are in fact comparing the

Internet to the kind of surfing you get in North Cornwall. You spend a fortune on equipment, there's lots of hanging around for very little excitement and every now and then something really disgusting bobs up to the surface.

Afghan hounds welcome; Afghan people join the back of the queue

29 February 2000

Yesterday the first pet passports came into effect. Around the country dogs have been hopping into photo booths and trying to look as relaxed as possible, which is not easy when you know you are not allowed on the chair. In Britain's airports, dogs have been boarding planes bound for Europe, one item of mouth luggage only, and have then spent the entire flight staring at the passenger next to them with a look that says, 'I'll have your biscuit if you don't want it.' Thirty thousand feet up dog owners have been asking the flight attendants, 'Can we open the window? He always likes to put his head out of the window . . .'

Animals have had to wait over a hundred years to get their own passports, which is only slightly longer than a lot of people have had to wait recently. Not one voice seems to have been raised in objection; not even Ann Widdecombe has accused this government of being 'soft on rabies'. *La rage* used to be this terrible plague that would sweep across Britain as soon as the first rat came through the Channel tunnel. Ministers would warn that if the disease came to Britain, all of England's foxes would have to be shot. 'Shame!' shouted the backbenchers, thinking of how that would deprive them of all the fun of ripping them to pieces with packs of dogs.

Quarantine conditions were so harsh and so expensive that every year hundreds of pets were smuggled into the country hidden away inside large consignments of cocaine and heroin. Every summer British children suffered dislocated arms as nervous parents yanked them away from patting harmless poodles in the Dordogne. It was all a nonsense of course; nobody on the continent gave a second thought to rabies. Anyway racehorses were always exempt from the laws and could come in and out of the country as they pleased, unless of course they broke their leg at Becher's Brook in which case they were fed to all the dogs in quarantine.

Now at last we have got over our irrational fear of rabies and all mammals can pass through customs without fear of being caged for six months. All mammals except asylum seekers that is. So that's why they are abolishing quarantine for pets; they need all the cages for refugees. Afghan hounds are welcome, Afghan people get a bone and bowl of water and are told to sit and stay.

What is it about the English that makes us love animals and dislike foreigners in almost equal measure? Why is it that the transport of veal calves in tiny crates prompts open weeping from demonstrators, and yet when the victims of political oppression are packed into prison ships it is described as luxurious first-class accommodation paid for by Britain's taxpayers? (It's a shame none of the asylum seekers ever murdered thousands of political opponents in Chile or we could have put them up in a luxury mansion next to Wentworth golf course.)

The fear that we used to have of rabies was out of all proportion to the reality of the problem. The same is now true of asylum seekers. There is a madness that has swept this country, but you don't get it from a dog bite, you get it from listening to politicians debating refugees. Britain is not suffering a terrible wave of immigration from bogus applicants who are sneaking past unnoticed while customs officers are patting all the labradors now coming through the barrier. We currently take fewer refugees per head of population than most countries in Western Europe and the idea that Britain is 'soft on asylum seekers' is not only incorrect, it is also a nauseating response to the wrong question. The issue should be, why are we not doing more to help those who have been the victims of oppression? It seems that we don't mind dropping bombs on the Balkans, but ask us to pay £3 more council tax to help the refugees from that corner of Europe and the tabloids splash it across the front page as if this was the end of civilization as we know it.

John Major resisted pressure to play the immigration card at the last election, presumably deciding that if you are definitely going to lose, you might as well do it with a modicum of decency. The early signs are that the next election will not be so clean. Perhaps all these dogs arriving at our Channel ports will give more ammunition to the politicians. Ann Widdecombe will say that many of them are in fact Albanians wearing golden retriever costumes. Perhaps Jack Straw will feel compelled to make another bizarre outburst, this time about how these foreign dogs have smelly breath and keep urinating in public places. On second thoughts it is unlikely. The British would never talk like that about animals, not when there are asylum seekers to have a shot at. This week our siege-like island mentality took a very small step in the right direction: we have stopped being paranoid and have opened up our borders to pets. Everyone seems very relaxed about this; not even Ann Widdecombe or Jack Straw is concerned about rabies. But this is because since immigration returned to the political agenda they're both foaming at the mouth already.

Bet your bottom billion dollars . . .

7 March 2000

The first Europeans to reach the Pacific coast of North America observed a bizarre custom practised by the Kwakiutl Indians in which tribal chiefs would challenge each other to what was called a 'potlatch'. This involved the two chiefs going to the cliff edge and throwing items of immense value into the sea to demonstrate their village's enormous wealth. Blankets, copper pots, weapons; they took turns to chuck away everything that they needed to survive as their two tribes looked on and gasped at their leaders' courage. The first one who ran out of valuables was the loser. And the explorers watched all this and thought, 'Great – that's how we'll choose our president!'

Today is Super Tuesday in the United States of America. The only accurate part of this description is that it is indeed a Tuesday. It's not really that 'super' that a number of states hold primary elections on the same day. 'Tiresome Waste of Money Tuesday' might be a better name, or 'Let's Bore Everyone to Tears Tuesday', because it is the day when the pretence of American democracy reaches its inane anticlimax. Call me a sceptic, but it cannot be a good thing that the leader of the free world is chosen on the basis of who has the most balloons.

The battle for nominations and the race to become president now involve a permanent cycle of massive fundraising and profligate spending, and as Bush has demonstrated yet again, the candidate who accumulates the most dollars wins his party's nomination. Why can't they just be honest about it? Instead of spending months flying around the country accusing each other of being soft on crime or dithering on abortion, why doesn't Bush get his wallet out and say to McCain, 'OK, let's get this over with – how much have you got?' Then Bush could take the stand and shout, 'God Bless Money!' as everyone whooped, clapped and held up banners saying, 'Whoever's richest for the White House!'

Al Gore seems to have already wrapped up the Democratic nomination on the basis that while Bill Clinton was president, he was right by his side. I only hope he averted his eyes on occasion. But he too has spent tens of millions of dollars and will spend as much again when the election proper gets under way. When Lincoln dedicated the cemetery at Gettysburg, his address was only slightly wrong: 'These dead shall not have died in vain – that this nation under God shall have a new birth of freedom and that government of the billionaires, by the billionaires for the billionaires shall not perish from this earth.'

John McCain effectively lost his battle to become the Republican candidate last October when a bill he had co-sponsored to limit spending in US presidential elections was defeated in the Senate. Amid accusations of dirty tricks, a filibuster to prevent proper debate on the bill was passed by just five votes and so the twentieth attempt in the last twelve years to reform financing of elections was thrown out. Yet again America's super-rich are free to throw money at the candidate they think least likely to take any serious money off them once they are in the White House. It's as if the head of the Broadcasting Standards Council was funded by Chris Evans. Meanwhile the majority of poor Americans, who are offered nothing by either party, take no part in the whole process and an apartheid of apathy is created.

Imagine if the same system was used to appoint the British head of state. The Queen's fortune would be used up in a couple of months buying television prime time to persuade us that the Windsors really were one big happy family and that Philip was not going to go all liberal on gun control. Once the cash had run out she would have to have fundraising dinners with various showbiz millionaires, pretending to be amused when Gazza put a whoopee cushion under her throne. And, worst of all, I'd find myself posting a small donation to her campaign as she emerged as the only candidate who stood an outside chance of beating Richard Branson.

Fortunately in this country we have far fewer elections and manage to be slightly more democratic. At least most British citizens actually take part in a British general election, even if you can hear them making their choice in the polling booths by saying 'Ippy-dippy-dation, my operation, how many people at the station . . .' But, as ever, the trend is towards the American way. At the last election the Conservatives spent (or arguably threw away) twenty million pounds without shifting their poll position one iota. Labour cannot pretend that relying on donations from the likes of Bernie Ecclestone has exactly helped their credibility. There is an inevitable equation that states that the more money political parties require, the less democratic the political system will become.

It is because today's American presidential hopefuls are so beholden to their financial backers that there could never be a candidate with a real programme to tackle America's huge inequalities. The people who need representing the most will not be voting this supine Tuesday. And because of the narrowness of the remaining constituency, none of the candidates can suggest any vaguely sensible policies like introducing gun control or abolishing capital punishment. And so it is that the United States is lumbered with politicians who would not only be prepared to sell their grand-mothers but, in George W. Bush's case, to electrocute them as well.

Ecumenical with the truth

14 March 2000

Most of us find the act of apologizing an awkward and embarrassing experience, but being infallible for two thousand years can't make it any easier. On Sunday Pope John Paul II shocked his congregation by breaking with centuries of tradition and saying sorry. He apologized for the persecution of the Jews, he apologized for the oppression of women, he apologized for the use of violence and torture down the centuries and he apologized for the time he reversed the Popemobile into another car and didn't leave a note.

Worshippers knew that something was up when the pontiff arrived at St Peter's dressed in purple. The colour signifies penitence and contrition, so they thought either he's going to ask forgiveness for something or he's now got so old that he's completely lost any sort of dress sense. Of course it is possible that the whole thing was a spontaneous aberration, brought about by the stress of giving up the fags and booze for Lent. But his apologies on behalf of the Catholic Church were widely welcomed. Apparently the Reverend Ian Paisley said, 'Oh that's all right, mate, don't worry about it.'

Now that the Vatican has sought forgiveness for the sins committed in its name surely it is time that the Church of England followed suit? The Archbishop of Canterbury must apologize at once for the misery caused by the Young Christians' Good News Coffee Morning. He must seek absolution for the torture that was the Harvest Festival Bring and Buy Sale. He must apologize that we have all been embarrassed into self-consciously mouthing half-remembered hymns at weddings and christenings. I have no fear of hell now that I've heard a group of thirty-something atheists mumbling their way through 'I Know That My Redeemer Liveth'. For some the suffering has been even greater. Many of my contemporaries have been forced back to church and now kneel in the front pew deep in prayer: 'Oh Lord, please let the vicar notice me here, so that I may get my kids into the local Church of England primary school.'

There are of course some genuine atrocities that have been committed in the name of religion by the British since the Reformation, not least in Ireland, but the Vatican represents a much older and more popular church and can therefore boast a far more impressive list of historical outrages. The Pope was indirectly apologizing for just about everything done in the name of the Christian religion since St Peter first went round knocking on people's doors asking them if they had heard the good news about Jesus. It must have been a great comfort to those witches burnt at the stake to think that in four hundred years' time someone was going to say sorry for it all.

The way things seem to work in the Catholic Church is that it doesn't matter how heinous your sins are as long as you acknowledge them. On Sunday the Pope effectively went into confession and asked for forgiveness for persecuting millions of people for countless centuries and the priest replied, 'Oh well, my child, it was all a long time ago. Say a couple of Hail Marys and be on your way.'

This is a great scam that Catholics everywhere should now start trying themselves.

'Forgive me, father, for I have sinned. My great-great-grandfather on my mother's side took part in repressing the Indian Mutiny.'

'Are you sure there is nothing else more recent you want to confess?'

'Well, yes, there's my granny of course. She originally defended Stalin's persecution of the kulaks.'

It's easy to apologize for atrocities that happened hundreds of years ago like the crusades and the conquistadors and Barbara Cartland's first novel. The point is that there are terrible things happening today which the Pope has the power to change. While the AIDS epidemic sweeps through Africa, the Vatican has decreed that the provision of condoms in the area would be a sin. An incalculable number of unnecessary deaths occur every year because of this one tenet of outdated dogma. If the Pope is trying to tell us that religious doctrine does not continue to cause suffering he is being ecumenical with the truth. Will we have to wait five hundred years before Pope Gladys V admits that this was wrong or will today's Vatican look to their own sins rather than those of their forefathers?

Of course it is possible that by then there will be no organized Christian religion. Now that the Vatican has unpicked one of the central tenets of Catholicism, the whole edifice of the church could begin to crumble. In that sense Canterbury is centuries ahead of Rome, for the Pope is acknowledging things we have taken for granted in this country for years. And now the new national religion of Britain is agnosticism. Every Sunday morning millions of English worshippers head down to Sainsbury's Homebase. There they pray that the special offer on the Black and Decker Trim 'n' Edge still gets them loyalty points on their reward card. On the Sabbath evening the family come together and watch the *Antiques Roadshow*, and on each holy day they get in the Mondeo and make a pilgrimage to Lakeside Thurrock shopping centre. Since we began to doubt the word of our own religious leaders, Britain has turned into a nation of agnostic fundamentalists. It almost makes you nostalgic for the Spanish Inquisition.

I give you my heart (and my kidneys and pancreas)

21 March 2000

For years I have carried a kidney donor card in my wallet. Part of me wanted to scribble a couple of preconditions on the back of it, but the chances that any of my internal organs might be required by Mrs Thatcher were so slight that I thought it not worth mentioning. However, now I learn that just carrying a donor card is often not enough; the hospital will still seek permission from my relatives. And, unsurprisingly, breaking the news of someone's death and adding, 'Oh, by the way, can we have his pancreas?' has sometimes proved a little awkward.

Different societies have found different solutions to the shortage of human organs for transplants. In China it is common practice to use the organs of executed prisoners. So every Chinese jail has a little counter where you can go in and say, 'I'll have two lungs, two corneas and a liver please.' Then you watch the telly up on the shelf for a bit, read the free local newspaper and ten minutes later they come out of the back and pass over your order in a little tin carton.

Until recently, in India it was not only perfectly legal but also quite routine for people to sell one of their kidneys when they needed to raise a little extra cash. They had a special section for it in the Indian *Exchange and Mart*, between keyboards and kissograms. And if you were in need of expensive medical treatment you could do a part exchange; it was just a question of haggling.

'Ooh no, I can't give you that much, I'm afraid,' the surgeon would say. 'You see, this kidney was originally one of a pair. It's not worth much without the other one.'

'Oh well, I'd really like to hang on to one of them if it's all the same to you.'

Hopefully nothing like this happens in this country, although I have always been rather suspicious of those people who wear badges saying, 'Lose weight now, ask me how.' Perhaps the British government might be tempted by the idea of selling kidneys on the open market. At last, a way for graduates to pay off their student loans!

In Belgium and Spain the shortage of organs is being tackled by a system that is termed 'presumed consent'. This means that there is a national register where you can specify that you do not wish any of your organs to be removed after your death. Otherwise it is assumed that you have no objection to saving someone else's life when your own is over. There are some people in this country who would recoil at this idea; if you put a Belgian kidney in the body of a Tory Euro-sceptic, the body would instinctively reject it. But now the British Medical Association has come out in favour of this system and is campaigning for a change in the law.

The problem with our system as it stands is that it is simply not working. Fewer than one in five people carry an organ donor card and the gap between demand and supply is growing all the time. Some hope that the shortfall will be made up by organs taken from animals, but this solution is still many years from being realized and brings its own problems. Will there be a choice of animal for the recipient? Will it be like choosing the fish in a French restaurant? 'Er, I'll have the heart of that piglet there, please . . .' And I suppose it also raises the question, 'Do animals have the ethical right to refuse their consent?' If I was a pig living in a pen marked 'To be slaughtered for organ transplant' I think I might be quite keen to join the register saying I'd rather not, thank you very much.

Countless deaths every year are caused by the unnecessary shortage of organs for transplant. This is such a scandal that it should be on every front page, but unfortunately it has been overshadowed by more important stories like David Beckham having his hair cut. The government should have the courage to follow the advice of the BMA and change the law to presumed consent. Yes, it is a moral and ethical minefield, but if you weigh up the possible distress of a family who learn that their recently deceased son had his kidney removed before he was cremated, compared to the distress of the family who have to cremate their son because no organ can be found for a transplant, then it seems to me that the choice is clear. One scenario concerns a death which has already happened and the other is a death which was easily preventable.

In the countries that operate presumed consent, the issue has been handled with sensitivity and they have witnessed a marked increase in the number of lives saved. I, for one, would hope that if I lost one of my relations, doctors would not need to ask me if the internal organs could be used to help someone else. Although after last weekend, what with St Patrick's Day and Ireland winning the rugby, I wouldn't wish my dad's liver on anybody.

And the award for the best awards ceremony . . .

28 March 2000

There were some fantastic actors up for an Oscar this year. You only had to look at the generosity of their smiles as they applauded the person who'd just beaten them to appreciate what brilliant performers they really are. The Oscars is without a doubt the biggest awards ceremony in the world; somehow the knife-edge decision over who will get the Nobel Prize for Chemistry has failed to capture the public imagination in quite the same way.

Oscars night is now the occasion at which Western society honours its greatest heroes. In the old days celebrities didn't get awards; instead the Pope would just create some more saints. At the annual sanctification dinner at the Vatican, Philip the Good would have to smile and applaud while inside he was spitting with jealousy that Joan of Arc had been made a saint while his Treaty of Arras had been completely overlooked by the judges.

Today there are awards ceremonies for virtually everything. For example, the comedian and writer

Tony Hawkes recently found himself hosting the British Flooring Awards, which apparently saw great excitement as guests wondered who would win Best Adhesive-Backed Linoleum. Among the other genuine awards ceremonies that are held every night in the hotels along Park Lane are the Heating and Ventilation Awards, the Catering and Hotel Keeping Awards and the Handling and Storage Awards. Perhaps there should be an awards ceremony for the best awards ceremony: 'And the winner is *this awards ceremony*!'

More and more professions are realizing that this is a way of raising their profile and keeping their work-force motivated. Soon hundreds of people will arrive at the Grosvenor House Hotel suitably done out in stripy jumpers and eye-masks for the Burglar of the Year Awards:

'My fellow burglars, this award doesn't belong to me . . .'

'Well no, Nobby, you just nicked it off Brian.'

Or live from Tehran, the International Terrorist Awards: 'And the nominees are Shining Path of Peru, ETA and the Animal Liberation Front!' And right across middle England fingers will be crossed for that elusive British win, although, as Jonathan Ross points out, just being nominated is in itself a great honour for the plucky animal lovers from Devon.

One of the last gaps in the market for an awards ceremony was filled last year with the inauguration of the Political Awards. It was felt that politicians do not get enough free publicity or go to enough drinks parties, so another beano was organized in their honour. As one of the few people who had written a political book I found myself automatically among the nominations for Political Book of the Year and so I went along wondering how my book about losing all those elections to the Tories would get on. It lost to a Tory. I wouldn't have minded but I lost to Ted Heath of all people, and that was the first thing he's won since the 1970 general election. I suppose it's just as well he beat me in the ballot, he would only have gone off and sulked for another twenty years.

Because our vision of awards ceremonies has been so influenced by Hollywood, all the other awards ceremonies are produced along the lines of the Oscars format. Ted Heath rather failed to play along with this; he singularly refused to burst into tears, thank his mum or hug me meaningfully back at the nominees' table.

The problem with awards is when people start to take them seriously. Increasingly, in the arts, prizes are taken as proof of merit. This year *American Beauty* won five Oscars so it is therefore a great film. But *The Straight Story* got nothing so it is not. In my opinion they are both excellent, but there's no objective way of measuring the best of anything in the arts. Nothing is definitely good and nothing is definitely bad – Michael Winner's films excepted.

Prizes for art and culture are of course part of a marketing scam just as much as they are in the heating and ventilation industry. In America at least they accept and understand this and no film that had completely bombed at the box office would be likely to win an Oscar. But in class-ridden Britain with all our snobbery and intellectual posturing the opposite is true; over here if a piece of culture is hugely popular it is presumed that it must automatically be rubbish. Art has to be difficult and inaccessible in order to be considered worthy of award status. If the Oscars were organized in the UK, the winner would be an obscure art film that nobody had liked or gone to see, but that got a few London film buffs very excited by its inversion of narrative form and the fact that everyone was talking in Esperanto.

So the next time the critics use the occasion of the Oscars to bemoan the lack of a British film industry, they should look to their own snobby prejudices that have helped separate the words 'popular' and 'culture'. It is no surprise who gets the prize of all the British talent that is put into great films. A nervous hush falls across the room as the envelope is opened . . . 'And the winner is . . . Hollywood!'

Snobs' borstal, only £15,000 a year

4 April 2000

If you live in one of those streets that are so posh they have residents' parking for their wheelie-bins, you may have noticed some strange children in your neighbourhood this week. Don't be alarmed, that couple unloading their new four-wheel drive don't make all their money by kidnapping children. Believe it or not, those kids are their own; they've just been to pick them up from boarding school.

This week, thousands of children will have returned to their 'homes' for the first time since Christmas. They'll be seeing their pets, playing with their toys, sleeping in their own bedrooms and for a few weeks experiencing something approaching normal family life. But just when they start to adjust, a few belongings will be packed into a trunk and they will be exiled to snobs' Siberia all over again. Whenever I worry that I may produce screwed-up kids, I console myself with the thought that at least I'm not spending thousands of pounds a year just to make really sure.

The fact that it is routine practice to separate children as young as seven from their parents should be a national scandal. Call the police, call social services – a child has been abandoned! But somehow it is unacceptable for a penniless refugee to keep her child with her as she begs on the street, but it's considered a social status symbol to be able to dump your children in a posh borstal for eight months of the year. Call me a wet liberal but there is more to parenting than sending off a parcel containing a Dundee cake and an Airfix model once every term.

Just as children who were beaten may themselves become violent parents, so Daddy will put his son down for his old school on the day that the poor child is born. I don't know why these parents don't just dump the baby in a telephone box and have done with it. In Aztec society, children were occasionally sacrificed at the age of seven. On the given day, a child was taken to the top of the pyramid and then hurled to his or her death. And the Aztec dad pompously told his wife that it was for their child's own good while the mum tried to put a brave face on it by saying to herself, 'Well, they do have splendid cricket facilities in the Kingdom of the Sun God.'

The range of activities they offer is the most common defence of these institutions. Well, they may have more rugger pitches and their own theatre and a brand new science lab and twelve computers for a class of twelve but without wanting to sound like a Country and Western song, what they don't have is *love*. When a child is at boarding school there is no one there who loves them. There is nobody who will be on their side no matter what, and whom they can just go to and cuddle whenever they feel like it. In the old days they had a boy for whom they fagged of course, because there was no one you would rather put in charge of your eleven-year-old than an abandoned sixteen-year-old who has been bullied for the past five years. What better way for a young boy to learn respect for his elders than by being buggered by them?

By sending away your children, you are separating them from the most important thing in their life, the most crucial factor in their development as fully rounded human beings. I have never understood why posh people always feel the need to possess so much stuff – horses, boats and holiday homes – yet when it comes to their own offspring they prefer to lease them on an occasional basis. Of course there are plenty of children who go to boarding school who may not be emotionally scarred. One of my best friends had a father in the RAF who was constantly having to move and so from the age of eleven she shared a dorm with eight other girls. She is one of the most balanced, warm-hearted people I have ever met and apart from the fact that she likes the Carpenters does not seem to have been psychologically damaged in any way. But for every person like her there are countless dysfunctional adults who were denied proper role models, who have problems communicating with the opposite sex or, worse, have grown up believing that the boat race is an interesting sporting event.

If you have just brought your children home and this is the first you have seen of them since Christmas, don't take them back in four weeks' time. Don't send them the subconscious message that you do not want them around, that they are not welcome at home. Tell them you love them so much you want to see them all year round. Tell them you will undertake yourself to teach those important social skills like talking too loudly and throwing bread rolls around in restaurants. And think of the money you'll save; you can put it in a savings account for your children. They'll need it when the time comes to dump you in an old people's home.

Greenham pleasant land

11 April 2000

A momentous event took place at the weekend. A man from West Berkshire District Council took a pair of wire cutters and snipped through the fence surrounding Greenham Common. It was not reported whether this local government official had a rainbow painted on his face and whooped like an Apache before symbolically burying a placenta under a peace tree, but somehow I doubt it. The former American Air Force base, the old front line in the battle against nuclear weapons, is just an ordinary piece of common ground once more. It brings a patriotic lump to my throat. Now it can be used for more traditional English pastimes like scattering pornographic magazines about or pretending not to notice that your dog is going to the toilet.

I have seen first-hand the misery that nuclear weapons can cause. I once stood in the rain outside Greenham Common, holding hands with a peace studies lecturer from Bradford. But though the battle for the land has now been won, the principle for which so many women gave up their homes, jobs and fashion sense has not. Britain still has nuclear weapons. And just as the peace camps have disappeared, so the issue has vanished from the British political agenda. The Cold War may be over, the world may have changed, but we are still spending billions on an independent deterrent that was originally 'justified' on the grounds that it would prevent a Soviet attack on Western Europe. Today we could stop a Russian invasion by telling the AA not to answer breakdown calls from any tanks west of Moscow.

So why do we still spend billions on nuclear weapons? The answer is of course for the same reason as before; it has nothing to do with military strategy and everything to do with political expediency. Because no political party dares to present the British electorate with the unpalatable truth that we are not an important enough country to warrant having the bomb. Ever since the end of the Second World War the British have been living under a massive self-delusion about our relative significance as a world player and key to this has been our possession of nuclear weapons. We have been like a family struggling to make ends meet in a council tower block in the West Midlands. As they sink deeper into debt the wife tentatively suggests to her husband, 'Well, we could always get rid of the yacht . . .'

'Get rid of the yacht? Are you mad?'

'But it's costing us a fortune, dear, and we don't sail or live by the sea or anything.'

'But what would the neighbours think if we didn't have a yacht? We'd be a laughing stock.'

There are plenty of things we believed in during the 1950s that we now realize are simply not true. The royals are not the perfect family unit, the police are not always 100 per cent honest and Arthur Askey's 'Bumble Bee' song was not a hilarious tour de force. But the British people still cling on to the idea that Britain is a major military power and so no politician dares suggest we give up our nuclear weapons. We might all be driving around in German and Japanese cars, but hey, we've got the bomb and they haven't. There must be cheaper ways of making ourselves feel superior to the Germans. Practising for penalty shoot-outs would be a start.

In fact the billions that we have spent over the years on our nuclear white elephant is partly the reason why we have less economic clout than many of our neighbours. Imagine if some of that money had gone into education and industry. What use are atom bombs when BMW close Rover? We can't nuke Munich, even if there are some in the Conservative Party who would argue otherwise.

This week it was reported that Britain would actually need several days to get its missiles ready to fire. Presumably that's the time it would take for the US President to return Britain's answerphone message asking for permission. In a parliamentary answer the Defence Secretary revealed that Britain's cash-strapped nuclear submarines were on a reduced state of alert in order that they could concentrate on 'secondary tasks'. In other words, 'Trips around the lighthouse £1, children 50p.'

Our Trident submarines could never fire their missiles independently of an American military operation. So it makes no more sense for Britain to spend billions to have its own deterrent than it would for the state of North Dakota. We are part of a military alliance completely dominated by Washington; our 'independent' deterrent is in fact just part of the American nuclear arsenal, the only catch being that we have to pay for it. Perhaps that's why it's called a 'special relationship'. Though the US will always be a nuclear power, today there is less reason than ever before for Britain to live in penury so that we can keep paying our subscriptions to the nuclear club. The bomb is an irrelevant status symbol from another age.

It's like those platform shoes that we all wore in the '70s. We felt great because they made us feel so tall. It was just a shame they prevented us from doing anything useful like walking.

The anti-disestablishmentarianists spell it out

17 April 2000

Last week a report commissioned by Jack Straw challenged the ancient constitutional links between church and state in this country as the government took the first tentative step along the road to the disestablishment of the Church of England. The exciting news spread quickly through Britain's factories and housing estates.

"Ere, Brian, have you heard? A Home Office report has suggested that minority faiths may be historically disadvantaged by the preservation of a Protestant hegemony.'

'At last! The politicians are finally tackling the concerns of ordinary people.'

The survival of a national religion may not be the question that will set alight the next election, but it is every bit as symbolic of Britain's outdated institutions as hereditary peers and repeats of *Last of the Summer Wine*.

There are people in our society who feel passionately about this subject; nothing angers the *Telegraph-*

reading religious right as much as a perceived attack on the church or the monarchy. So it seems the case for disestablishment just gets stronger and stronger . . . Most other Western democracies do not have one religion enshrined above all others in their constitution, and it is all the more bizarre that this should be the case in Britain when we are one of the least religious countries in the world. The most popular denomination in this country is, in fact, 'Dunno really . . .' If pushed, most people would probably say they were C of E or, to give it its full title, 'Church of England, I suppose'. But despite this, as in Iran and the Vatican, the head of state is also the head of our church.

At the moment this passes unnoticed because our monarch is a typical English church-goer; she's an old lady in a funny hat. But one day Charles will become king. Not only does he not seem like natural C of E material, he has a Catholic girlfriend, and under English law no monarch may become a 'Papist' or indeed marry one. Charles also decided to cause a little controversy a while back by suddenly announcing that he does not wish to be *defender of the faith* but *the defender of faith*. At which point everyone scratched their head and said, 'Sorry, I think I missed something there.'

If the monarch is genuinely to represent the religious orthodoxy of the nation then the Queen should go to church only once a year, to midnight mass as a drunken afterthought when the pubs are closing; where she can stagger in late, eat her kebab and sing, 'Hosanna in ex – CHELSEA!' The rest of the year should be spent reflecting the multicultural nature of our society. We are now a nation of many faiths and the Queen should take turns to be the figurehead of all of them. This would mean a spell of Her Majesty becoming a Muslim, a Hindu, a Rastafarian, and maybe an hour and a half as a Zoroastrian.

Then finally she can end the year as a Jewish mother, using the Queen's Chanukkah broadcast to introduce her son: 'He's done so well, he's going to be king, you know . . .' Maybe the Duke of Edinburgh could try his hand at Buddhism, explaining the wonders of reincarnation to animals before he shoots them.

In this era of constitutional modernization it's very hard to see any reason why we should continue to hold up one particular religion as the accepted national faith and thereby marginalize and denigrate other beliefs. It seems central to the concept of religious freedom that church and state should be separated. What is so surprising is that a government that has shown no ideological aversion to selling off nationalized industries has been so slow to spot the last great privatization staring it in the face. First there was Telecom, then BP, British Gas and now finally the privatization of the Church of England. There will be a high-profile advertising campaign: 'If you see God, tell him!' There will be a spectacular unveiling of the share price – perhaps the clouds could part and a couple of angels could descend with harps, halos and the freephone hotline for share applications. Lots of private investors will pocket a few hundred quid and then in a few years' time there will be complaints that these new contract vicars who were hired on the cheap from Heathrow Cleaning Services are nowhere near as sensitive and spiritual as the old ones.

The disestablishment of the Church of England will have to come sooner or later and it would be better to tackle it now before it is forced upon the government in a constitutional crisis. The reform would chime with the spirit of modernization under New Labour. It would be a kind of theological devolution, with religious control being released from the centre so that everyone could feel equal worshipping the God of their choice. As long as that God has been formally approved by an interview at Millbank, obviously.

Though change is long overdue, in a way you have to feel sorry for the traditionalists. It's not as if they can organize any protest against the reform. Because every time they organize a demo the whole thing is ruined. One of the anti-disestablishmentarianists shouts, 'Gimme an "A!" . . .'

Charity begins a long way from home

20 April 2000

You could tell the people running the London Marathon for charity. They were the ones carrying plywood Spanish galleons strapped over their shoulders. 'In aid of the British Heart Foundation', said their T-shirts as they lay wheezing on the roadside while St John's Ambulance checked to see if they'd given themselves a coronary.

For some reason it has become the accepted convention that people raising money for charity are compelled to dress up in stupid costumes. Why is it that giving up time or money also requires us to surrender our dignity? 'Thousands are starving in Ethiopia so I'm going to sit in a bath full of baked beans and do a sponsored singathon of Abba hits.' The Bible does not say what Jesus was wearing at the feeding of the five thousand, but I can't imagine he dressed up as a pantomime dame, with two balloons stuffed under his shirt while all the Romans looked on with a smile, saying, 'It's all right, it's for charity.'

Perhaps being madcap and bonkers is a way of

coping with the awfulness of the suffering to which we are drawing attention. Occasionally, as with the current crisis in Ethiopia, the problems seem so huge that we just want to put them out of our heads altogether. We pretend we're doing enough for charity by buying a lottery ticket, and reassure ourselves that if we won the jackpot we'd give a lot more.

The fact is that most of us won the lottery on the day we were born. We rubbed the little silver bit on the scratchcard of fate and it came up with 'Middle class, England' and we punched the air and shouted, 'Yes!' The bloke next to us rubbed his coin on his scratch-card and saw that he'd got 'Peasant, Horn of Africa'. 'Oh, bad luck, mate. I might as well take that coin off you before you go.'

But despite our enormous good fortune some of us are still reluctant to give away a little of our comparative wealth. This might be because we have an aversion to medical students collecting for rag week dressed as characters from *South Pacific*. But it is more likely that we have a deep-seated fear that we may get taken for a ride, that we may be giving a pound which won't reach its intended destination. But isn't this a risk worth taking? Even if it was true (which it is certainly not) that only a fraction of third world aid gets through to those who really need it, a mere ten pence would still be worth much more to the intended recipient than the original pound was to us. In fact, with emergency relief every penny generally goes straight to the famine-hit areas. The Red Cross, for example, are currently running daily flights carrying maize and soya directly into the worst-hit areas. (The airline food stays on the plane; the Ethiopians have already suffered enough.) The Oxfam fact sheet in front of me says that £2 buys enough seed to plant a whole acre of sorghum in the Sudan. This is an incredible fact. OK, I don't actually know what sorghum is, it could be local slang for cannabis, but it

134

still sounds like a bargain. What else can you get for two measly quid? Seven minutes' parking in central London. A disappointingly small packet of cashew nuts. One unfunny greetings card. My kids are currently stuffing their faces with an Easter egg that cost £3. The same amount could pay for a girl in Bangladesh to go to school for three months. Admittedly the girl in Bangladesh would much rather have the big chocolate Easter egg, but that's beside the point.

Yet many people will only give to 'good causes' if they can personally witness the benefits of their own largesse. In reality the good cause is their own ego. A friend of mine showed me his latest copy of the magazine sent to alumni of Westminster School. It proudly reported that a former pupil has just given one million pounds to his old public school. 'Hmmm . . .' this old boy must have thought. 'Who can I think of that really needs a million quid? Starving Ethiopians maybe? Flood victims in Mozambique? Children with leukaemia? No!' he decided. 'Clearly it has to be Westminster School, where all those poor children of merchant bankers and Tory MPs are currently having to get by with Internet access limited to off-peak hours only.' What more deserving cause could there be?

But unless thousands of emaciated refugees are massing on the cricket pitches of your old public school, I urge you to make a donation to Ethiopian famine relief now. Don't make excuses to yourself, nothing but good can come out of any donation you make. Remember, £1 keeps distress at bay for a whole day, £10 will pay for a whole week of smugness, £50 guarantees a whole year of sanctimoniously refusing other charities. So ring that helpline now. And remember this is for charity, so don't forget to put on your Widow Twanky costume before you make that call.

Apathy in the UK

2 May 2000

Millions of homes in this country will have recently received a polling card. These have a variety of uses; you can put them by the phone and use them to scribble down numbers, you can fold them and stick them under wobbly tables or you can tear them up and use them for making joints. If you are really adventurous you might actually use yours to go and vote on Thursday, although tragically you would be in the minority.

Participation in British elections is bad and getting worse. At the last Euro elections the turnout was so low that when a candidate asked for a recount the returning officer said, 'All right then – OK, I've finished!' Perhaps there should be more incentive to go and vote, a *Readers Digest*-type prize for the person who turns up with the lucky magic polling number. Since the main political parties feel compelled to offer bribes at election time, I sometimes wonder why they don't just have done with it and stand outside the polling station shouting, 'Vote Conservative and get two hundred pounds cash, a new DVD and a night out with Ffion.'

The sad truth is that people don't value the fantastic prize that has already been won for them – the right to vote. It is only within the lifetime of many older voters that we have obtained universal suffrage in this country, and yet when our polling cards land on the doormat we regard them with about as much respect as minicab cards and the leaflet from Speedy Pizzas. Emily Davison lost her life jumping in front of the King's horse at the 1913 Derby so that we could live in a democracy. Maybe that wasn't her motive, maybe she just had two bob to win on the horse that was running second. At this very moment there are people in jail for the crime of advocating democracy. They dreamed of a society in which every citizen had the right to vote. As a member of Amnesty I have sent postcards to such political prisoners, though I decided it probably wouldn't be very tactful to tell them we'd achieved their vision of utopia over here, but found that people generally prefer to stay in and watch *East-Enders* on a Thursday.

There are all sorts of reasons why people feel it's not worth bothering to struggle down to the polling station. One is that we have a voting system which disenfranchises millions of people. 'What's the point in voting?' says Tony. 'Whatever I do, that Ken Livingstone will get in.' Another is that most people still have very little power over their own lives; they feel excluded by society and so turn their back on the narrow choices offered to them. This is a symptom not of a failure of democracy per se, but of a democracy still in its infancy. And when our 'democratic' society fails to live up to its promise, the reaction varies from apathy to anarchy. The anti-capitalists who now regularly choose to celebrate May Day by getting smashed over the head with a police truncheon will cease to be a fringe novelty unless political power becomes genuinely devolved from the centre and people are routinely involved in decisions that affect their lives, nationally and locally and in their work-places. The alternative to real democracy is a society in which political opposition is regularly expressed through rioting, looting and throwing custard pies in Ann Widdecombe's face. It is not a pretty sight. And the custard pie doesn't help either. (Actually it is probably rather cheap and sexist to make jokes about Ann Widdecombe's appearance. What we must ask ourselves is whether she is a lovely person on the inside. And the answer is no, unfortunately.) Violence against individual politicians or world capitalism cannot be the way to construct a fairer, more democratic society. Tempting though it might be to vent our anger by hitting out at the symbols of the establishment, the only way forward must be to try to make the world a better place through the existing political system. We have sufficient freedom to go on and achieve real freedom, as Trotsky said to his friend with the ice-pick.

The establishment of the Scottish and Welsh assemblies and the chance to vote for a mayor of London are small steps in the right direction along this very long road and we all have a responsibility to take part in the political process in a constructive way. Democracy is a precious and fragile thing and we cannot allow it to be threatened by anarchy or apathy in the UK. But just in case you disagree, Ann Widdecombe's book tour continues for another week or so and custard pies are available in most good bakeries.

Ship of fools

13 May 2000

They have given up trying to find the Lost City of Atlantis. The unpaid council tax has been written off, the telephone code remains unchanged and Atlantis will soon have to surrender its city status to either Reading or Croydon. But now someone has finally come up with a replacement. Across the Atlantic, work is beginning on the construction of the world's first floating city; a huge ocean-going society with permanent residential accommodation for 40,000 people, with its own schools, hospitals, offices and, of course, shopping malls. The entrepreneurs behind *Freedom Ship* believe that thousands of people will buy 'properties' and then live and work on this sea-borne city; that they will run businesses and bring up families while the giant vessel sails endlessly back and forth between the hottest parts of the world in search of sun, sea and skin cancer.

It is *Brave New World* meets *The Flying Dutchman* – except that Wagner would probably have been a bit liberal for the residents of *Freedom Ship*. The name itself immediately marks the project out as deeply suspect – the word 'Freedom' with a capital 'F' is generally used only by nutty right-wing organizations and the makers of sanitary towels. The liberty to which it refers is of course freedom from taxes. The ship will be an enormous floating tax haven – like Jersey, but without the radical edge. In fact *'Freedom' Ship* will be a dictatorship run by the captain, but who cares about that when all the alcohol is duty-free and you are on the world's longest booze cruise.

The project's promotional material does everything it can to suggest that a life at sea is a healthy one. While I'm forced to concede that Cap'n Birds Eye is definitely looking younger than he did, there is more to health than a bit of sun, a gymnasium and a few cycle lanes. There is your mental health and nothing is more guaranteed to drive you off your head than living for ever in a society made up entirely of the people you met on holiday. Apparently the ship will boast a multi-language library – so you can choose between Dick Francis in English or German. The website does not mention whether this particular city will have a red-light district, but since they're hoping that entrepreneurs will start up their own businesses on board and they are promising extensive landscaping you might keep your eyes open by those bushes behind the tennis courts.

The really fascinating thing about *Freedom Ship* is what it tells us about the psychology of those who seek to establish a capitalist utopia by starting all over again somewhere else. They think that society's problems are nothing to do with them; that the unpleasant experiences of people begging, stealing or charging them VAT are random bits of bad luck that have happened because of their postal address. They imagine that you can leave all human ills behind in the same way that you can sail away from cold weather. The project is a logical progression from those high-security private housing developments with electric gates and CCTV – private solutions to social problems for which we are all responsible. *Freedom Ship* will apparently be such a perfect society that they are going to have one security officer for every twenty residents. How reassuring, being stuck on a boat with 2,000 bored private security guards made up of failed policemen and sacked bouncers who needed to get away from their own countries in a hurry.

The marketing material also boasts that thanks to a unique system of separate tanks the world's largest ship will be completely unsinkable. Which is a great line but one I'm sure I've heard before somewhere – I think it was followed by Kate Winslet nodding nervously and noticing how few lifeboats there were. Apparently the vessel is so large and stable that you wouldn't know that you were at sea. So it's worth all that effort then.

If *Freedom Ship* doesn't sink it will probably be captured by Indonesian pirates or there will be a mutiny by passengers driven insane by years spent watching CNN and playing quoits. But you can be sure that something will go wrong because the words capitalist and utopia are incompatible. That's not to say that some form of perfect society is not possible because after the launch I really can foresee it. Imagine a city ship floating around on the other side of the world with the likes of Margaret Thatcher, Paul Daniels, Norris McWhirter, Jim Davidson and all the other soulless right-wing cruise-ship customers permanently on board. Of course it would be a living hell – it would be the worst society imaginable. But wouldn't it be paradise back here without them?

Gawd bless yer, ma'am

17 May 2000

The government have announced that they are to charge £500 to guests wishing to attend the Queen Mother's hundredth birthday party. It's a desperate measure but it's the only way they could be sure of keeping Fergie away. Of course £500 is only for starters; guests will be even more out of pocket by the time they're sorted for Es and wizz.

The Conservatives are outraged about this vulgar plan to claw back some of the cost of the celebrations; Ann Widdecombe praised the Queen Mother as 'a long-established institution' which sounds as if she may have been mixing her up with Strangeways. The royalist right had barely recovered from the *Daily Mail* front-page headline 'How dare the BBC snub the Queen Mother', under which a corporation that is usually lambasted for screening dull, unpopular programmes was criticized for not filming a few soldiers marching around Horse Guards Parade being waved at. If it was such a great programme Sky would have bought the rights ages ago.

The BBC will be criticized whatever they do. Way

back in 1923 the progressives were angry that there was no radio broadcast of Elizabeth Bowes-Lyon's wedding to the then Duke of York. This was refused because it was feared (and I'm not making this up) 'that disrespectful people might hear it whilst sitting in public houses with their hats on'. God forbid that anything so discourteous should come to pass today, although the *Eleven O'Clock Show*'s photomontage of the Queen Mum's head on a naked pensioner's body must come close.

In providing a completely pointless thing about which to be outraged, the Queen Mother is of course fulfilling her historic duty. The reason that she has been built up to untouchable iconic status is so that subscribers to *Majesty* magazine have something to tut about when we only say she is 'lovely' five times over instead of the statutory twenty-seven. The BBC is actually spending a million quid covering her hundredth birthday, which sounds like plenty, and if it's any consolation somebody might point out to her that they definitely intend to provide live coverage of her funeral. And the government is in fact spending £400,000 on the celebrations, which is more than most pensioners have managed to get out of them recently. But still the Tories are furious at the lack of enthusiasm. This week they criticized British involvement in Sierra Leone on the grounds that the army might not have sufficient manpower to carry out more important duties elsewhere. Now we know to what they were referring. Never mind preventing genocide; we need the army band back here to play 'Happy Birthday'. All sorts of other festivities are planned. For example, one royal press release announces that on 2 June in St Paul's Cathedral the Princess Royal 'will unveil the bust of the Queen Mother', which is not an image you want to dwell upon. On 12 April she was presented with the citizenship of Volgograd (formerly Stalingrad) for her work for that heroic city during the war. Although I have read *Stalingrad* I must have missed the chapter in which she led a Soviet tank division and isolated von Paulus's Sixth Army from the rest of the Third Reich.

Of course *the war* is the reason why it is outright treason not to love the Queen Mum. As we have been told a thousand times, she opted not to go abroad during the blitz even after her home received a direct hit, only half a mile from her bedroom. To reflect this, her birthday celebrations include an appearance by Dame Vera Lynn and a fly-past of Second World War aircraft (which will then fly over the Channel for a re-enactment of the bombing of Dresden). This is all part of the attempt to portray her as an ordinary patriotic citizen who toughed it out during Britain's darkest hour with all the other cockneys. The really popular superstar royals like the Queen Mother and Diana are not royals at all, but have merely married one – and these icons are served up as one of us. 'I mean your Queen Mum, she was just born in an ordinary castle, weren't she, I mean she's not posh like the rest of 'em, is she; look at her mum and dad – ordinary working-class geezers, they were, old Lord Claude Bowes-Lyon and Cecilia Cavendish-Bentinck.'

What is completely bizarre is that a huge section of the British population still apparently feel such enormous love for someone about whom they know so little. She may have a nice smile and an ability to wave, but then so have the cartoon characters walking round Disneyland. Personally I cannot get excited about an elderly aristocrat's birthday, and if it were down to me the celebrations would be even more low key. The important thing with old people is not to put them under too much stress. What could be worse than organizing a hundredth birthday extravaganza and having her die in the middle of it all? Perhaps they should cancel those plans to give her the bumps as well.

*   *   *

NB Since this was written Buckingham Palace have of course given up pretending that the Queen Mother was still alive. For those who are still traumatised by this shock news, I would like to apologize for the extreme poor taste of all the above jokes. The old lady who lives in my road was so upset by the sad passing that I got her some flowers. I didn't buy them, I just found them lying around outside Clarence House.

There's a Freedom of Information Bill (and that's all they're prepared to tell us about it)

24 May 2000

I'd much rather road signs in Dorset spared me the information that I was now entering Hardy Country. We can get by without an electronic voice telling us that 'lift doors are opening', as that is generally something you can't help but notice when you're standing in a lift. When I buy a packet of peanuts I have already made certain assumptions that are not shattered when I read the warning 'contains nuts' on the side of the packet. In every walk of life we are given more information than we need; we are bombarded with stupid pointless facts to the extent that we are now suffering from total information overload.

Except in the one area where it really matters, in the area of government and the law. In London SW1, the information suddenly dries up. There is a culture of instinctive secrecy and evasiveness in our government that makes Whitehall behave like a reticent teenager.

'So – where have you been today?'

'Out.'

'Did you do anything nice?'

'Nope.'

'Erm, have you given any more thought to compensating victims of Gulf War syndrome?'

'OH LOOK JUST GET OFF MY BACK OK?!' and the door slams and it's another month before you dare broach the subject.

The last Conservative government was consistently secretive, but then they did have a lot to be secretive about. It's an approach they have continued in opposition by keeping the public from discovering the identity of most of the shadow cabinet. But when Labour was elected with a commitment to introduce a Freedom of Information Bill, there was optimism that things might begin to change. Unfortunately, the first opportunity for a generation to change Britain's culture of secrecy is not being taken. Unlike Ronseal Quick Drying Woodstain, the Freedom of Information Bill does not do exactly what the name suggests.

The legislation currently going through the Commons is there as a nod to an outstanding manifesto commitment but you can tell that their heart is not in it. It's as if the government introduced increased benefits for deaf people but only announced it on the radio.

The Bill basically says that all information should be in the public domain, unless it is something the government or local authorities would rather not tell us and then they don't have to. Since the promising white paper the liberal principles of the legislation have suffered a death by a thousand caveats. Information can be withheld by the newly appointed 'information commissioner' if it is 'commercially confidential', if it would 'prejudice the effective conduct of government affairs', if it is related to the formulation of government policy or if the person making the

147

enquiry has any letter from the word 'mackerel' in their name. Obviously I made the last one up but Jack Straw will probably add it in if he reads this.

The Bill reinforces the sense that information which affects how we are governed is for the authorities to release when they see fit, rather than ours to know automatically by right. Not only is this against the spirit of democratic government, it also increases the cynicism towards politicians about which this government so often complains. And it is an unnecessary backward step because usually there is absolutely no need to be so secretive in the first place. Most classified information is like those plates of seafood you get on holiday in Brittany. You spend hours battling away with nutcrackers and tweezers, and when you finally get something out you think, 'Oh, is that all there was inside?'

In fact the worst thing you can do with government data is to make it twice as compelling by refusing to disclose it. It'll probably leak out anyway, but by then everyone will be under the illusion that it is actually of some interest. No one would have read *Spycatcher* if they had been allowed to. The trick with awkward or sensitive information is to be completely open and honest, but to get the most boring person you can find to take ages going through it all in laborious detail. This was a scam that the Thatcher government tried during the Falklands War. Every time the British army suffered a setback, an anonymous civil servant with glasses was wheeled out before the cameras and would then list the dramatic casualties of battle with all the excitement of a geography teacher describing drumlins.

On this basis my nomination for the new information commissioner is Sir Geoffrey Howe. The government could then confidently disclose all the details of arms sales, covert operations by Special Branch and even who it is that goes around putting solitary gloves on the railings by bus stops. All secrets would be safe. But the government won't be as subtle as this. They will of course keep their promise to appoint an information commissioner – someone you are supposed to approach when you wish to get some facts from a government department. The only catch will be when you ask for the information commissioner's name and telephone number. 'I'm sorry,' they'll say, 'that's restricted information.'

The gravy train is now leaving platform one

31 May 2000

This week it became apparent that Railtrack were pulling out of the planned £5 billion upgrade to the west coast main line. They have effectively driven a steam train through the rail network's modernization plans. And the fact that it was a steam train just goes to show how little money's been spent on investment recently. No formal announcement was made, unless of course they got the station announcers to relay this embarrassing information over the tannoys so that no one would have the faintest idea what was being said. But we should not be surprised that they don't want to fork out £5 billion to improve the railways; you'd have to sell several Casey Jones all-day breakfasts to recoup that sort of money. Railtrack believes that this sort of capital investment should come from the government. That's how things work on the railways since they were divided up by the Conservatives. One half, the private sector, collects the money; the other half, the taxpayers, are expected to dish it out. No wonder Railtrack's profits have increased every year. The gravy train is now leaving platform one.

Railtrack are like those passengers who spread their bags and coats across a double seat while you walk up and down the carriage looking for somewhere to sit. It's not illegal, it's just greedy. Last year's profits reached £428 million after generous wages were paid out to the board. Presumably there were no more improvements that needed to be made to Britain's rail network or the left-over money would have been spent on that. We all get annoyed at being ripped off, but at least when you pay £40 to watch Manchester United you know that Sir Alex Ferguson doesn't then expect the taxpayer to cough up for two new strikers and some more executive boxes. It's not as if Railtrack even had to pay the market value of the infrastructure in the first place. Luckily they had a family railcard and it was after 9.30 at a weekend so they got the whole rail network for half price. And now, just to show their commitment to an integrated transport system, they are trying to sell off station car parks to private developers. Given half a chance they'd probably flog off those strips of land with those funny metal rail things on them as well; there'd be an attractive mews development with private pool and gymnasium stretching all the way from London to Glasgow.

This country has to have an effective train network. But the longer it is in the private sector, the more money that is paid out to shareholders and executives, then, as sure as leaves are going to land on the line in the autumn, the worse that service is going to be. There are some national institutions that you just cannot expect to run at a profit, such as the health service, the education system and Princess Margaret. The same is true with our railways; we need more investment, cheaper fares and the banning of the word 'customer'.

So a really bizarre and novel idea has just occurred

to me. Why not have a railway system that is owned and operated by the state? I can't believe that no one has thought of this before. If it was all the property of the British people then the profit that comes from selling tickets and scalding hot tea with UHT milk could all be ploughed back in. There would be no conflict between safety and profit and the fat cats who run the rail companies wouldn't have to pretend they travel by train any more. I know it has become politically unfashionable to defend state ownership, but if flared trousers can make a comeback then why can't nationalization? Of course, anyone trying to sell the merits of this idea to the government could never call it nationalization; you'd have to give it a modern, business-sounding name like 'Towards a Stake-holding Community' and then you'd have to say the words 'Internet' and 'millennium' a lot. Call me a dangerous radical, but if the taxpayer is forking out for the investment in the railways then the profits should go to the exchequer as well.

The failure of the rail companies to manage without state support should be a source of great satisfaction and encouragement to the left. Privatization doesn't work. The private sector can't hack it. When John Major and Norman Lamont broke into the signal box and started desperately pulling levers, the rail industry was sent hurtling off in the wrong direction and eventually it will have to be brought back. Since then Railtrack have consistently dumped on the taxpayer, and haven't even waited till the train pulled out of the station. The railways should be brought back under state control and compensation should be as under-valued as the original sell-off. Railtrack wouldn't have to provide any service or worry about safety or have anything to do with trains ever again. The trouble is they'd probably expect the government to step in and pay them huge profits anyway.

*   *   *

This piece was written before the Hatfield train crash and the subsequent collapse of the railway timetable which made Railtrack Britain's least popular company since that medieval pet shop started selling imported brown rats just before the Black Death.

The war is over

7 June 2000

This week is the anniversary of the D-Day landings. Last week it was the anniversary of the evacuation of Dunkirk. Next week is probably the anniversary of the first broadcast of *'Allo, 'Allo* and Prince Charles will unveil a memorial to all those actors who died on set. In Britain there is always a reason to look back at the Second World War. One of these days an explorer is going to land on this island and shout, 'The war is over!' and everyone will emerge blinking from the undergrowth where we've been hiding in our tatty uniforms since 1945. As far as the British people are concerned, the history of planet Earth goes like this. 1) The Earth cools. 2) Primitive life forms emerge. 3) Britain wins World War Two. Apart from that, nothing much of any importance has happened, with the possible exception of England winning the World Cup and the Beatles going on the *Ed Sullivan Show*.

Anniversaries are a way of cherry-picking our history and avoiding the complex and sometimes unpalatable truth. For example, this year is the hundredth anniversary of the end of the Boer War but where are the celebrations of Britain's invention of the concentration camp? There ought to be pages about it in the *Daily Telegraph*. 'Typical! Britain invents something and then the Germans and Japanese go and do it better than us!'

Or what about commemorating Britain's defeat in the Cod War (twenty-four years ago this week)? Where is the march past of veteran fish? Where are the films recounting how our plucky fishermen and the Royal Navy tried to liberate the oppressed cod from the tyranny of the Icelandic jackboot, so that they might be welcomed back to Blighty as Birds Eye frozen fish shapes?

When we do focus on a piece of our history it is not to understand it better, but to mythologize it yet further. Why is it that we still cling to the legend of Dunkirk? Perhaps because it is the only time in our history that we have got to the beaches before the Germans. My father was at Dunkirk; while thousands were fighting to get on a ferry, he was the one looking for the duty-free shop. It is understandable that his generation still see the war as the defining experience of their lives. But what depresses me is seeing the twenty-something English football fans being interviewed in the run-up to Euro 2000 whose perceptions of mainland Europe are still based on a distorted history of the Second World War. 'Well, Britain like, stood alone, against Hitler who wanted to close down the Rover factory but he was stopped by Bobby Moore and er . . . Captain Mainwaring and I'm really proud of how Britain stopped the Nazis and that's why we're all going to invade Holland and Belgium, give the fascist salute and beat up loads of foreigners.'

Like much of the popular understanding of World War Two, our interpretation of Dunkirk is a triumph of spin. As in any war the real story is complex and chaotic. But the British army was not rescued by an armada of little pleasure boats; 300,000 English squaddies did not come back across the Channel on pedaloes. The British army was in fact saved by a gross tactical error by Adolf Hitler who halted his generals when they were on the verge of capturing the entire British Expeditionary Force. He then went on to increase our chances of survival yet further by invading Russia and declaring war on the United States. His generals were furious with him but decided that he wasn't the sort of bloke to whom you could say, 'You've really cocked up big time here, Adolf.'

It was necessary at the time to build up the symbolism of little Englanders standing up to the German Wehrmacht, but by allowing the myth to endure and grow we have done ourselves nothing but harm. Britain standing alone in 1940 was the consequence of a military disaster in which we failed to prevent the fall of France – it is not a basis for anti-European foreign policy sixty years later. Furthermore, by distorting our historical status and pretending that we fought World War Two all on our own, we have inevitably created a sense of frustration when Britain then consistently fails to dominate the world in politics and sport in the way that we've been encouraged to believe it's our right to do. The backlash then comes at events like Euro 2000.

So stand on the white cliffs of Dover and wave off the little ships as they sail to Dunkirk to re-enact Britain's finest hour. But leave the boats over there for a week or two, because we're going to need them to bring back all the disgraced English football fans. And then the news reporters will ask, 'Why is it that these thugs hate the German supporters so much?' before they head off to film the next anniversary of a war that ended over half a century ago.

Microsoft world

14 June 2000

Included free with Windows 2000 will be a computerized edition of the game Monopoly. In this version Microsoft already owns every property from Old Kent Road to Mayfair and you just go round and round giving them lots of money. You try to tell yourself it's not fixed but when Bill Gates wins second prize in a beauty competition you can't help being suspicious.

Over the past two years, in a legal battle even more difficult to understand than the Microsoft user's manual, the computer giant has been found guilty of anti-competitive practices and abusing its monopoly power. Considering how aggressively Microsoft has consistently stamped on any competition, their lawyers really should have seen this lawsuit coming, but then this is the company whose computers failed to foresee that the year 2000 would follow 1999, so you can't presume anything. Now an American judge has ordered Gates to spell out in detail how he is going to break up his company, which should be interesting. After four hours the judge will stop him and say,

'Sorry, just going back a bit there, can you explain what you mean by "software" again?'

Since losing the case Bill Gates has seen his personal wealth drop by around $25 billion, so he's had to postpone the loft conversion he and his wife had been saving up for. Internet Explorer will probably no longer be given free with Windows, which means that poor Internet users like me will end up having to pay more to write reviews of our own books on Amazon.co.uk. It is of course true that Microsoft have stifled competition – but just a moment, who is it that is saying this sort of behaviour is unacceptable? The United States government! This would be like Gates telling Clinton he's a bit nerdy. There are a number of monopolies in this world but the US has a monopoly of all of them. Of course, this case is not really about free trade. It is a battle between the world's most powerful country and the world's most powerful company. It is the first flashpoint in the new cold war between nation states and corporations. More battles between the giants will follow: Japan v Sony, Korea v Daewoo, Britain v Top Shop. America won the first cold war on behalf of capitalism. And what thanks do they get? Capitalism then proceeds to push America aside and the next struggle ensues.

Bill Gates should now hit back by counter-suing the United States for operating anti-competitive practices. He would have a very good case. As a government, the US have consistently stifled free trade. Tiny independent operators like Cuba and Nicaragua have been virtually forced out of business and all sorts of international laws broken in the process. With the kind of breathtaking arrogance you get only from the leaders of world superpowers and seventeen-year-old public-school boys, America actually attempted to make it illegal for European countries to trade with Cuba; the case against America is even greater than the one against its richest citizen. Like Microsoft, the US has a variety of operating systems; in the Balkans they used NATO, but the World Trade Organization, the World Bank and even the United Nations itself have all been called into play at various times to ensure that the odds are always stacked in favour of American interests. This will probably be the last European Football Championship in which a team from Europe is allowed to win.

Any fair-minded judge would have to agree that, like Microsoft, the United States has abused its monopoly of power and must therefore be broken up. It has refused to operate a level playing field and so must be separated into its constituent parts. Dividing it between North and South is one option but this was tried before apparently and caused all sorts of problems. You could split it between Democrats and Republicans or Pepsi and Coke drinkers or between the pro- and anti-gun lobby, though this might be a bit unfair if another civil war broke out. But the American courts have ruled that monopolies should not be allowed to dominate and so the US must be as good as its word. If Microsoft Windows is not allowed to give you free bundled software, then each Americanized country should not automatically get a McDonald's in every high street and Jerry Springer repeats on their TV channels.

There must be a way of dividing America up so that we continue to get *Seinfeld* and *ER*, but are not compelled to get the rest of the American culture that is bundled in with it. Can we have the films without having to watch the acceptance speeches at the Oscars? Can we have the music without the graffiti on our subways? The break-up of America will be such a complex job that somebody will have to design a computer program to do the job. If only Microsoft hadn't been fragmented. They probably had a free program on Windows 2000 that could have done it all for us.

A midsummer night's Dome

21 June 2000

Today is the summer solstice and the most important
date in the calendar for pagans, druids and the man
who tears off the little tickets at Stonehenge car park.
For as long as anyone can remember, Stonehenge has
been witness to an ancient midsummer ceremony in
which hippies try to approach the stone circles and are
then ritually whacked over the head by policemen in
traditional riot gear. This year, however, with a callous
disregard for our prehistoric customs, English Heritage
has opened up the site and encouraged people to
witness the one day of the year when the rising sun
lines up with the hele stone, the slaughter stone and
the English Heritage souvenir shop. Every effort is
being made to recreate Bronze Age Britain including
putting out traffic cones to block off the A360 at the
junction with the A303, as archaeologists believe this
was how it must have looked back in 2000 BC.

These days Stonehenge is a massively popular
tourist attraction with more visitors than the site can
cope with. Which is ironic really, because when it was
built between 3000 and 1700 BC it was ruthlessly

criticized as a Neolithic PR disaster and a waste of Bronze Age lottery money. Many of the primitive Beaker people who inhabited England at the time felt that the money could have been much better spent on other things, such as beakers and – well, er, more beakers.

For Stonehenge was of course the original millennium dome. The rulers of ancient Britain decided that to celebrate a certain date on the calendar they should construct a huge circular monument which would be a source of great national pride and inspiration. Visitors would come from miles around and see real bodies being sacrificed in the Body Zone. They would understand the working of the sun and the stars in the Learning Zone. There was probably even an Environment Zone although I'm sure no mention was ever made of how they managed to get planning permission to erect sixty four-ton stones in the middle of Salisbury Plain.

But then things started to go wrong for the Stonehenge Experience Consortium. High-flying druids were delayed by security on the opening night. The projected twenty million visitors failed to materialize, unsurprising when the population of Britain was only a few thousand. 'Fifty-seven bronze ingots for a family ticket!' exclaimed the local peasantry. 'And that doesn't include having to buy egg, chips and mammoth at the Little Chef on the way down.' And all this after it had taken over a thousand years to complete. Archaeologists are divided as to whether this was due to shifting religious and cultural pressures or simply because the builders kept disappearing to work on another job. 'Sorry, mate, we're still waiting for those bloody rocks to be delivered from the Preseli mountains. Of course we could have finished it last week if you'd let us use a concrete lintel from B&Q, but if you will insist on having traditional bluestone . . .'

Thousands of years have passed and Stonehenge has completely recovered from its shaky start and is now an enormously popular attraction. But its modern-day equivalent will not have five millennia to prove itself. This week it is halfway through its short life and now has no chance of meeting the original estimates for visitor numbers. To appease the modern-day gods of corporate sponsorship, Jennie Page and Bob Ayling have already been dragged to the slaughter stone and publicly sacrificed. Before long Greenwich will become a mysterious historical site where archaeologists will debate the cultural significance of the building that once stood there. Was it a temple? A solar calculator? Or some sort of educational and cultural theme park thingy?

As someone who generally puts off doing anything until the last possible moment I will probably get round to going to the Dome on New Year's Eve; but until then all I can say is that everyone I know who's been along there seemed to enjoy themselves and come away impressed. But you don't need to go through the Learning Zone to understand that the Dome was tainted from the outset by politics. Everyone who dislikes this government was determined to hate the Dome with or without ever going there. And just as you could gauge the movements of the sun and the stars at Stonehenge, you could measure the waxing and waning of the government's popularity by reaction to the Millennium Dome.

The trouble was that everyone knew the government really wanted you to go there. Nothing could be worse for attendance figures. For years Stonehenge was officially out of bounds and people were desperate to get in. Now the razor-wire fences have been taken away from Salisbury Plain and access is permitted. But they should hang on to that fencing and put it up around Greenwich. Tony Blair should go on record saying that we cannot have members of the public wandering all over this historical site – in fact the government should make it illegal to trespass on the Millennium Dome. Attendance figures would double overnight.

Who wrote the book of life?

26 June 2000

I was instinctively against the idea of GM crops until I heard that they've managed to isolate the gene that makes mangetout vaguely posh. Soon it will be possible to ask for mangetout in the greengrocer's without feeling a bit stupid.

What has already been achieved with vegetables will now be possible with humans. We could find the gene that makes people in restaurants pretend to actually taste the wine before they say, 'That's lovely, thank you.' The gene that makes us keep looking round at our new cars when we've just parked them. And of course the gene that makes us lose concentration when we read about the linear sequences of amino acids in the synthesis of proteins. Judging by some of the rubbish that has been written about DNA this week, the leap from vegetable to human is not such a great one. Pages and pages have been churned out by pompous leader writers hailing this incredible scientific breakthrough and using the word 'millennium' a lot. Why can't everyone just be honest about it; put their hands up and say, 'Sorry, I haven't the faintest bloody idea what these scientists are talking about, but they tell us it's important so I suppose we'd better take their word for it.' Most of us were completely baffled by Monday's breakthrough in genetic decoding.

'I thought they'd just closed down DNA?'

'No, that was C 'n' A, wasn't it?'

We are told that the Book of Life is the most complex sequence of letters ever written, though whoever said that never took *A Hundred Years of Solitude* on holiday.

'Let us be in no doubt about what we are witnessing today,' proclaimed Tony Blair. 'A revolution in science that far surpasses even the discovery of antibodies . . .'

I wish that instead of nodding wisely and trying to look moved, the journalists had asked him, 'So could you explain it a bit further please, Tony?'

'Er – well – erm . . . there's your chromosomes and er – genes and DNA and stuff . . . anyway must dash, nappies to change and all that.'

Bill Clinton wouldn't take questions either. His advisers were worried that journalists asking about DNA storing vital information might set him off denying having sex with Monica Lewinsky all over again.

'DNA on genes, you say? I could have sworn it was on her dress . . .'

Now the debate has quickly moved on to the predictable second stage – the ethical and moral debate. This discussion is as old as science itself. When the first caveman invented the wheel, an anxious discussion no doubt ensued as to what terrible uses this 'wheel' might be put to – a nightmare which finally became reality in the 1970s when the first Austin Allegro rolled off the production line. But you can't attack the pioneers for the social consequences of their work; Captain Cook discovered Australia but you can't blame him for *Neighbours*. If there are discoveries to be made then people will seek them out. Of course there are dangers. We must not have people being discriminated against because of their genetic inheritance – Carol Thatcher excepted. We cannot allow the insurance companies to demand genetic testing. They should continue to refuse to pay out to everyone on the same equal basis. The risks are not from science itself but, as always, from the way we have constructed our society. You don't have to have read the Book of Life to know that unless they are restrained some individuals will try to use this week's breakthrough to greatly increase their own wealth and power at the expense of others.

There may well be areas of human endeavour that are best left to the private sector, like cosmetic surgery and pizza deliveries. But the future of the world's health, the right to patent and profit from human genes, to ultimately redesign and alter our species is not something I would want to entrust to the good people who run the multinational drug companies. Yesterday's *Times* argues that without the profit motive the next stage of scientific development would happen more slowly. As if we are all impatiently sitting around saying, 'Come on, boffins! The rate of scientific change at the moment is nowhere near fast enough!'

We have to take control of what is happening. How is it that we are able to decode the entire genetic make-up of human beings – something it would take one person fifty years to type out (or longer if they had to keep stopping to overrule their Spellcheck) and yet we are already admitting defeat at the comparatively minor challenge of regulating and legislating to ensure all this work is put to the best use? The prize of conquering susceptibility to so many diseases is too precious to surrender to the inherently discriminatory free market. This information belongs to us all – our politicians need to work as fast as our scientists to make sure it stays that way. And while we are at it, we need to find and isolate the gene that means some people are motivated only by the lure of enormous personal wealth. A billion dollars for the first one who finds it.

No left turn ahead

5 July 2000

We live in the Age of Irony. It is apparently all right to make sexist jokes if you do it ironically; it's fine to do gags about gays if it's done with a knowing wink. But now I've suddenly realized that we are living through the biggest satirical wind-up of all. This government is being *ironically* right wing. All this reactionary talk about single mothers and asylum seekers and on-the-spot fines – it's OK; it's all ironic. The Labour government's style says, 'Yeah, yeah, obviously we're in favour of all that old equality and redistribution of wealth stuff; but we've come through all that and this is the next stage.' They're not New Labour but Post-Modern Labour.

This weekend the cabinet, Labour MPs, MEPs and trades unions will all descend on Exeter University to thrash out the policies that will form Labour's next manifesto. I hope all those ministers enjoy Exeter University as much as I did when I was there, though it's hard to imagine John Prescott and Margaret Beckett skinny-dipping in the river Exe and then getting out of their heads on magic mushrooms. If, as looks likely,

Labour wins the election then who knows, this week-end could end up being a turning point in the history of this administration. Because hundreds of Labour MPs will demand that Labour's second term is more radical than the first and Tony Blair will enthusiastically endorse a socialist manifesto for the next general election. I can see it all now. Or perhaps those magic mushrooms take longer to wear off than I thought.

Three years ago when Labour finally came to power we all felt like Nelson Mandela must have done after he was released. An enormous euphoria that quickly disappeared when he realized that now he had to live with Winnie. Tony Blair's first term was all about making people believe that Labour could look like a government. Unfortunately, because the governments of the previous eighteen years had been full of deranged right-wing psychopaths, Labour's task occasionally involved postures and policies that would have made Norman Tebbit blush. Now when Jack Straw gets a taxi, the cabbie ends up saying, 'Well I wouldn't go that far, I mean I think some of them are genuine refugees and, er, live and let live and all that . . .'

But Labour's mission has been accomplished. They look comfortable with the reins of power and, for the first time in Labour's history, a full second term looks within its grasp. This was arguably Tony Blair's top priority for his first period of office and maybe for some of those heading down to Devon this would be enough for the second. In which case the next manifesto will read, 'If elected, Labour will seek to be elected again. Because without power, Labour can never achieve its goal of being in power, and if we fail in this ambition we believe the voters will throw us out of office. No, hang on, will have already thrown us out of office.'

The top brass gathering at Exeter University are the luckiest Labour Party members ever. They have the greatest ever majority. They look set to be the first ever Labour government to win a full second term. And to cap it all, the Student Union building has two pool tables and sells cheap cider. Are they going to let the next election pass by without seizing this chance to win with a manifesto that would really attack the inequalities in this country? Will they be satisfied with more of the same? In years to come, will they sit their grandchildren on their knee and say, 'Aye, the party had never been stronger and the Tories had never been weaker and oooh, you should have seen what we did with all that power! Why, the ordinary folk were dancing in the street when we granted independence to the Bank of England!'

After a hard day's debating, on Saturday evening the ministers and MPs will all sit down to a slap-up meal. Dinner will consist of a couple of eggs, still in their shells, rolling around on the plate. It's what's known as a New Labour omelette. Labour were cautious with their last manifesto, which is kind of understandable when they had failed to win a workable majority for seven elections in a row. But the time has come to break some eggs. We cannot reach the end of a second Labour term with the health service still underfunded, with a failing education system, with a growing underclass and high unemployment. For once in our lifetime Labour can win on a radical programme. Historic opportunities such as the next election are as rare in politics as witty Ulster Unionists.

The Prime Minister told us he wants to think the unthinkable and rewrite the rule book, so how about this for a radical idea: a Labour government that moved to the left once it was in office. That really would be a completely New Labour.

Missile impossible, part two

12 July 2000

It has been a difficult few days for Lieutenant General Ronald Kadish, director of America's Ballistic Missile Defence Organization. At the weekend he invited a load of friends over to show them his new Intercontinental Missile Defence Shield and – isn't it always the way? – the bloody thing didn't work. A Minuteman II was fired from Southern California. Another missile was fired from 4,500 miles away in the middle of the Pacific Ocean to intercept the oncoming warhead but apparently the necessary electronic signal was not received at the correct time or something. That'll teach him not to read the manual beforehand.

It all happened so quickly; suddenly the missile was careering off target, billions of dollars of military hardware was heading in the wrong direction at 16,000 mph and Ronald was frantically skimming through the chapter entitled 'Care of your Minuteman missile system'. Then his wife had a better idea: 'Quick, phone the helpline!' And while the President was demanding to know what was going on, the poor general was stuck listening to a recorded message that said, 'Thank you for calling the ICBM helpline. If you wish to purchase other Minuteman missile systems, press 1. If you are phoning about our direct debit payment plan, press 2. If your intercontinental missile has malfunctioned and is hurtling towards Southern California, press 3 and hold for an operator.' And then they played a tinny version of 'Bolero' as the general watched a hundred billion dollars going up in smoke.

It was the most expensive firework display of all time but, like our own 'River of Fire', it was a bit of a disappointment. They all went 'ooohhh' but there was no 'aaahhh'. Not even Mrs Kadish's delicious mulled wine and the packet of sparklers could offer much consolation. Hundreds of people covered their eyes in embarrassed disbelief. It was like the premiere of John Travolta's *Battlefield Earth* all over again.

This is not the first time America's missile systems have missed their target. During the Gulf War, a great deal was made of the Patriot missiles' ability to knock out the oncoming Scuds. The Patriots were declared a huge success because out of 22 Scuds fired, 21 were intercepted. But this is where the US military use a different language to the rest of us, because as everyone remembers lots of Scuds got through and caused enormous damage. So a Pentagon spokesman was eventually forced to explain (as if we were all really slow and stupid) that when they said 'intercepted' they meant that the path of the Patriot crossed the path of the Scud, *though not necessarily at the same time*. So 'intercepted' means 'missed'. He was later heard on the phone saying, 'Darling, I'm going to be late home tonight because I've intercepted my train.'

If modern defence strategists had planned the D-Day landings, the Allied forces would have found themselves wading ashore at Torremolinos. Despite the

United States spending $122 billion on missile defence systems, they have yet to develop anything which actually defends anyone against missiles. Perhaps I'm being over-picky, but you would have thought that this wasn't really good enough. And even though it is no longer clear who is going to declare war on the world's only superpower, the man who may well be the next president, George W. Bush, remains a great supporter of the Star Wars project. America may have token enemies like Iraq and Libya but they're no more likely to launch intercontinental missile attacks than Darth Vader himself. Instead of spending these unfeasibly large amounts of money on the unworkable National Defence Shield, the Pentagon might as well buy a Super Soaker XP 2000 (slogan, 'Wetter is Better'). Admittedly it is unlikely that this water pistol would actually intercept any incoming nuclear missiles but it's got about the same chance as anything else they've tried so far while having the advantage of being considerably cheaper. Even if the Pentagon eventually upgraded to the more expensive Super Soaker Monster XL with multiple nozzles and extra large reservoir, they'd still save a fortune.

But of course, when it comes to military spending the cash is always available. They could launch an aircraft carrier that didn't float and they'd still get the funding to build another one. Why is it that enormous amounts of taxpayers' money are always available for defence spending and yet if it is education or health we always have to help make up the shortfall ourselves? You don't get soldiers' wives organizing summer fetes to raise money for much-needed nuclear warheads. 'Tank rides round the square 50p.' 'Throw a wet sponge at the general – three goes for a pound.' I suppose the sponge would only fly off in the wrong direction and land on the napalm barbecue. If the smart bombs were that smart they would decommission themselves and redirect the much-needed funding towards health, education and overseas aid. Because it wasn't the missile that missed the real target this week. It was all that money that went up in smoke with it.

New balls please

19 July 2000

This week English sports fans witnessed a sight even grimmer than the acrylic jumpers on *A Question of Sport*. England's Davis Cup team lost to Ecuador, a country whose tennis facilities are so restricted that their training schedule was limited to playing swing-ball in the coach's back garden. You could tell they'd been underfunded because every time the ballboys threw them another tennis ball they got out a marker pen and scrawled their initials on it. Wimbledon has now become a consistent source of embarrassment for the British. When the sun is out our best players get beaten by unseeded teenagers and when it's raining Cliff Richard stands up and sings 'Living Doll' in front of the world's media.

This latest sporting humiliation comes after England's dismal showing in Euro 2000 and years of failure in cricket, rugby and just about every sport that has ever been devised. Our golfers consistently come a poor second and then blame the American golf courses for their lack of little windmills and helter-skelters. Our rallycross team spent four hours in a lay-by arguing with the AA about their expired membership. Our Olympic orienteering team couldn't find the stadium. Our ladies' swimming champion kept tutting because the German in the next lane was splashing too much and wetting her hair. When it comes to picking the world's great sporting nations, Britain is the fat kid with asthma left standing against the wall.

There are all sorts of reasons why we underachieve on the sports field. If you read the *Daily Telegraph* you will discover that it's all down to those loony lefty councils who banned competitive sport and forced our most promising athletes to channel their energies into lesbian peace workshops. But obviously it is in fact all the fault of the Conservatives, who presided over the selling off of school playing fields, under-investment in education and a failure to provide the sort of training facilities that are available in more successful sporting countries like, er, Ecuador.

Perhaps there is something in our national character that makes us not want to appear too pushy. When two British football players are going for the same ball, is there a nagging doubt at the back of our minds that we ought to be saying, 'Oh, I'm so sorry – no, no, after you'? Our sportsmen and women are supposed to provide us with role models – to reflect Britain's international status and importance in the world. And in consistently underachieving and disappointing us they have been doing a fantastic job. What foreign athletes fail to understand is that it is not winning but losing dismally that counts.

When I was at school, the people like myself who were not very good at sport adopted a sneering contempt for anything vaguely athletic, so that we could pretend that it was simply beneath us. This is the only way for England to salvage any dignity from the next world cup. The Neville brothers should hang around behind the changing rooms smoking, spitting and occasionally flicking their ties at all the better players as they turn up.

'Oi, Zidane, you goody-goody! You don't actually *like* games, do you? Ugh – look, he's putting shorts on, the big nancy.'

Then when the referee demands that the English players get changed, they can wave a tatty forged note from their mum under his nose and claim, 'I'm excused games, I've got a verruca.' Some of our most revered sportsmen already behave like this; I remember seeing Paul Gascoigne staggering around with a can of lager in one hand and a kebab in the other. I wasn't surprised when he was taken off at half time.

There was of course a brief period in history when Britain was unbeatable on the playing field, but we achieved this with the rather crafty trick of inventing all the sports ourselves to give us a head start. This has to be the way forward once again. We should examine what it is we are good at, develop these pastimes into fully fledged sports and then dominate them for a few decades. For example, it's all very well throwing a shot-put a long way, but no one can throw a plastic chair from a Belgian café as far as an England soccer fan. Soon we will hear Des Lynam promising a great evening of sporting action: 'Tonight on ITV, high-lights of last night's thrilling clash between the Belgian water cannon and Fat Degsy from Millwall. We have a chance to see Britain's gold medal hopefuls in the synchronized rioting and then it's over to court number one for the Police v Innocent Deported Soccer Fan.'

All these new events will be organized into a special international tournament at which Britain can show-case the sports that will dominate the new century. It is our chance to be first once more. Except, as they say on *A Question of Sport*, 'What happened next?' It's obvious of course – at the last moment our bid to host the games will be beaten by bloody Ecuador.

School's out for summer (and most of autumn too)

26 July 2000

The current parliamentary term ends this Friday. MPs will be allowed to bring in games for the last day, and will be dropped off at the gate with all sorts of cards and presents for Mrs Speaker. Then they'll fly off for a few weeks' lying in the sun to get away from all those months of lying in the *Sun*. Gordon Brown has been down to W.H. Smith to choose his summer reads. There's nothing better than stretching out on the beach with a copy of *Whither Global Economics?* Tony Blair is constantly setting himself tougher targets, so this summer he'll be fathering triplets and rescuing an entire team of drowning synchronized swimmers. John Prescott will make do with a week at Blackpool but will be the only person at the funfair to insist on two dodgem cars. William Hague and Ffion will spend the summer on their own and far away from the crowds as they undertake another Meet the People Tour of Britain. Likewise for Conservative shadow ministers like Gary Streeter and Edward Garnier it will be a relief just to enjoy a few weeks out of the limelight.

But then it's straight back to work as MPs return to Westminster at the end of the summer on, er – 23 October.

It has been suggested that, when the rest of us take a fortnight off, fourteen weeks might be considered a little excessive. Obviously our politicians won't spend all their holidays staying in luxury hotels and drinking too much; there's the party conferences to fit in as well. But it's hard to sympathize with successive governments complaining that they cannot bring in all the measures they would like due to a lack of parliamentary time when one quarter of the year is used up with the summer holidays alone. The government remind me of those students who used to get up at two o'clock in the afternoon and say, 'When am I supposed to fit in writing this essay?'

The length of the summer recess is just one of the ridiculous anachronisms that alienate ordinary voters and increase cynicism and antipathy towards those who govern us. Like the anti-social hours and the myriad of obscure parliamentary conventions, it gives the impression that our politicians are from a different planet to the rest of us, which apart from anything else is unfair on the MPs, John Redwood excepted.

Many of these traditions go back hundreds of years; their origins lost in the mists of time, like Edward Heath's grudges. But that doesn't make them sacrosanct, and so when this government was elected it resolved to bring things forward a couple of centuries to somewhere in the mid-1800s. Sadly, parliamentary convention dictates that the new Modernization Committee is allowed to meet only once a year on Michaelmas Eve, and then only if the member for Old Sarum is wearing a hat. But they have managed to put an end to late night sitting despite fierce Tory opposition; for some reason MPs like Ann Widdecombe and Michael Howard prefer to come out at night. And experimental morning sittings have now been tried and deemed a great success; the chamber was just as empty before lunch as it usually is the rest of the time.

Another improvement has been Prime Minister's Questions. For no better reason than tradition, members could only put the PM on the spot with a supplementary question, so they always had to precede their interrogation with an enquiry about his engagements that day. This convention was done away with to prevent Tony Blair finally losing patience in the way that any ordinary member of the public would. 'Are you completely deaf or wot? You are the sixth bloody person in a row to ask me my engagements for the day. Why don't you try listening for a change, you stupid cloth-eared bastard!'

But the problem is that the modernization of Parliament has only been nibbling at the edges. Instead of coming back in late October, the MPs should never come back at all. In place of a Parliament in Westminster, the MPs should meet in cyberspace; we should have a virtual House of Commons to represent our virtual democracy. Like a video conference call, debates could be carried out without MPs ever having to leave their constituencies. It would be the Internet equivalent of a late night radio phone-in, though the quality of debates would probably not be quite that liberal and sophisticated.

Of course Parliament will never radically change its ways, because the mystique and conventions are all part of a protective shield. The day we understand everything that is being said there will be the day we realize that the policies don't make any sense either. So nod and smile when politicians say that Parliament really has to close for three months. The truth is we allow our politicians to have such long holidays for the same reason that we put our senile old relatives into homes. It's not for their benefit, it's just to give the rest of us a break.

Clone-age man

2 August 2000

This week the government gave the go-ahead for the cloning of human embryos. To illustrate this story the newspapers published the magnified image of a fertilized cell, prompting a flurry of calls from Downing Street to check that it wasn't an intrusively early photo of Leo Blair. The decision was announced by science minister Lord Sainsbury, and after a quick glance over the press release, journalists carelessly dashed off the surprising story 'Sainsbury's to make human embryos available'.

This was an announcement that has been coming ever since the birth of Dolly the Sheep. Dolly, as the first sheep clone, caused a media sensation a few years back, but has since rather failed to keep hold of the public's attention. She's just sacked her publicity manager and is planning a relaunch once she gets out of the Betty Ford Clinic. As soon as the concept of cloning human embryos was given the green light, the church-going conservatives started foaming at the mouth, while the producers of the *Moral Maze* simply passed out with the excitement.

Opponents of these developments warn of a nightmare world in which whole groups of people would be exactly the same. It's almost impossible to imagine – benches of Conservative MPs where they are all identical merchant bankers in their forties. WI meetings where the women are indistinguishable and hold exactly the same views. Squaddies who all have the same physique, tattoos and moustaches. It doesn't bear thinking about. 'God in his wisdom made each of us totally unique,' said every single religious leader last week.

In the 1970s film *The Boys from Brazil*, it transpires that Nazi scientists have cloned a whole batch of young Adolf Hitlers whom they're grooming to become the new führers to take over the entire world or, failing that, the Lambeth Parking Permits office. The film was a sombre warning as to how science can go badly wrong, causing people to talk in unconvincing German accents and grow bizarre wonky moustaches. But who else might be recreated now that this technology is genuinely available? 'The Girls from Grantham' has a chilling ring to it. Perhaps in our lifetime we will be able to visit a historical theme park where cloned figures from history will show us round the attractions. 'Welcome to the Gettysburg Experience!' the clone of Abe Lincoln will say. 'No photos please; if you want any souvenirs just ask Genghis Khan there in our gift shop.' Perhaps Marilyn Monroe will be on the till, if she's not locked in the storeroom with the clone of John F. Kennedy.

Of course any talk of the imminent cloning of humans to follow in the footsteps of Dolly the Sheep is scaremongering, and the cloning of humans remains illegal. The biologists making these breakthroughs are motivated only by a desire to save human lives. Many of them feel they have been misrepresented in the media, though when I phoned one of them about this, his assistant Igor said the master was busy up on the roof with the lightning conductor. Their great break-through was apparently the discovery of stem cells. These are the cells that give chemical messages to other cells telling them to develop into a particular type of tissue. This is less reliable with male cells as they always forget to pass on the message. Some cells turn into bone, some cells turn into brain; the unlucky ones turn into that bit of skin on your Adam's apple that you always cut when you're shaving. Soon biologists hope to be able to inject the appropriate cells to help the body produce its own tissue of exactly the desired type. This has the potential to help everyone from diabetics to people with damaged internal organs. Even new limbs could be grown, although it may be too late to help the current England football team.

The scientists are using fertilized cells that would perish anyway to help people who are already alive. An embryo is not a foetus, which is not a baby. The moment of fertilization is just one milestone in the creation of human life; it is one of the stages in a long and gradual development to that joyful moment when a baby pops out and keeps you awake for two years. The embryos used in this research are less than a week old. Most couples will have lost fertilized cells without even knowing it before one finally attached itself to the wall of the womb and made its host start bursting into tears and eating pickled onions and ice cream. The people who find the whole idea of cloning human embryos distasteful would probably prefer to put Alzheimer's and cancer to the back of their minds as well. This is a huge leap forward and the church's reaction was depressing in its predictability. Now I understand why they were always against the cloning of Dolly. We don't need any more sheep when we already have the religious right bleating the same old objections.

The Broadcasting House make-over show

8 August 2000

Later this month Greg Dyke will be making a major speech on the future of the BBC at the Edinburgh International Television Festival. Given the usual manic atmosphere of the Edinburgh Festival all he needs to do is open his speech with a couple of good gags and he'll land himself a job presenting a new panel show on Channel 5. The new Director General's plans include two new BBC channels to supplement BBC1 and BBC2. After a long and expensive consultancy by media strategists it has finally been decided that these channels will be named BBC3 and BBC4. They will incorporate BBC Choice (which most of us are unable to choose) and BBC Knowledge (which no one knows about), forming two exciting new specialized youth and culture channels.

Why is it that we have to have all programmes of a certain type bundled together on theme nights or on designated channels? If I ever have a programme controller to dinner I'm going to announce, 'It's pudding night at John's house! Tonight's sumptuous four-course meal starts off with rhubarb crumble and custard. Then the main course, apple pie and cream – and that's followed by jam roly-poly and then bread and butter pudding to finish off.'

If you read the BBC's original charter you will see that it states the corporation has a duty 'to provide a properly balanced service consisting of a wide range of subject matter'. It goes on to say, 'Oh, and the BBC must also give Noel Edmonds a job for life,' though many suspect that this second bit was scrawled in later by a bearded man in a Mr Blobby costume. If the BBC goes down the road of specialized channels it will be in danger of losing the universal appeal that justifies the licence fee. We don't need one channel for every type of programme, as BBC News 24 has clearly proved. It's still not clear whether the '24' refers to hours broadcast, millions spent or total viewers.

The debate on the future of broadcasting is hotting up because this autumn the government will be publishing a white paper on the future of communications. Submissions have been made by everyone who is concerned about the future of quality television and Denise van Outen as well. All the BBC top executives were invited to give their thoughts, but most failed to read the letter because it was not headed 'Proposal for new celebrity gardening quiz hosted by Carol Vorderman'. Meanwhile members of the Commons select committee on broadcasting have been spending a lot of time seeing how the BBC works at close hand; for example, that was actually Gerald Kaufman inside the Tinky-Winky costume. One of the most controversial proposals being mooted by the government was the abolition of the BBC Board of Governors. This has now been shelved, though it's been suggested that the board should contain more people with direct experience of broadcasting. So out would go Baroness Young of Old Scone and in would come Charlie Dimmock, Sabrina the Teenage Witch and Wolf from Gladiators. Perhaps the answer would be to make the BBC Board of Governors justify themselves in terms of viewer appeal. Instead of meeting occasionally in a posh boardroom, they should all have to live together *Big Brother* style, locked inside one communal house with fly-on-the-wall cameras everywhere. Then as well as watching them discuss the future of public service broadcasting, we could also see who gets off with whom. 'Midnight on Day 3 and Baroness Hogg is tiptoeing across the corridor into Sir Christopher Bland's bedroom.' Viewers could then vote to have members thrown off the board if they didn't have enough tattoos or hadn't been helping with the washing up.

This approach has to be the way forward. Instead of spending lots of time and money changing the corporation, the process of reform itself should be made into a whole new raft of BBC programmes: *TV Regulators from Hell*, *Have I Got Select Committee Reports for You* and then finally *Ready Steady Murdoch!* That way the reinvention of the corporation will be left to the programme makers. This will culminate with BBC1's most ambitious make-over show yet. Carol Smillie will introduce two teams who will have just one weekend to transform the BBC from a bureaucratic old public service broadcaster into a dynamic modern communications provider using a bit of MDF and some stencils from Sainsbury's Homebase.

'OK, Red team – how are you getting on?'

'Well, we found this cellar full of archive sports programmes so we've knocked up a little channel called BBC Sports Gold.'

Perhaps this will be the big idea that Greg Dyke will unveil at the end of the month. Sadly, most of us will never find out. Even if his ideas are announced on his own network, his exciting vision of a popular and commercial BBC will be completely upstaged that weekend. It's the start of the football season and everyone will be watching the new *Match of the Day* over on ITV.

Hoarding the countryside

30 August 2000

Wordsworth's famous lines will soon need to be updated. 'I wandered lonely as a cloud That floats on high o'er vales and hills, When all at once I saw a huge billboard telling me to fcuk fashion.' The government have announced that advertising hoardings will now be permitted across most of the English countryside. Clearly the millions of visitors to our shores this summer were disappointed that the views across rural England were not obscured by enormous posters and so the government have stepped in to put this right. The abolition of controls originally brought in under the Attlee government follows intensive lobbying from that great lover of our natural heritage, the Outdoor Advertising Council. We are assured that we will still see beautiful scenery in the English countryside, but only as featured on the poster advertising the new Vauxhall Astra.

Now the chit-chat on *The Archers* will be changed for ever. 'Ooh, I've got terrible problems; no rain for a month, winter cabbage gone to seed and the focus group has revealed that the branding concept on my poster sites is failing to reach the targeted C2s.' Once farmers have got the advertising bug they might find other ways to get the message across. The sheep in *One Man and His Dog* won't just be herded into a pen; the collies will have to arrange them on the hillside to spell out 'You can't get better than a Kwik-Fit fitter'. Bright yellow mustard will be planted in such a formation that airline passengers flying overhead will see the Nike logo. Bored-looking cows will stand around in fields holding placards that say 'Massive golf sale – 100 yards on left'.

There are always more places in which commercials can be sited. Soon it won't be possible to have a hearing aid fitted that doesn't contain a tape that plays you the Shake and Vac jingle every five minutes. Or what about advertising during the Queen's Christmas message? 'At this festive time one's thoughts turn to the Commonwealth, but also to the fact that the World of Leather sale starts 9 a.m. Boxing Day at Lakeside Thurrock, Bluewater and Purley Way, Croydon.'

The trouble is of course that the more advertisements we are exposed to, the less effective they become. The first piece of junk mail was probably read quite carefully. John Prescott giving permission to increase the number of poster sites won't result in a corresponding rise in consumption of all the products advertised. We are still only going to buy one car each, John Prescott excepted. Advertising might persuade us to switch from Coca-Cola to Pepsi but it won't make us spend money we haven't got on things we don't want. However many times I watch the videos standing in the post office queue, I am still no nearer to buying myself a Stannah stairlift.

The proliferation in advertising is steadily eating away our quality of life and is becoming increasingly ineffective as it does so. And the idea that the financial crisis facing British farming can be solved with roadside posters is clearly ridiculous. The farmers in greatest need live in the remotest areas and have no sites of any value. It is true that the more accessible areas of rural England do receive thousands of visitors every year but it is precisely because they are unspoilt. The act of erecting poster sites will in itself help make the sites valueless. Somehow I can't imagine myself driving down to Somerset to look at the view of Chris Eubank sipping a mug of Nescafé.

The way forward is to combine two countryside problems to create an overall solution. While it is banning fox-hunting the government should add an amendment legalizing the hunting of advertising executives. Yuppie account handlers will be strolling around the countryside checking out their new advertising hoardings when suddenly the horn will sound and packs of hounds will descend upon them snapping at their Armani suits as red-coated huntsmen gallop across the fields in pursuit. It will become one of the beautiful traditional sights of the English countryside. It's a shame that the billboards will prevent anyone from actually seeing it.

NB The government later reversed their policy on this issue, but were only just dissuaded from putting posters up all over Dartmoor to advertise the fact.

Chris Woodhead, he doesn't know his three Rs from his elbow

5 September 2000

Every summer the scene is the same. The Chief Inspector of Schools nervously waits for the exam results. The letter lands on the doormat. His parents stand over him as he opens the envelope.

'Well, dear, what does it say?'

'Oh no!' says Chris, completely mortified. '200,000 grade As. The best results ever,' and he bursts into tears of disappointment.

'Never mind, dear. Maybe some of them could do retakes and try and get lower grades.' But it's too late. Chris has already run up to his room, slammed the door and put on Radiohead at full volume.

It strikes me as completely bizarre that our Chief Inspector of Schools is concerned that the number of grade As at advanced level is too high. 'An education system must involve failure,' he said on Monday. 'Life involves failure.' Life also involves illness and injustice, but that doesn't mean we should give all our kids malaria and put them in prison for the Great Train Robbery. Perhaps Chris Woodhead ought to be appointed manager of the England football team. 'I am delighted with the way the lads threw away a two–nil lead over Portugal. Fingers crossed, we now have every prospect of being knocked out of Euro 2000 in the first stage.'

The subtext of his ' "A" levels are too easy' message is 'Ooh, it were harder in our day'. Because these young kids today, they don't know they're born. When I were a lad, you couldn't just point a remote control at the telly, you had to get off the sofa, walk all the way across the room and press a button next to the screen. Aye, and you couldn't just listen to an album all the way through, no, you had to get up and turn it over. Boy, did we have it tough.

'A' level results are higher because students and teachers are doing better. Mightn't it be more appropriate to give some credit where it is due, instead of undermining the achievement of everyone involved? More and more athletes are able to run the four-minute mile, but we don't say, 'Yes, well, miles are much shorter than they used to be.' I never got a grade A in any exam I took; I even managed an 'unclassified' in my metalwork 'O' level after the examiners failed to understand the abstract sculpture that was my interpretation of a small engineering project. What Chris Woodhead is saying is that we need more results like this. So English students should be urged to describe the poetry of Shakespeare based on their readings of Brodie's Notes. History students should be encouraged to revise only half of the syllabus, so they have to begin 'A' level essays by saying, 'When examining the reasons for the repeal of the Corn Laws it is interesting to look at the causes of the American revolution . . .'

The alternative of making 'A' levels harder would be grossly unfair to anyone who ended up failing an exam which they would have passed a few years earlier. They would be competing for the same jobs as slightly older candidates who were no brighter but seemed to have better qualifications. Maybe the solution is to follow the Scottish example and just lose the exam results altogether.

The real problem with our education system is the same as it always was. School involves spending years learning stuff we never use again. To get my maths 'O' level, for example, I spent two years grappling with the most impossible mathematical problem of all time: 'What is the point of slide rules?' Logarithms, quadratic equations, matrices; I eventually understood all of them, but while a cheap pocket calculator was burning a hole in my pocket I failed to solve the impossible mathematical conundrum of 'Slide rules, why?' And so now, instead of teaching our children about oxbow lakes and the Whig hegemony, we should be teaching them stuff they can use when they get to our age. How to get peppercorns into the pepper grinder, for example. 'A' level eating spaghetti in a white shirt. GCSE staying awake during Nationwide Football League Review. How to say 'No thank you' to squeegee merchants in such a way that they will take any notice. How to open a door for someone which opens away from you. There are hundreds of skills that most of us still haven't mastered.

And just as our education should better prepare us for adulthood, so the Ofsted regime of regular inspection should be extended to our life after school. When Trevor McDonald reads out the evening news, there should be someone sitting behind him, tutting slightly and making notes whenever he mispronounces *Slobadon Milosovech*. When flight attendants have finished giving the safety instructions before take-off, they should be told that they were failing to engage the passengers in an exciting and challenging way. Even Chris Woodhead should not be immune. An inspector from 'Of-ofsted' should observe him for a week or so and if he was deemed to be failing then it should be reported to the Chief Inspector of Schools. And after his comments this week, surely he'd have to close himself down.

Political football

13 September 2000

Tony Blair and Gerhard Schröder had high-level talks about the problem of football transfers last week. This was, of course, the official spin to cover up the embarrassing outburst which always happens when English people start arguing with the Germans about football; namely that Tony Blair drank too much lager and stood on the table singing, 'Two world wars and one world cup, doo-dah, doo-dah!'

With every politician finding it necessary to have an interest in the sport, football is in danger of becoming, well, a political football. Soon William Hague will be claiming he's always loved soccer-ball, that when he wasn't downing fourteen pints he was on the terraces supporting Liverpool United. And just to show that he's still in touch and is concerned about standards, he'll suggest the introduction of league tables for football clubs.

The latest story to concern our MPs is the impending abolition of transfer fees, which threatens to have very serious consequences for Britain's smaller clubs. This issue is like those maps of flooded Britain after the polar ice cap has melted. Your eye goes straight to the bit where you live; you see that your house will still be on dry land and then you stop worrying about it. As a Fulham supporter I used to worry about the status of poor clubs like Fulham, but now I can't help but be pleased when every change benefits the rich clubs like Fulham. Most people support big clubs and only pay lip service to the wonderful work done by the likes of Brighton and Hove Albion. With the outcome of the next election being decided in places like Brighton, it's important that the government doesn't upset all the football fans who live in such towns and acts in the interest of their favourite team; namely Manchester United.

The issue is that the system by which players are transferred from one club to another is apparently in breach of EU employment law. We are told that workers are not sold from one company to the next in any other area of commerce; you don't get labourers being sold from one building firm to another, say the critics. But of course footballers are not like builders. I have never seen Ryan Giggs beat three defenders and then suddenly leave the ball in the middle of the goal mouth to go and play in another game over the other side of town.

Football is more than just a business in which brands are competing in the market place. You don't get thousands of Pepsi and Coke drinkers chanting abuse at each other: 'You've got no teeth any moooore!' Fathers don't say to their sons, 'I'm taking you to Sainsbury's on Saturday, son, because this family has shopped at Sainsbury's for three generations.'

Maybe the way forward is not for football to become more like other businesses, but for the world of commerce and politics to become more like football. Important economic and political issues should not be settled by Commons divisions or shareholders' meetings but by penalty shoot-outs. At last the issue of monetary union would get the attention it deserves. 'And you join us here at Old Trafford at a crucial moment in our economic history where Britain's adoption of the euro is about to be decided on penalties. The very existence of the pound now depends on the goalkeeping skills of young William Hague as Peter Mandelson bravely steps on to the spot for the first kick.'

And like Arsene Wenger or Gerard Houlier, Blair should be able to sign the best politicians from Europe and the rest of the world. Then Andrew Marr could stand outside Downing Street in a sheepskin coat with a couple of young fans waving at the camera behind him as he brings us exciting news of the latest signing: 'Joining the cabinet this week, Blair's record £5 million signing from the French government, Lionel Jospin, who'll be making his debut today as Minister for Defence.' English front-bench politicians like Francis Maude or Peter Ainsworth who have failed to make their mark in the top flight over here could be sold to foreign parliaments and would find their natural level by joining the opposition in Cyprus or Slovakia.

Perhaps these were the changes discussed last week by Tony Blair and Gerhard Schröder. But somehow you get the feeling that whenever politicians kick around the subject of football it's in the hope that some of the popularity of the beautiful game will rub off on them. Any way that you look at the figures, more people tune in to Sky Sports 2 than the Parliament Channel.

So maybe it's for the best that the cultures of politics and football do not grow any closer. Otherwise we might get to a situation where politicians were only motivated by money, where winning was all that mattered and where members of the House of Commons started to behave like some sort of unruly rabble, jeering and shouting abuse at supporters of the other side. And that would be too awful to imagine.

Tories ahead in polls shock!

20 September 2000

History is full of examples of politicians who were dismissively mocked before they came to power. Richard Nixon, Ronald Reagan, Margaret Thatcher . . . Nobody ever thought Ethelred would make it to king. 'He'll never get his act together,' they said. And suddenly the political joke who leads today's Conservative Party isn't so funny any more. While the petrol stations were empty, William Hague was the only person collecting premier points. The party that want to keep us out of monetary union are ahead in the polls for the first time since the day they blew £15 billion trying to keep us in.

Finally we are forced to give some real consideration as to what a Hague government would be like. For a start government policy would not be formulated by think tanks or cabinet committees, but by the demands of angry callers to late night radio phone-ins. 'You're listening to Prime Minister William Hague, taking your calls through to midnight here on Radio Bigot FM. And the next caller is Brian on line three; what can I do for you, Brian?'

'Well Prime Minister, I went to the doctor's, and he was an Indian bloke, right, and he used all these foreign words like gastro-enteritis and endoscopy and what I'm saying is if they can't talk proper, they should be made to have English lessons.'

'OK, Brian, you've got your request – though I'm afraid all the teachers are tied up at the moment learning how to teach kids to hate homosexuals.'

People used to laugh at the Tory leader because he was a bit of a train-spotter, but he's worse than that, he's a bandwagon spotter. Hague is dispensing with the Tories' battle-bus and in the next election he'll travel round the country by jumping from one bandwagon to the next. If the *Daily Mail* called for a return to burning witches, he'd be out there collecting firewood.

In Hague's first hundred days all the progress that we already take for granted would be done away with. The literacy and numeracy hours would be replaced by Heritage Hour in which children learned that Germany is a country that we beat in World War Two and that the British Empire was very big. The Right to Roam would be replaced with the Right to Shout 'Get orf my land!' and the ending of the ban on land-mines would encourage landowners to enforce this as vigorously as they liked.

Under a Hague government, the tobacco companies would encourage smokers to picket corner shops to protest at the high cost of twenty Silk Cut. Hague would agree with them and cut the tax. Then winos would blockade the off-licences demanding a reduc-tion in the price of Special Brew. Hague would agree with them and cut the tax. Since he's already promised to cut income tax *and* public spending as well, he'll need all the alcohol he can get as he despairs of the mess he's got himself into. Anyone who doesn't believe that Hague ever drank fourteen pints hasn't looked at the sums in this month's Conservative pre-manifesto.

If Hague actually came to power, Britain wouldn't just grind to the temporary standstill that his supporters engineered last week; it would roll rapidly backwards into the chaos of economic mismanagement, mass unemployment and European isolation, all topped off with a sprinkling of pernicious saloon-bar bigotry. Pensioners would lose the winter fuel allowance and their free TV licences so they'd have to burn their tellies to keep warm. Our children would have to endure the twin burden of cuts in school spending and having Ann Widdecombe as a role model.

A Tory government is once again a genuine prospect that we have an urgent duty to prevent. So now is the time for everyone on the left to focus on returning a Labour government next year. To all the people who supported Ken Livingstone, all the people who backed Labour in opposition but would rather snipe from the sidelines than be tainted by support; all the people who vote Liberal, Green or Socialist Labour, the time for such luxuries is now over. Close your eyes and imagine William Hague waving on the steps of Downing Street and then remember how impossible it is to shift the Tories once they are in power. Remember, next time round not even a revolution would get them out. Because who's going to start throwing petrol bombs at 58p a litre?

Political exhibitionists

26 September 2000

Wherever great political parties come together, eager businesses large and small will flock round and set out their stalls as if taking part in some enormous corporate car-boot sale. A political conference without an exhibition centre would be like a leader's speech without a standing ovation – it's just against the laws of science. It has always been this way; if you look carefully at footage of the Nuremberg rallies you can see people wandering around at the back, browsing at the stand promoting timeshare apartments in Stalingrad.

In the old days of Labour Party conferences, the stalls were more in keeping with Labour's lowly status in seemingly permanent exile from the corridors of power. You could wander around and buy a packet of Nicaraguan coffee and a badge that said, 'Nuclear power? No thanks!' in a choice of thirty-seven different languages and it sounded just as wet in all of them. But now it is business-friendly New Labour and the wobbly trestle tables have given way to high-tech presentations aimed to persuade us of the merits of

201

Internet banking or digital television. 'Hello, have you thought of the opportunities for your business in switching to intel-wap-34zs integrated software?' says the keen young rep, handing out a leaflet to the bemused delegate from the National Union of Miners. Of course there are still a few stands hired out by charities or pressure groups, but every year the stalls representing persecuted minorities or endangered species are pushed further to the brink of extinction by the huge brash stalls from the multinationals.

Cynics cite the party's willingness to invite the capitalists into their parlour as further proof of Labour's abandonment of its socialist principles, and most years there is a minor scandal when it's revealed that there's a stall promoting an Iraqi arms dealer or some private health company selling internal organs stolen from Brazilian peasants. For some New Labour MPs the exhibition area is like a red-light district for weakening lefties. They walk around trying to avert their eyes as stallholders call out to them, 'Hello, darlin', fancy getting into bed with big business?'

'No, no, I can't – I'm married to my socialist principles.'

'Go on, have some fun. Just a quick bit of online share dealing, no one would have to know . . .'

And he takes the leaflet with all the furtiveness of a man collecting the grubby cards stuck up inside a telephone box.

The stallholders seem to believe that once they have handed you a leaflet their mission is accomplished. The whole operation seems to be constructed on the wildly optimistic presumption that people do not receive enough junk mail in the course of their everyday lives and so will go out of their way actively to search out some more. 'Hello, would you like a chance to read more about Powergen?' says the young man handing you a glossy piece of paper as you rush past. Well, this is too exciting an opportunity to miss. 'A chance to read more about Powergen, you say? Well, I was halfway through the new Stephen King novel, but I'll put that to one side now that I've got the chance to read more about Powergen!' Obviously no one actually ever reads any of the bumph. The stallholders from British Nuclear Fuels ought to give out a leaflet that says, 'Just to let you know that all our power stations are going to explode on Thursday,' and see if anyone notices.

For delegates and journalists alike, the stalls are a place you wander round when you are bored, and incredibly they manage to leave you even more bored than you were when you sat in the hall listening to the speaker from Batley and Spen CLP advocating composite 27 on Nagorno-Karabach. But that is the whole purpose of the place. It's all an elaborate ploy designed to keep the delegates in their seats for the entire week. There are plenty of other ways that the Labour Party could use the exhibition halls to make money: install a temporary multi-screen cinema, organize a four-day beer festival or turn the whole place into an amusement arcade. But the trouble with all these ideas is that they would risk being too popular. We couldn't have Tony Blair speaking to an empty conference hall while all the delegates were gathered around the screen of the Alien Megadeath Videogame, trying to see if John Prescott could beat his all-time-high score blasting away the droids from the planet Krall.

So Labour happily takes lots and lots of money from all the capitalist businessmen who in turn are happy to pay it because they know they are reaching members of the party that holds political power. It's all rather flattering really – that these business people should imagine that we ordinary activists from the labour movement could have the slightest influence upon a Labour government. Somehow it's all the wrong way round; the people with access to those in power are lobbying the people without. So next year it's going to be a bit different; the Labour Party delegates will be the ones handing out the leaflets to all the businessmen. 'Hello there,' we'll say. 'Erm, next time Tony invites you to Downing Street for a business breakfast, is there any chance you could remind him about implementing socialism?'

Laboured conference

27 September 2000

The Labour Party was created a hundred years ago. It was formed on a Tuesday at three o'clock and at five past the first person resigned because Labour had moved too far to the right. Back in 1900 the conference itself was not much different to today's. Security was as tight as ever of course – police checked everyone entering the conference centre to make sure they had a big moustache and a hat. Keir Hardie gave a powerful speech and during the standing ovation Mrs Hardie came up on to the stage and, to the shock of delegates, they engaged in an intimate handshake. But sadly the whole event was knocked off the front page of *The Times* by lots of small advertisements for snuff and domestic servants.

Labour began the last century with virtually no representation and enters the new century with its largest ever majority. This is an amazing political achievement in one hundred years; it's just a shame that the first ninety-seven years were a bit patchy. The delegates in 1900 sought one goal above all other – to get Labour representation in the place where it mattered, in the House of Commons. But isn't it always the way – now that this ambition has been achieved and Labour totally dominate Westminster, we find those crafty capitalists have moved the goalposts and real power has shifted elsewhere.

Why else would Gordon Brown spend only a couple of days at Brighton before flying off to the IMF to lobby and speak at the conference that really mattered? Back at Labour's annual get-together, delegates continue debating the National Policy Forum and passing resolutions while the onward march of world capitalism makes nation states and their political parties increasingly irrelevant. Still, there's always the compensation of seeing Margaret Beckett singing, 'Yes sir, I can boogie' at the Emily's List Karaoke Night.

Our increasingly powerless political structures continue to operate in the same way as Keir Hardie's because we don't know any other way. That's not to say that big business doesn't need national governments; they've got to have someone to blame when the oil companies put the price of petrol through the roof and still haven't mended the car wash.

But what are we supposed to do now the rules have been changed? None of us goes into politics thinking we can change the world on our own. When special bins for dog mess were introduced on Clapham Common, I wrote to the council and suggested that another bin was needed on the patch of grass between the church and the library. The council officer responsible wrote back and said they agreed with me and an extra bin full of dog crap now stands as a monument to my own political influence. This is the only thing I can say I have definitely achieved in my twenty years as a political activist and I hope it brings great pleasure to all who use it. The trouble is I'd like to write to someone asking for the abolition of world poverty and injustice as well, but I'm just not sure which council department would be able to fix that for me.

The Labour MPs and delegates at Brighton all feel this same sense of frustration. Yes, we can achieve a lot with a Labour government but, in the grand scheme of the world economy, Labour MPs are just writing letters to their local council. Perhaps that is why the electorate are becoming so disillusioned – there are parts of the country where more people took part in the *Big Brother* phone vote than exercised their democratic right to elect their representative to the European Parliament.

What we need is an annual conference held by all the people who really run the world. 'Mr Speaker – although we have done very well to win power without ever winning any elections, this is no time for complacency. We must not rest until every rain-forest is chopped down, every twelve-year-old in Africa smokes sixty fags a day and every street corner has an abandoned McDonald's chocolate shake leaking across the pavement.' The delegates' hearts would be filled with pride at such lofty ambition.

And our elected politicians can stand outside the conference centre, waving their placards from behind the crash barrier, demanding to be listened to. Gordon Brown can shout, 'What do we want?' and Lionel Jospin can refuse to join in because he didn't shout in French. And the riot police will fire tear gas and Bill Clinton will show everyone how not to inhale.

We might not get back power overnight but neither did Labour's first conference. I'll start with a letter to the council and see what happens. A century is a long time in politics.

For you, William Hague – opportunism knocks!

4 October 2000

Since the advent of televised politics, no bald politician has ever won a British general election (with the exception of Mrs Thatcher of course, but she always kept her wig on for the cameras). When I told my brother I was writing about William Hague this week he said, 'That's easy – just put *bald-headed prat.*' This gut reaction probably sums up why many British voters will not vote for him at the next general election, but it's not Hague's lack of hair that is his problem, it's his lack of anything else. In an age when leaders need charisma, the Tories have chosen someone with 'char-isn't-ma'. He has stumbled on to the national stage like a nervous TV game show contestant, blinking under the glare of the spotlights as the host shouts, 'For you, William Hague – opportunism knocks!'

After a week of non-stop exposure which will climax with his leader's speech we can finally see what William Hague stands for, and the clear answer is nothing. At last – all the Don't Knows have a politician to stand up for what they believe. The only conviction you'll see in today's Tory Party will be when Jeffrey Archer gets sent to prison. Now we can really look forward to reading the Tories' manifesto. It will be full of blank spaces for people to scribble in whatever they fancy that particular week. 'The next Conservative government will be committed to being tough on . . . whatever's in the news.' It's not that Hague doesn't stick to his guns. He just waits for farmers to shoot young offenders and then sticks to theirs. He thinks that 'principles' is a shop where Ffion buys her dresses. During the fuel protest he said he wouldn't change policy today because of a protest yesterday. Technically he was as good as his word; he waited two days and then changed his policy. The promised cut in fuel duty was as shameless as it was uncosted, but this has since been followed up with lavish promises to top whatever Labour spends on pensions and the NHS. He's not saying, 'Labour aren't spending enough, here's what needs to be spent and this is how we'll raise it.' He's saying, 'If Labour promise the moon, we'll promise the moon and sixpence.'

The net effect of all these knee-jerk pledges is to reveal that when it comes to Conservative Party policy, William Hague is making it all up as he goes along. Like a teenager trying to impress his friends he is rashly making claims that will not stand any close scrutiny. The fifteen-year-old boy will boast that he's actually got pots of money and then he'll fantasize out loud about how he's going to spend it. If he gets really carried away he might even claim he drank fourteen pints as well. William Hague can promise whatever he wants because deep in his heart he knows he will never be in a position where he has to deliver it.

The only explanation I can make for William Hague's disastrous leadership is that he is secretly working for the other side. Like some East German spy, William Hague has actually been a Labour Party mole for the last twenty-five years. When he was a teenager he wandered into the Labour Party offices wanting to do whatever he could for the cause. 'Infiltrate the other side,' they said to him. 'Work your way up through the organization and do your utmost to damage the Conservatives from the inside.' He bought a blue tie and a Barbour raincoat and mingled unnoticed at Conservative bring-and-buy sales. He got up at the 1977 conference and did a crude parody of a Tory boy and to his astonishment he was applauded as having great promise. Finally he became an MP and started to do some real damage. When Norman Lamont was persuaded he should blow £15 billion in one day, who was his parliamentary private secretary? Why, Secret Agent William Hague of course. On Black Wednesday, Hague was the Chancellor's extreme right-hand man; when Lamont sent £15 billion up in smoke William was the one handing him the matches. Then Hague was given his own job as a minister. Here he served his beloved Labour Party beyond the call of duty; on the day that he ended his period of office as Minister of Wales, the Tories lost every single seat in Wales. 'Excellent work, comrade. Are you sure the capitalist dogs of the Conservative Party still suspect nothing?' 'No, comrade,' said William. 'In fact they are thinking of making me their leader . . .' and the sound of laughter could be heard echoing from the Labour Party headquarters. Perhaps this year he will use his conference speech to finally come clean. The trouble is that even if he did, nobody believes a word William Hague says any more.

Vous êtes dans l'armée maintenant

11 October 2000

This week it was proposed that the Royal Air Force would soon be engaging with the German armed services. Lady Thatcher must have thought it the best birthday present she could have wished for, until someone explained, 'No, Margaret, we mean British and German forces *on the same side.*'

The idea of a European Rapid Reaction Force has been gaining ground ever since the debacle of Kosovo, even though the words 'European' and 'rapid' do not normally sit that comfortably together. The reasoning is that with the Americans becoming less willing to finance military interventions, the European Union should have its own defence capability based in Brussels, to operate independently of NATO which is based in, er, Brussels. Then European military powers like Britain and France could combine to launch operations without having to seek the approval of the United States. Well, it worked so well in Suez, why not?

It is claimed that language would not be a problem – apparently European soldiers would find the British officer class just as incomprehensible as English squaddies always have done. But it's hard to imagine that in the heat of battle the odd second might not be lost. A British soldier would shout, 'Enemy fire! Take cover!' and then all the continental troops would get out their Petit Larousse English/French dictionaries and eventually smile and reply, 'Yes, I am liking the Beatles also.'

The British government is actually one of the leading advocates of the so-called European Defence Identity, although if it came to any major conflict it might be politically difficult for our leaders to appear too enthusiastic. We would probably opt out of the single European army until the conditions were right; Labour would insist that we would not join any war until the five military tests were met, while the Conservatives would say that Britain would not invade anywhere for the lifetime of the next Parliament. The outbreak of war would then be delayed while each of fifteen member states organized a referendum.

In fact the Conservatives want all military operations to remain under the command of NATO, by which of course they mean the Americans, since NATO is basically the United States plus the skinny kids who hover behind the legs of the biggest bully. The establishment of a European Defence Identity would at least bring military decisions back to the countries deploying the troops, but because the European Union does not have a single president or prime minister, any military intervention would have to be agreed by committee. Why on earth would fifteen different European heads of state want to use military force at once? They couldn't all have elections coming up at the same time. Any declaration of war would have to be organized like the Eurovision Song Contest: 'United Kingdom, Royaume Uni – can we have your vote please?' Gerhard Schröder would say into the microphone as Terry Wogan jested about the early casualty figures coming in from the front.

With the planned expansion of the European Union to eventually include Turkey, Chad and Australia, it's hard to know against whom the EU could launch an attack. If I was a soldier in Switzerland I would be getting very nervous around now, especially since the Swiss army only have those little penknives with which to defend themselves.

'Er, sarge, do any of these blades fold out into an anti-tank missile launcher?'

'Um – I don't think so – but there's a little pair of nail scissors there, you could really hurt someone with them.'

The deeper problem of course is not how to organize military intervention but whether it generally works or not. The people of Serbia did not overthrow Milosovich because NATO dropped bombs on them a few months back. And if NATO was sincere in its claim that it bombed Belgrade for humanitarian reasons, let's now see the same countries spend more on helping rebuild Serbia than they spent on the bombs that helped destroy it. Any new force will soon learn that military action is always easier to embark upon than it is to curtail. Throughout history political leaders have gone to war and found themselves in a longer conflict than they had expected. When poor Edward III got embroiled in the Hundred Years' War he said, 'Blimey, I didn't think it was going to go on this long,' and his advisers said, 'Well, the actual name of your war might have raised the odd suspicion, Your Majesty.'

If there's to be a European Rapid Reaction Force then its use must be limited to emergency and humanitarian aid. They could try developing a full-blown European army but there'd be only one outcome. As the various units sought to wield military power without clear political leadership, arguments would break out among the various European ethnic groups. Minor skirmishes between British, French and German troops would escalate, nation states would mobilize, and Europe would once more be plunged into all-out war. Still, I suppose it would save us having to make a decision on monetary union for another few years.

A man is robbed every twenty minutes (and he's getting pretty fed up with it)

18 October 2000

Politicians from all sides have been discussing the new crime figures this week and the statistics make depressing reading. When talking about action against burglars, use of the word tough has increased 57 per cent. But when referring to violent crime, incidents of politicians saying 'tough' has gone up by a massive 71 per cent. We are more likely to be assaulted by the phrase 'more bobbies on the beat' than at any time in the past twenty years and millions now live in fear of the trauma of waking up to discover that Jack Straw is talking on the *Today* programme.

Meanwhile the British Crime Survey has actually revealed that crime itself is going down. There are fewer burglaries, except in the areas where people keep leaving the house to attend Neighbourhood Watch meetings. There is a reduction in motor vehicle crime which is attributed to car alarms; while the increase in parked cars being attacked with a sledgehammer in the middle of the night is also attributed to car alarms. Apparently we are more likely to be robbed and assaulted by strangers, but this is hardly surprising – if you're going to mug someone you'd have to be pretty stupid to try it out on your best friend.

Ann Widdecombe will be disappointed that the crime figures have fallen, despite all the efforts of her Conservative colleagues in getting themselves arrested on a regular basis. One of the few perks of being shadow Home Secretary is being able to point to the inexorable rise in recorded offences and using this to attack your opponent. But now as she peeks out from behind her net curtains she will realize that she too has been the victim of a crime. When it comes to the law and order issue Labour have stolen the Tories' clothes (although the image of Jack Straw in one of Ann Widdecombe's dresses is not something you'd want to dwell upon). While her own pronouncements are greeted with stoned giggles from her colleagues in the shadow cabinet, Labour can point to solid social and economic policies that have helped bring crime down. The massive reduction in youth unemployment, for example, must surely be a factor; quite how the Tories imagine that scrapping the new deal and the minimum wage would help reduce youth crime has not been explained. Maybe Ann had an explanation for this but it was nicked from her briefcase.

Although the figures are falling, a huge percentage of crime continues to be committed by young males. There is a simple way of rectifying this imbalance; the government should introduce lots of new offences for everyone else. All sorts of anti-social behaviour continues to go unchecked in our society. For example, if you are in a long queue it should be unlawful for the person right in front of you to be suddenly joined by lots of friends. It's no good them just thinking up something completely inconsequential to say about having parked the car, just to show you that they know each other. Then if you arrive in the cinema after the film has started, it should be an offence not to duck slightly as you walk across the front. If the film ends five minutes before last orders it should also be against the law to sit there in deep contemplation, waiting to see who was Key Grip while everyone else on your row has stood up and is desperate to get out and grab a swift pint.

Leaving the scene of a jammed photocopier should be a criminal offence. And there should also be a new offence of corporate stalking. I have been stalked by British Telecom for several years now. They keep sending me letters and ringing me up when I least expect it, saying they know who my friends and family are and then threatening to change them.

Of course it could be argued that we don't need any new offences when there are so many crimes that are ignored already. None of the reporting on this week's crime figures made any reference to city fraud or big business tax evasion. Where are the interviews with old ladies saying how they are afraid to go out lest they should be offered a tip for some insider trading? Where are the big yellow signs in the City of London saying, 'Appeal for Witnesses – Fraud. Did you see anyone skimming the remainders fund, selling currency forward and then buying it spot fixed overnight? And more to the point, can you explain what this means?'

There are all sorts of reasons why crime has fallen and many voters will be alienated by anyone trying to score party political points on this issue. But before the election Tony Blair promised to be 'Tough on Crime and Tough on the Causes of Crime' and the latest crime figures suggest his approach may be working. OK, so he nicked the phrase off Gordon. But you can't blame Labour for that; the Tories were in power when it happened.

Shadow of a shadow cabinet

25 October 2000

Earlier this year I went to a social event organized by the Fabian Society in Westminster. After the wine had been flowing for a couple of hours, a game evolved in which some of the guests started reversing the bit of card in their name badges and writing down the names of members of the shadow cabinet. Ordinary Fabian members mingled around the House of Commons terrace pretending to be Tory Agriculture spokesman or shadow Leader of the House and the wonderful thing was that people who were not in on the joke had no way of knowing whether or not they'd really just met a Tory frontbencher. You could see them glancing at the job title on the name badge and then stiffening slightly as they realized that they were chit-chatting with a leading member of the opposition. Then they'd attempt to exude a casual 'of course I recognize you' air to the smart young Asian woman who was apparently the Tories' shadow Minister for Defence.

Sometimes I wonder if the current Tory front bench are all former SAS officers whose identities have to be kept secret for security reasons. It is hard to think of a more anonymous bunch. Does William Hague have the same problem as the rest of us when he holds meetings of the shadow cabinet?

'Er – you, thingy, whatsyername, what do you think we should do?'

'I dunno, mate, I'm just the bloke who's come to mend the photocopier.'

'Oh, sorry. Actually, you don't fancy being Environment spokesman, do you?'

Hague must take much of the blame for the anonymity of the team he has built around him. He chose new faces as a way of saying to the voters, 'Look, you don't have to elect anyone connected with the last Conservative government.' To which the logical response must be, 'Good point, I'd better vote Labour just to make really sure.'

Apart from the unholy trinity of Hague, Portillo and Widdecombe whom we got to know in the Major years, the *Observer's Book of British Conservatives* says sightings of other shadow cabinet members are extremely unlikely. So who are the poor conscripts who found themselves suddenly promoted to generals after the massacre of May '97? They're all listed on the Conservative Party website where their faces stare out at you like the sad photos from an appeal for missing persons. First up is Francis Maude, who is apparently now shadow Foreign Secretary, but the Tories might as well go to a temp agency on the continent to hire a real foreign secretary for all the impact he has made. Likewise James Arbuthnot, David Willetts, Andrew Lansley, Bernard Jenkin, Denis Kindel, Peter Ainsworth, Edward Garnier, Andrew Mackay . . . I couldn't put a face to any of them. Most of us could name more Pokémon characters than Tory frontbenchers. Shadow Chief Secretary to the Treasury is David Heathcoat-Amory. At last, a Tory name I vaguely recognize! Oh no, I'm thinking of the other

219

Heathcoat-Amory, aren't I? The one who was Chancellor in the 1950s; that was probably David's uncle or something . . . Then there's Liam Fox. He used to be a doctor so he's been given the Health portfolio. Actually he was once an army doctor, so he may well be Shadow Minister of Defence as well. Oh no, apparently Defence is Iain Duncan Smith – because he used to be the publishing director of *Jane's Defence Weekly*. I suppose if Jane had gone into politics they would have given the job to her.

And the remarkable thing is that these people must be the best of the bunch; the Conservative crème de la crème. The other hundred and fifty Conservative MPs have not made it to the front bench because they have failed to make as great an impact as Gary Streeter. (No, I hadn't heard of him either. He's shadow International Development apparently.) If they ever became the government they would do for Britain's profile what they have done for their party's. Today's leading Tories are the contestants in a political version of *Stars in Their Eyes.* They are complete nobodies who brave the spotlight and have a crack at pretending to be one of the Tory superstars of yesteryear. 'Tonight, Matthew, I'm going to be . . . Margaret Thatcher!' says David Willetts as he steps forward and trots out all the old lines about Europe and the unions. I don't know why he doesn't go the whole hog and put on a blue dress and blond wig – at least then he might stick in the memory for more than five minutes.

There was a time when, if you were a potential high-flyer, the Conservative Party was a promising career ladder. But today, if you are smart and ambitious, years spent on the opposition benches do not look like a very attractive or lucrative option. The result is that today's Conservative Party is filled with an evangelical rump of MPs who are not only second rate but who *actually believe* all that mad right-wing stuff. Misguided and incompetent – it's a fairly terrifying combination. John Major may have imagined the answer to Britain's problems was a traffic cone hotline, but at least he remembered to put a telephone number on the signs.

One last thing I ought to mention – one of the names of the various shadow ministers I listed above is completely made up. It's actually the name of the reserve goalie for Doncaster Rovers. So now it is competition time. If you can spot the imaginary leading Conservative, fill in the form below and hand it in at Politico's bookstall in the conference centre. The first correct answer out of the hat will get £25 worth of book vouchers. Entries from the reserve goalie for Doncaster Rovers will not be accepted. And I was also going to say that this competition is not open to members of the shadow cabinet. The trouble is, how would any of us know . . .

This piece was initially published in the Labour Party conference brochure and featured photographs of the various shadow ministers. Unfortunately two captions got mixed up and so the wrong name was put to two of the faces. Fortunately not a single person noticed.

Things can only get wetter

1 November 2000

Few of us will forget the extreme conditions we experienced this week. For hour after hour we were battered with relentless press coverage of the storm, and clichés rained down as tabloid readers were forced to wade through pages and pages of storm supplement extras. Brave commuters battled through anecdotes about their journey to work, sometimes taking several hours and often involving huge diversions to recount how they managed back in 1987. Power lines were down in some areas, though not enough to stop millions having to endure Trevor McDonald's Storm and Travel Special. The travel report on the radio was actually shorter than normal. They just said, 'Travel news now – you can't travel anywhere.'

Journalists have a special computer programme for this sort of news event called Microsoft Hack. You type in the word 'weather' and then you're presented with the options, 'hot', 'wet' or 'cold', and the story just writes itself. There were one or two early editions yesterday where journalists using Microsoft Hack had clearly experienced software problems: 'In the wettest

October day since records began, tarmac melted from the heat as sheep were rescued from snowdrifts and whole reservoirs dried up, bringing volunteers to airlift fish to safety from the rising floodwaters.'

The only thing that any visitor to Britain needs to understand about a crisis like the one we experienced this week is that *we just love it*. A drama that involved everyone rallying around, making cups of tea, rescuing animals and talking about the weather to boot; the British were in pure heaven on Monday. 'It was just like the blitz,' said one commentator, although this time if people spent all night in the underground it would have been because their trains were stuck in a tunnel on the Northern Line. The railways did remarkably well in that the service was barely changed from the one they'd provided in the week before the storm. There was the same excuse for cancellations that we get every autumn, although to be fair this year the leaves on the line still had the rest of the tree attached to them. Ferries were unable to dock at the Channel ports causing serious shortages of smuggled cigarettes. The damage to property ran into millions of pounds which means that the insurance companies may end up having to pay out anything up to £17.50.

Labour ministers might try pointing out that though the experience of Monday's storm was distressing, the hurricane that we suffered under Mrs Thatcher's government was in fact a lot worse. But of course there is a real political point to be made. There have been floods all over the world in the past few years. Four thousand people killed in China, thousands made homeless by mudslides in Venezuela, devastating floods in the Italian Alps and western United States; these events put a few ruined carpets in Somerset into some sort of perspective. But now there's another storm on the horizon. The People's Fuel Lobby are planning to bring the country to a halt all over again. Never mind that petrol consumption is considered a major factor in the world's climate changes, never mind that half the country will be permanently underwater in fifty years' time; as long as it doesn't cost too much to get out the Land Rover Discovery and run Hermione to her gymkhana, that's the main thing. So that's why so many Conservatives own those huge four-wheel drives. OK, so they may use up more petrol but that doesn't matter because when the ice cap does melt, the status symbol jeep is just that bit better at getting through the flood water. I suppose that's why they all have little bolt-holes in the Cotswolds as well – when London is finally completely underwater, they can just escape to the cottage in Gloucestershire until the government sorts it all out.

After the burning of fossil fuels, our second greatest source of greenhouse gases is apparently the methane from cows' bottoms. But with the amount of bullshit coming from the fuel protestors at the moment this figure looks set to rise as well. I just wish that their deadline had expired on Monday; it would have been fun to watch them out in the storm trying to bring the country to a standstill as hurricanes and floods completely upstaged them. The People's Fuel Lobby would be better off threatening *not* to bring the country to a standstill; that would really be depriving the British people of the thing they love the most. 'Oh please,' the papers would say, 'please give us another crisis; we can't bear to go back to moaning about the Millennium Dome.'

Yes, there is a problem with petrol prices. They are just not high enough. Either we stop using our cars so much or the permanent flooding of half the country will mean that we stop using them altogether. They used to give out free glasses with petrol. They should start giving out sandbags and life jackets instead.

Waste of space station

8 November 2000

The first residents of the new international space station have just completed their first week in orbit together and already the tensions are beginning to show. Yuri isn't putting the milk back in the fridge but that's not as annoying as that funny whistling-through-his-teeth thing that Sergei does all the time. The American Bill Shepherd is trying to hold it all together, but he's been on the defensive since that argument on the first morning which ended with him saying, 'How was I to know I wasn't supposed to put the cat outside at night?'

The three astronauts will be cooped up together until February with no option of leaving or seeing anyone else, though Bill has yet to break it to his parents that they probably won't be able to come and stay for Thanksgiving this year. All flatshares are a strain, but one which involves being locked in a space pod for eighteen weeks sounds like hell on Earth without the 'on Earth' bit.

Eventually there will be accommodation for residents from all the sixteen countries who are funding this project and presumably Channel 4 are now planning the space age follow-up to *Big Brother*. TV phone votes from around the world will determine who stays in the house and who gets cast out into the void of deep space.

At least if it produced a TV show we might be able to understand what the point of it all was. It has already cost sixty billion dollars, which makes it the second biggest waste of money of all time after the American presidential campaign. Do we really have to spend that much just to learn that men from planet Earth have problems using a gravity-free loo, when after thousands of years they still can't aim properly at the ordinary toilet bowl in their bathrooms.

The history of space exploration is littered with bizarre projects that cost a fortune for no discernible benefit to us down here on Earth. Somewhere up on the moon is still parked the world's most expensive car, the Space Buggy, which was driven around for a few miles and then just abandoned; a sort of lunar equivalent of joyriding. In the 1970s we marvelled at the technology on this amazing car because eight-track music systems seemed quite impressive back then. There was Skylab – an orbiting science laboratory which conducted experiments such as observing how a spider made a web in space. Which sounds like an elaborate cover-up for the fact that they'd used those cheap contract cleaners before take-off. Then there was the Hubble telescope, pictures of outer space which took two weeks to be beamed back to Earth, and then another two weeks to be developed at Foto-Kwik. Next there is talk of a manned space trip to Mars, which seems like trying to run before we can walk. A successful manned rail trip to Birmingham New Street might be a start.

People who defend space expenditure always point to the incidental by-products of the programmes to justify the enormous cost. 'We'd never have got the non-stick saucepan if it hadn't been for the moon landings,' they always say. Surely a programme that had been specifically designed just to develop non-stick saucepans might have achieved the same end at marginally less expense.

This latest project is the international equivalent of a timeshare apartment. Sixteen countries have been conned into paying their bit towards a half-built orbiting holiday home. Their government representative went along to the presentation because you got a free Sony walkman just for turning up, but before long he found himself persuaded of the merits of his government having a little place of their own that they could use any time of the year (as long as it was for a four-month spell in three years' time). Like all holiday homes it is more use as a status symbol than somewhere you'd actually want to live.

But Daniel Goldin, the head of NASA, has defended the project by saying that now, 'Instead of pointing missiles at each other, we'll be learning from each other.' Perhaps this gives us a clue to the method behind all this madness. Maybe future residents of the space station will not be astronauts but political leaders. If Yasser Arafat and Ehud Barak cannot learn to get along after they've been trapped together in a tiny space capsule for four months then we can be sure they never will. David Trimble and Gerry Adams, Robert Mugabe and Ian Smith, Liam Gallagher and Robbie Williams; the place is going to be packed out in no time. And then when all the political leaders and celebrities have promised to get along, they'll radio down to mission control and ask which button they press to come back again. And only then will we say, 'What do you mean, "come back"?'

The forty-third President of the United States is – er . . .

18 November 2000

I cried on the day President Kennedy was shot. I was lying in my cot and I'd dropped my rusk through the bars. Next week sees the anniversary of that infamous assassination, and America looks set to commemorate it by killing off another rightful president. For years the debate will rage – was the Florida judge acting alone or was it part of some wider conspiracy? Was there a second judge hiding behind the grassy knoll? Show that film again – there's definitely a second hole going into that ballot paper.

There is of course a difference between Kennedy and Gore. Kennedy won the presidency by only 100,000 votes, whereas Gore beat Bush by more than twice that. We keep being told that America is the greatest democracy in the world. Well, yes, apart from the minor quibbles that less than half of the electorate voted and the bloke who got fewer votes looks set to win. Soon the billions spent on the election will be as nothing compared to Jeremy Paxman's hotel bill for his extended stay in Washington.

Immediately it became apparent that neither candidate had won decisively, all sorts of accusations and recriminations started being thrown about. Gore was told he blew it by not being enough like Clinton. Instead of going around shaking people's hands he should have locked himself in the stationery cupboard with his secretary. Then it was claimed that some ballot papers were so confusing that less intelligent electors voted for the wrong person. So at least Al Gore got Bush's vote. Meanwhile careful analysis of the figures shows that the Governor of Texas has been seeking to gain an unfair advantage over the past few years by executing more Democrats than Republicans.

It must be said that political dynasties don't come much less glamorous than the Bush family. If the original President Bush had been a film, would anyone have bothered with a sequel? But now in the land where anyone is supposed to be able to reach the White House, the son of the last Republican President looks set to inherit it because of dubious electoral practices in the state where his brother is Governor. So that's why George W. Bush went into politics. He wanted to spend more time with his family.

There must be a simple way to sort this all out. Can't we get Anne Robinson to ask both candidates a few general knowledge questions and then say, 'George W. – you're the weakest link – goodbye!' Or maybe a more American way would be for the two candidates to fight it out in the style of the World Wrestling Foundation. Al 'the jogger' Gore v George 'the executioner' Bush. It would still look less fixed than the result in Florida.

'It could never happen here of course,' we all say smugly. Except it has happened here twice since the war, most spectacularly in 1951, when Attlee's government got the highest percentage poll of any political party since the advent of universal suffrage and yet Labour were thrown out of office. And who can forget the things that Churchill's 1951–5 government then

229

did without a proper mandate? Well, we all can as it turns out, but that's not the point.

Events across the Atlantic should make us look again at our own political system. We can hardly laugh at the Americans when our own head of state was chosen by dint of being the elder daughter of an accidentally crowned king, descended from a foreign prince who was brought in at the last minute to keep out the Catholics. (I don't see why the Tories are so paranoid about us being ruled by the Germans, when they've been sitting on the British throne since George I.) Maybe in this area we should seek to be more like the Americans – the Queen and Prince Charles should have televised debates to decide on the top job. Charles would be accused of being pro-gun control as the Queen shouted, 'God bless the good ol' United Kingdom!' and everyone would whoop and cheer as red, white and blue balloons descended from the ceiling.

The unsettling reality is that it is in exactly this type of constitutional deadlock that the Queen would wield genuine political power. And you could bet your bottom euro that the people advising her would be arguing for a Conservative administration rather than Labour. The American constitution might be showing its age this month but at least they've actually got one. We still have an unelected second chamber, an un-representative House of Commons and a voting system that leaves millions of people feeling that their votes simply don't count. We'll realize how deeply flawed our political system is only when William Hague walks through the door of 10 Downing Street after most people have voted against him. And then we'll wish we had a more liberal and intelligent leader – someone like George W. Bush.

London dungeons

24 November 2000

There has always been a chronic accommodation problem in the capital. If you look up the part of London where I live in the Domesday Book, you will see the village of 'Claphamme' is described as 'being a parish of five oxen, seven horse to plough and three oak barns, currently being redeveloped as exclusive loft apartments; ready Christmas 1089'. A thousand years later the property pages of the *Evening Standard* are eagerly flicked through to see which is the latest old building to be converted into luxury housing.

'Oh look, Rupert, they're converting Great Ormond Street Hospital into twenty-five maisonettes.'

'That's terrible. Why only twenty-five?'

The demand for yuppie flats cannot be infinite; surely sooner or later they must run out of yuppies. What will they do then, start converting all the properties back again? 'Yah, we got rid of the extra bedroom at the top of the house and had it converted back into a traditional loft. It cost a fortune but we covered up the skylight, put in a rusty water tank and rolls of itchy insulation felt and then filled it all up with old school reports and broken Christmas-tree lights.'

I have never understood how London continues to function when three-quarters of the accommodation is permanently beyond the reach of most Londoners. And why is it a good thing when house prices go up? 'There was a double dose of bad news on the economy today. Inflation was up and, to make things even worse, house prices are still falling.'

The person who resolves to live their entire life in London has to go through various distressing stages. Phase one is the nightmare that is the flatshare. This is the period early on in your adult life when you permanently fall out with your friends by living with them. The only way to get the government to understand the seriousness of London's housing crisis is to force the cabinet themselves to flatshare. They should all have to live together in a poky five-bedroom house in Willesden.

'All right,' says Tony, opening the fridge in the morning. 'Who's been eating my guacamole?'

'Your what?' says Prescott, sitting there in his vest reading the *Sun*. 'I thought those mushy peas tasted a bit funny. Oh, by the way, Gordon – you owe me three quid for the milk bill.'

'What!' explodes Gordon. 'Look, just because we have seven thousand pounds in the food kitty doesn't mean we can afford to go off buying luxuries like food. And Mo, do you mind not smoking at the breakfast table? Why does she keep giggling at the family on the cornflakes packet?'

Eventually flatsharers separate off into couples and lock themselves into their bedrooms to bitch about the others. At this point the 'luckier' ones scrape together a tiny deposit to buy a rabbit hutch in the outer suburbs. Even a tiny two-bedroom leasehold rabbit hutch without a little glass water dispenser will set them back £150K. And they pay a fortune in service charges and still no one cleans out the straw. Many

232

people feel compelled to buy because of the social stigma that has become attached to renting. In most European cities renting remains a sensible and respectable option, but ever since Mrs Thatcher went down to Sainsbury's Homebase to buy a new door for 10 Downing Street, anyone who does not own their home is looked down upon. I blame all those colour supplement features in which minor celebrities describe 'A Room of My Own'. Why can't the Sunday papers feature ordinary Londoners in 'A Room of My Landlord's'? Scruffy students could then be photographed slumped in dingy bedsits, describing how the swirly brown carpet was chosen to match the brown stains on the walls. 'Of course this sofa is genuine Dralon,' says Degsy from Dollis Hill. 'And I'm particularly fond of this dangerously wired water heater . . . I keep it in the hope that it might electrocute some of the silverfish that live in the cutlery drawer.'

Eventually the new homeowners feel compelled to try to buy a larger family house with a separate bedroom for the kids, but such is the financial burden that one of the parents ends up spending the entire night at the office anyway. Journalists in the third world write moving accounts of how Londoners are sold into slavery by taking out endowment mortgages. 'These poor English families remain bonded in debt to the building societies for the rest of their lives. Despite working from morning till night they are told that their debt is actually larger than it was when they originally took out the loan.'

In order to keep London's properties at the sort of prices where ordinary people can afford to buy, I think each of us has a duty to lower the tone of our neighbourhoods. If you see an estate agent showing a posh couple a house in your road, wander out on to the pavement wearing only your pants and polythene pac-a-mac and offer them a taste of one of your home-made bovine spine-burgers. 'Hello, are you thinking of buying the old used needles recycling centre? Apparently the garden's still full of them.' They'll try and drive away as fast as they can, until they discover that the neighbours on the other side have already stacked their car up on bricks and nicked all the wheels.

We have to do something to bring down house prices because the alternative is a city in which the demand for cardboard boxes in shop doorways will become so overwhelming that estate agents will end up featuring them in their windows. 'Compact, bijou starter home, close to shops. Well, in the doorway to be honest.' And for the average Londoner, the property pages of the *Evening Standard* will be more valuable than ever. Not to find a home that they can afford, but as blankets for when they've given up even trying.

Dome alone

29 November 2000

If you thought the festivities on the night of the Millennium were impressive, they'll be nothing compared to the party that's planned for 31 December this year. On the stroke of midnight twice as much champagne will be consumed, more fireworks will light up the sky and the cheering will be ten times louder. And all these celebrations will be coming from one little office in Westminster where Lord Falconer is jumping up and down shouting, 'Hooray! I don't have to be minister for the bloody Dome any more!'

However, Falconer might need to be kept in his job because the problem of the Dome is not going to go away. The National Audit Office has just announced a second inquiry, this time into its actual sale. The first buyers pulled out when they realized that the estate agents' blurb ('Unique spacious property with views over Thames. Security recently upgraded.* Reduced

*There had recently been an attempted diamond robbery at the Millennium Dome. A gang of armed robbers crashed through the gates at high speed, thereby doubling that month's attendance figures.

for quick sale.') did not tell the whole tale. This week's new bidder is planning a high-tech e-commerce park inside the Dome, although if past history is anything to go by, half the e-mails sent to Greenwich will probably decide, 'Oh, I can't be bothered to go all the way out there.'

So just because the cabinet look set finally to be shot of the place does not mean that it will disappear as a political issue. Because for anyone looking for a way to bash the government, there is a mind-numbing inevitability that their first stop will always be the Millennium Dome. So Tony is sitting at home having dinner with the family and he says, 'No, Euan, you can't have Playstation 2 for Christmas – it's too expensive.'

'Well, maybe you could have afforded it if you hadn't spent so much money *on the Dome*!'

Then Cherie sips the wine and says, 'Yuk! Maybe you could have bought a decent bottle of plonk if you hadn't spent so much money *on the Dome*!'

And the man selling dusters knocks on the door and Tony says, 'No, thank you' and the man says, 'Yeah, you won't buy a duster, but you don't mind spending all that money *on the Dome*, do you?' It must be starting to drive him a little bit mad, but now it's time to take this wind-up to the next stage. If you are meeting with Tony Blair this week, when you talk to him try using only the word 'Dome'. So if you're a civil servant outlining a new set of figures, just say, 'Dome dome dome dome.' And the PM will turn to Alastair Campbell and say, 'What's he saying?' And then Campbell should say, 'Dome d-dome dome domey dome-dome.'

All governments have cock-ups, and the Dome is of course nothing as compared to Black Wednesday or Neville Chamberlain saying, 'Let's give this Hitler chap the benefit of the doubt.' In one sense the Millennium Dome has been a triumph. A British theme park should give us the chance to do the things we enjoy the most and the Dome has provided long queues and something to moan about all year long. All its problems stem from one crucial and overwhelming mistake – the projected number of visitors. The number of people who've been to the Dome has been very disappointing and he didn't even bring a friend. In actual fact the target attendance figures were set under the last government and much as the Tories love to see the Dome as a symbol of New Labour it started out as the baby of the last Conservative Deputy Prime Minister. That is not to say that this government should not have seen that the figures were crazy (and to their credit they have now admitted as much). But it's a little bit rich to suggest that the Dome would have been better run by a John Major government who were so useless they thought that 'incompetence' was something to do with weak bladders.

But for a project that was intended to entertain us, the entertainment has been non-stop. Ever since he took up the job Lord Falconer has been under pressure to resign, but that was of course the whole point of his appointment in the first place. The card in the Job Centre said, 'Fall guy wanted to take flak and get roasted on *Newsnight*. Temporary appointment only.' They could of course still sack him but they'd only have to replace him with someone else and Frank Dobson wasn't that keen for some reason. This has been the best idea to come out of the whole debacle – appointing a special junior minister to act as public whipping post for unpopular government policies. So Lord Falconer had better not get too drunk on New Year's Eve, because the next morning he'll be getting a very important phone call. 'Hi, Charlie,' the Prime Minister will say. 'I've got a great new job for you. How do you fancy being minister for petrol prices?'

French lessons

2 December 2000

Anglo-French relations took another turn for the worse this week. It began with John Prescott being a bit patronizing towards his French counterpart. As the UN talks on climate change fell apart she screamed, 'Unless we act now most of the world's land mass will be underwater, oxygen will disappear and the entire planet will suffocate!' And Prescott said, 'All right, love, all right. It's not the end of the world . . .'

Tony Blair tried to smooth things over by taking Jacques Chirac out to lunch at a pub in his constituency but things reached rock bottom when the French president was greeted with the words, 'Hello, have you been to a Harvester before?' It was of course a calculated piece of revenge by the British government. They could have retaliated to the French outburst by cancelling trade talks or banning French beef, but no, far more vicious to buy Chirac a glass of wine from a British pub. And then film him drinking it. 'Any more attacks on my deputy,' said Tony, 'and we're stopping at the Little Chef on the way back to the airport.'

Anglo-French relations have been precarious ever

since King Harold asked the Normans what they were doing in Sussex and they stuck an arrow in his eye, which is only marginally less co-operative than most of the French guards on the Eurostar today. The Normans then went backpacking round their newly conquered land, and if you look closely at the Bayeux tapestry you can make out lots of little figures spitting out warm beer and laughing at the primitive public transport facilities. Things got worse when Joan of Arc decided to drive out all the posh English people who had holiday cottages in Normandy. She was then burnt to a cinder by the English, to the horror of the French who thought that two minutes either side would have been plenty. After that the two countries fought wars with all the regularity of football tournaments, with the difference that the French didn't win quite so often. Henry V took a couple of thousand English troops over the Channel, who won a famous victory and then came back loaded up with lots of little bottles of French lager and a big piece of Brie for the missus. The last big bust-up ended with the Battle of Waterloo, precipitating a hundred years of unchallenged British supremacy and a number-one hit for Abba.

Except that is not how history is viewed on the other side of the Channel. I recently found myself chatting with a French woman and the subject turned to the French attitude to the US.

'I think the French feel hostile to the Americans,' she said, 'because before the rise of the United States the most powerful country in the world was France.'

There was a slight pause while I picked myself up off the floor.

'Sorry?' I said. 'When was this exactly?'

'Before America was the major world power, it was France.'

Obviously as a liberal and an internationalist I don't care who was the major world power before America, it just so happens that it was Great Britain, that's all.

239

She countered my amusing interpretation of history by reminding me of the French Empire in North Africa.

'That was all desert!' I exploded. 'Now yer British Empire, that was a proper empire. India, Australia, South Africa, Canada, why, the sun never set . . .' I went on as the strains of 'Land of Hope and Glory' rose behind me and Union Jack tattoos popped out all over my skin. European socialists have a duty to recognize the shameful inheritance of our imperialist history. But the French had better accept that we've got a bigger imperialist tradition to be ashamed of than they have.

The historical baggage that we British carry around with us is of course the real reason that we struggle to accept the increased status of the French in Europe. The tabloids and the Conservative Party have attempted to sustain the flattering fantasy that Britain's status in Europe is roughly unchanged since the happy days of World War Two as portrayed so accurately in 'Allo, 'Allo. And what's really underneath all this week's anti-French rhetoric is the nagging resentment that France and Germany are now the dominant partners in Europe. We have clung to an over-inflated view of ourselves which has left us as bit-part players in the shaping of the European Union.

A few years back there began an attempt to improve understanding between the two historical rivals by organizing school exchange visits, in which French teenagers were apparently supposed to endear themselves to us by wearing cagoules and wandering around Bournemouth shoplifting. The idea of the cultural exchange has now been extended into a scheme under which the French send us their brilliant football players and we send them bovine spongiform encephalopathy. Perhaps as part of the final stage of Euro-integration, this project should now be allowed to reach its logical conclusion and French and British cultures can become fully entwined. We will have to listen to their pop music, they will have to keep their pants on in the sauna. They will have to watch *Animal Hospital* but we'll have to let them eat any of the animals that don't make it. But we have no choice but to learn to get along. Racism can have no place in the future of Europe; and so let France and Britain lead the way in doing away with chauvinism and petty nationalism. And then the British press will proudly boast of how we built a Europe free of intolerance, xenophobia and bigotry, how we learned to love one another irrespective of race or creed. 'If racial prejudice is what you're into,' the tabloids will say, 'frankly, you'd be far better off with those bloody krauts.'

Only sixteen shoplifting days till Christmas

8 December 2000

When does the Christmas season officially begin? In the 1970s and '80s you knew the season of goodwill and joy to all mankind had arrived when the IRA started blowing up shopping centres. And we'd all tut and say, 'Honestly, the IRA's Christmas bombing campaign starts earlier every year.' But these days it's harder to know the exact moment when the festive season has really begun. Is it the day the Christmas lights are switched on in the West End? Or is it the next day when they break down again and some poor bloke has to go all the way down Oxford Street checking every single bulb? For some people it is the delivery of the first charity catalogue, when the family gather round excitedly to flick through this year's selection of raffia-work table mats. For others it is the first domestic argument about where they will be eating their roast turkey and chestnut stuffing.

'I am not spending Christmas Day at your brother's flat in Dudley.'

'Well, we're certainly not having your father here

again, not after last year with my sister. Mistletoe is not a licence for tongues.'

Of course moaning about Christmas starting too early is now part of the tradition itself. That's the wonderful thing about the festive season; the way it evolves and changes to incorporate new customs. And everything that now characterizes a modern Christmas will one day seem as ancient a tradition as the Yule log and Cliff Richard being number one. The new customs will feature on Christmas cards of the future; just as today we send pictures of rosy-cheeked Dickensian children singing Christmas carols in the snow, cards in the next century will depict nostalgic scenes of drunken clerks in nylon Santa hats staggering out of office parties and being sick on the tube on the way home.

The tradition of sending Christmas cards has evolved into a complex and subtle form of communication. Although the message usually says something like 'Season's Greetings', what this actually means varies according to the sender. Some cards say, 'I expect a Christmas tip'; others say, 'I still fancy you,' while one card I get every year says, 'You had a curry delivered from our tandoori once and we made a note of your address.' Then of course there is the mystery card. Somewhere in Britain there is a man with a very strange sense of humour who for years now has been sending cards to each and every one of us with the name of a made-up couple at the bottom: 'Merry Christmas from Roy and Jane'. 'Who the bloody hell are Roy and Jane?' you say. 'Was it that couple we met on holiday? No, it must be someone from your work.' 'Is that a "Jane" or is it a "James"? Do we know a gay couple called Roy and James?' and all the while the sender is chuckling to himself as he sends out another thousand cards from 'Lesley and Colin', 'Alan and Miranda' and 'Piers and Nicola', knowing that everyone will be worrying about who it is that they have left off their Christmas card list. It must be even worse for the royal family; they get thousands of cards. Prince Philip must say, 'We've got one from Edith Harris, 93 Station Road, Swansea.' 'Oh dear,' says the Queen, 'I don't think we sent her one . . .'

The royals have a lot to answer for when it comes to Christmas traditions. Quite apart from the Queen's Christmas message, which is unfair because ordinary people can't answer back, they are to blame for the practice of buying Christmas trees. Some people feel it is never really Christmas until they have driven across town with a twelve-foot tree sticking out of the side window knocking pensioners to the pavement. The custom was of course introduced by Prince Albert. His advisers were concerned that every high street in Britain seemed to have a boarded-up shop with a small disused car park out the front. 'I know!' said Albert excitedly. 'Everyone could use these abandoned forecourts to sell dead conifers!' and the ministers looked at one another anxiously. 'Yes,' he went on, 'then people can take these trees home and put them in the lounge for a few weeks until all the needles fall off and then they can be chucked into the front garden where they can stay for the whole year because the dustmen will refuse to take them!' And because Albert was a prince, no one had the nerve to tell him that this was a really stupid idea and so the convention survives to this day.

It was the royals who originally started the tradition of present-giving as well. Those three kings (who of Orient were) gave the first ever Christmas gifts to the newborn messiah. Of course if it was today he would have got a little bib with the slogan 'I dribble for West Ham' or a plastic Dinosaurs beaker from the Disney shop, but obviously it was early days for the Christmas gift industry so he had to make do with some last-minute frankincense and myrrh from the Bethlehem 7-11, while the gold was put in the junior savings account where Jesus couldn't touch it until he was twenty-one.

That was all two thousand years ago and the people who celebrate 25 December because it is Jesus's birthday have been waiting ever since for it to happen all over again. But they must realize that any chance of a second coming has been completely snuffed out. Because God must look down at the lametta and the spray-on snow, at the repeats of *The Great Escape* and David Bowie introducing *The Snowman*; he must watch all the dads moaning because the kids have nicked the batteries from the TV remote control to put in their new laser guns; he must see all the unwanted junk that is bought and then thrown away; he must note the tension that builds from the middle of November until the depressing anticlimax of Boxing Day, and all to the endless soundtrack of Slade singing 'Merry Xmas Everybodee' and God must say to himself, 'Second Coming? Nope, there's no way we're going to go through all that *twice* a year.'

Name, rank and ISBN number

9 December 2000

It was just another literary luncheon in Hampstead. Martin Amis and Melvyn Bragg were sipping Pouilly Fumé and discussing the Booker shortlist when suddenly there was a loud explosion and the French windows were smashed in. Smoke bombs and stun grenades rolled across the floor as three figures in black balaclavas abseiled in through the window. And John Mortimer looked up from his canapés and said, 'I think it's rather spoiled the atmosphere since all these SAS writers started coming along.'

The SAS kill-and-tell book is now established as one of the most successful literary genres of the last decade. Magical realism is all very well, but frankly the airport bookshops are hoping that Zadie Smith's next novel will feature a few more gory gun battles with Iraqi commandos. Earlier this year I found myself at a booksellers' dinner alongside Chris Ryan. You'd never guess he'd been in the SAS, I thought, as he tucked into his slap-up meal of two earwigs and a bit of moss, and then sent back his glass of water because it wasn't dirty enough. He shook my hand at the end of the evening and I still have the bruises on my fingers to prove it. There were plenty of other authors at the event but they never stood a chance; all the literary middle-class liberals who work in the bookshops were queuing up to ask Ryan what sort of gun he used when he killed all those Iraqis.

But at the SAS training camp they've stopped bothering with rifles and grenades. The new recruits stand to attention and give their name, rank and ISBN number. Then they demonstrate how to strip down a fountain pen and load a new ink cartridge in thirty seconds flat. Squaddies leap out of the armoured troop carrier at the top of Charing Cross Road, and have to sign at every bookshop in time to make their author talk at Waterstone's Piccadilly.

In fact, the market for SAS books actually peaked a couple of years ago, so now was the time the Ministry of Defence chose to take some legal action and give the genre the shot in the arm that it needed. With all the foresight that the MoD showed when it dropped the Bravo Two Zero team behind Iraqi lines equipped with only a cheese-grater and a 1960s street map of Kettering, they have tried to prevent the publication of the latest account of that mission, giving the book far more publicity than the publishers could have dreamed of. Now the British public will be denied the chance to buy it on Amazon.co.uk and will have to suffer the huge inconvenience of going all the way to Amazon.com instead.

The upper reaches of the British military disapprove of these books because they claim that they create a security risk. What is really at the root of their irritation is something far more ingrained than their concern for national security and that is good old-fashioned class prejudice. It's always been all right for the officer class to write worthy hardbacks to give to each other at Christmas. Ever since the Second World War officers have been writing books about the

SAS; there is even a biography of the regiment's founder by General Sir Peter de la Billière. He decided to write a hundred thousand words so he put his name at the top of the page and then found he was half-way there already. What rankles with the army high command is that these new chaps selling millions of copies are just ordinary soldiers. 'So leaving the armed services and ending up sleeping on the streets like all the others isn't good enough for them, I suppose?' If the new breed of SAS writers were not so successful, their superiors wouldn't bother doing anything about them.

Andy McNab's *Bravo Two Zero* is the best-selling war book of all time, and apart from anything else he has saved the army recruiting office a small fortune in advertising. Though these books may not be to the taste of many of the chattering classes they are reaching an audience which includes many people who might otherwise never think of going into a bookshop. Admittedly an eighteen-year-old squaddie is not going to put down *Immediate Action* and think, 'Blimey, I quite enjoyed reading a book. I think I'll try that Vikram Seth bloke next.' But he might read the next Andy McNab and then he'll find he has moved effortlessly from non-fiction to fiction and then the idea of regularly reading novels is not such an impossibility. And this of course is to be welcomed. Not just because we want a more literate society, not just because it will help make him a fuller person. But because this squaddie is going to need all the literary skills he can get in the future. The moment he's out of the army, a dozen publishers will be waiting for him. 'Right!' they'll say. 'All set to write us a book about it?'

I'm not a racialist, but . . .

16 December 2000

These days you can't even burn down a mosque without someone saying you're racist. You can't even put on a pointy white hood, set fire to a cross and hold a rally for the Aryan master race without the liberal elite suddenly deciding that this would somehow be 'politically incorrect'. Try and kidnap young black people from West Africa and sell them as slaves to plantation owners in the deep South, and suddenly you'll find yourself being accused of 'racial discrimination' by the PC police of Tony Blair's nanny state.

This was the essence of William Hague's speech on the Macpherson report. That yer anti-racism is all very well, but things have gone too far the other way. I'm sure I've seen that bald-headed bigot mouthing off about the blacks somewhere before? Of course, William Hague has turned into Alf Garnett. He sits in his armchair under portraits of the Queen and Churchill, ranting and raving and getting all his facts wrong.

'Yer crime is going up, right?'

'No, it's going down.'

'Shut up, Ffion, you silly moo! Yer crime is going up because yer police numbers is falling under Labour.'

'But police numbers have been falling since 1993 . . .'

'Exactly, 'cos yer bloody Macpherson says every one of 'em is racist.'

'But the report was only last year and it never said that anyway.'

'Look, shut up! And stop making out I'm racialist, you silly Welsh cow!'

What Hague was doing in his speech this week was shooting the messenger. What's more, Sir William Macpherson was an unarmed messenger, shot without provocation or warning, and no doubt Hague will be cleared of all blame when they hold an internal inquiry. Macpherson had only confirmed what we all knew anyway, that racism was rife in the police force and that the constant harassment of black people was counter-productive to the fight against crime. I remember how, after an IRA bomb destroyed the Baltic Exchange in the City of London, a 'ring of steel' was placed around the city and armed police were stationed at checkpoints where they stopped any car suspected of containing Irish terrorists. I had never realized that there were so many black people in the IRA. Every week I would drive over Blackfriars Bridge and see armed police searching the car of yet another black man thought to be a dangerous Irish republican. 'Here comes another Rasta, sarge! He looks like he's come straight over from South Armagh with a bootload of Semtex.'

But recently progress had started to be made. The police accepted the findings of the Macpherson report and the number of unnecessary 'stop and searches' of black youths had dropped dramatically. The fragile, painstaking process of rebuilding bridges between the police and the black community was just beginning.

Cue William Hague with his size ten Doc Marten boots. For the sake of perceived narrow party advantage between now and election day, he is prepared to stir up racism with a poisonous speech packed with prejudice, factual inaccuracies and straightforward lies. No wonder the father of Stephen Lawrence is so disgusted. The racists who regularly attack Britain's racial minorities need only the slightest encouragement to justify their actions. If the would-be Prime Minister says that blacks are getting away with crimes because the police aren't allowed to stop them, then young racists will interpret this as a call for them to step in and take action themselves.

The time has come for Sir William Macpherson to do another report – this time to uncover the institutional racism inside the Conservative Party. If Nelson Mandela had turned up at the Tory Party conference they would've asked if anyone ordered a minicab. The party that suggests it should govern multi-ethnic Britain does not have a single black or Asian MP. First we had Liam Fox stirring up racism by sounding off about Indian doctors who don't speak English properly and now William Hague is trying to equate crime with black people in the run-up to the election. Typical – you get one racist to move into the Conservative Party and then another racist moves in next door and before you know it the whole party's full of them. I've nothing against Conservatives myself – I mean they're good at sport and all that, Seb Coe and Colin Moynihan did us proud at the Olympics, but you have to admit that when it comes to crime, well, all I'll say is that without the likes of Jeffrey Archer and Jonathan Aitken the police wouldn't be under all this pressure in the first place.

And of course inciting racial hatred is against the law in this country but of course you're not allowed to arrest them for it – oh no, that would be politically incorrect. The Conservative establishment have made it impossible for the police to do anything about it. Real equality will have arrived only when the police stop and search William Hague for possession of an offensive speech every time he walks down the road.

Rollover Richard Branson

23 December 2000

You have to feel sorry for Richard Branson. What is he left with now? Well, all right, he has got his own airline, I suppose. And Virgin trains of course, and the financial services business, and a multi-million-dollar music empire and his own private Caribbean island – but apart from that, what is he left with now? He has spent the equivalent of a quadruple rollover jackpot trying to win the lottery, and has ended up with nothing. Perhaps Camelot ought to present him with a giant cheque for one pound just to make the symmetry complete. Somehow you can't imagine Branson ticking the box for 'no publicity'.

Branson likened the farce to the American election, but the comparison is a better one than he probably realizes. As with George W. Bush, we wanted Camelot to lose; but in both cases it was never a great choice in the first place. There should have been no winner – with the prize rolling over to next week. Yes, Branson's bid may well have meant a not-for-profit lottery; yes, his company might have injected new ideas and energy into the scheme, reviving sales and increasing donations to good causes. But set against this was the incontrovertible fact that awarding the licence to Branson would have given him another excuse to get his stupid beardy grin in the newspaper every week, and ultimately this was just too high a price to pay.

So once again the jackpot will be shared between several lucky winners who all live in the London area. You can tell the directors of Camelot are overpaid – every week their wages are presented to them by Jet from Gladiators. It's been pointed out in their defence that these entrepreneurs did originally take on a huge financial risk, because Camelot's precarious business involves collecting millions and millions of pounds from the British people and then giving only a fraction of it back. Amazingly they have managed to run this operation at a profit. With a financial expertise which borders on genius, they have succeeded in actually making money out of this crazy 'collecting-billions-and-then-keeping-lots-of-it' venture that they embarked on against all the advice of the accountants.

And because they have been so clever, over the past few years the directors have regularly awarded themselves huge bonuses. Every week we would choose the six numbers on our lottery tickets and they would choose the six numbers on their pay cheques. Camelot claim they are making efforts to reinvigorate the lottery, and to prove their point they have just come up with a new character to promote the latest game. After months of brainstorming they have named him 'Jack Pot'. Imagine the late nights they spent pulling their hair out before they came up with this one.

'What about Jim Pot?'
'No . . .'
'Keith Pot?'
'No, the Pot bit definitely feels good but we haven't got the first name right yet.'

'I know! Pol Pot!'

'No. Look, I think we'd better hire an expensive advertising agency and see if they can help.'

Camelot are a hangover from the sleazy mediocrity of the Major years and as soon as the way is clear they will start paying themselves huge bonuses all over again. Not 'Maybe, Just Maybe', but 'Definitely, Quite Definitely'. Chris Smith has had to take the flak for the decision to renew their licence to print money, although of course if the decision had gone the other way there would have been just as much criticism from people saying that Branson had got it out of some sort of favouritism. Somehow the government contrived a situation in which they weren't deciding who'd be awarded the licence but they would get the blame for whoever did. The 'fingers-crossed' logo is all very well but it shouldn't be the basis of government policy.

The question that ought to be staring a Labour government in the face is why does any private company have to be involved with the running of the lottery in the first place? We don't have any other taxes being collected by syndicates from the City of London who then hand over a mere one-quarter of what they collect to the exchequer. 'Remember that for every pound you give to Inland Revenue plc, twenty-five pence goes towards paying for schools and hospitals.' We don't get adverts in the paper from Customs and Excise plc explaining how hard it is to collect all that VAT and why this justifies huge bonuses for all the directors. No other country in Europe has a lottery run for private profit. The National Lottery should be just that – a lotto run for the nation and owned by the nation. Public ownership may have been out of fashion for a generation, but companies like Camelot and Railtrack have provided the left with an opportunity to seize back the agenda. So can we look forward to popping open the champagne when the next Labour government suddenly announces it is taking the lottery under state control? You don't have to be Mystic Meg to foresee that we've got more chance of winning a rollover jackpot.

2001 – an electoral odyssey

30 December 2000

Tomorrow night the Pedants' Society will be celebrating the dawning of the new millennium. 'Technically the new century doesn't start until 2001; *this* should have been the night there were parties in all the parks and sports stadiums,' the leader of the pedants will proclaim. 'Actually Brian, it's stadia, not stadiums.'

For the rest of us, the new year means something far more significant: general election time is upon us once again. When Stanley Kubrick envisaged the year 2001 he erroneously foresaw the wonders of interplanetary travel and the meeting of time and space. There was not one scene featuring Peter Mandelson speaking to prospective candidates in the key marginals on New Labour's priorities for a second term. Though I do remember a load of scary-looking subhumans smashing each other over the head, so at least the present Conservative Party got a look-in.

2001 will be a crucial year partly because the country will have to decide between Labour and Tory, but mainly because in the months beforehand the real choice between radical and conservative will have to be made by those drawing up Labour's manifesto. The discussion is already under way as to how bold Labour dares to be.

'Comrades, Labour is at a crossroads in its history. What are we to do?'

'Erm, change it into a mini-roundabout?'

First the manifesto will need a sprinkling of populism. One trick might be a promise to legalize the things that everyone does all the time anyway. Under the next Labour government it will be legal to feed your toddler grapes in the supermarket before they have been weighed and paid for. It will be legal to go the wrong way up a one-way street as long as you do it in reverse. Throwing an empty tin can on to the ground will still be a littering offence, but if the can is placed carefully on top of a post then that's all right.

Of course some new offences will have to be created. Fox-hunting looks set to be one of them; there may be many crueller things that happen to animals in Britain, but they are not done by such outrageously posh people, so hunting has to go. The populist persecution of the upper classes should then be taken to the next stage with punitive taxes on Pringle jumpers and the wearing of cravats to the pub on Sunday. The City of London should be incorporated into the borough of Tower Hamlets and there should be an extra tax for people with too many names. And if the trend towards building high-security private housing estates is to continue, then the maintenance of the electric gates should be handed over to Railtrack. That should keep a few cars off the road for a while.

One of the lessons of Labour's first term has been that the rich or right wing were never going to vote Labour and there was never any point in trying to get them on board. Nothing would have stopped the WI's slow hand-clap, short of Tony Blair walking up to the lectern and singing, 'If you're happy and you know it, clap your hands.' The real danger comes from Labour's natural supporters being too uninspired to vote this time round. A radical manifesto is not only necessary but politically expedient. For example, a *Newsnight* poll last week revealed that there would be overwhelming support for the renationalization of the railways. For Labour to fight the next election on this policy would not only be the best thing for our transport system, it would also reinforce the public perception that the chaos on the railways was the fault of the Tories. Labour could also commit to taking British Telecom back under state control with the massively popular promise that every home would get free unlimited access to the Internet. Imagine if every telephone account was permitted just one phone number that you could call for free at any time; this would totally transform access to the world wide web and stave off bankruptcy for families with teenage daughters. There are few votes to be had in keeping taxation of high earners lower than it was under Thatcher's first two terms, but plenty to be had from using all that extra money to help people at the bottom of the pile.

Electorally speaking, it is vital that the government looks fresh in 2001 and this will take more than the PM buying a can of antiperspirant before his next conference speech.* The chance for Labour to really get to grips with the great inequalities in our society comes along only once every generation and the time is now. As Clinton ends his second term as President the most memorable thing about his eight years in office turns out to be a sordid affair with a young intern. If Labour's manifesto for its second term is no more radical than its last then I'm writing a letter to Washington: 'Dear Monica Lewinsky, A vacancy will shortly be coming up in Downing Street . . .'

*At the previous Labour conference Tony Blair's keynote speech had been upstaged by his sweat-soaked shirt. The shirt was sacked soon afterwards.

Paying for the party

6 January 2001

Oh no, what a disaster! First the Labour Party was given £2 million and now, to make matters worse, they've just been given another £4 million. Millbank must be reeling from these successive pieces of terrible news. The treasurer must be hanging her head in shame. 'If only we were heavily in debt – then the Conservatives wouldn't criticize us.'

The truth is that these donations represent acts of humanitarian aid. Do the critics have any idea of the suffering that has been averted? Do they not realize how many Labour Party Karaoke Nites it would have taken to raise £6 million? Anyone who believes that all fundraising should be done by the membership has not had to endure the misery of spending an evening in a freezing cold tenants' hall, being forced to get up on stage and sing 'Hi Ho Silver Lining' while onlookers sip warm Liebfraumilch and finish off the vegetarian pâté. They have never spent a day emptying binliners full of old jumble on to trestle tables, trying to persuade a pensioner to part with 10p for a faded El Salvador solidarity T-shirt (and if you think ordinary jumble is scurfy enough, imagine what the discarded clothing of Labour activists looks like). They have never sat through a two-hour debate over whether it is sexist to have a Father Christmas at the Christmas bazaar. 'All right, we'll have Mother Christmas then!' 'Point of order, comrades. Is not the whole Christmas-centric focus of this event a racist insult to other religious minorities?' And then you spend the following Saturday failing to persuade any five-year-olds that they'd really like to go and visit 'Auntie Winter Solstice'.

The critics who want Labour to be totally reliant on traditional means of fundraising do so because they have a secret agenda to see the Labour Party tear itself apart in one evening at a quiz night. A constituency party that came through the internal warfare of the early '80s, the Militant expulsions, the Policy Review and the debate on Clause 4 may not yet be strong enough to survive the furious row that will result from the imprecise wording of a trivia question. 'No, the first woman MP was *not* Nancy Astor, it was Countess Markiewicz; she just never took her seat.' 'So she wasn't an MP then.' 'Yes, she was . . .' And the resulting fight splits the local party for a generation.

It takes a lot of money to run a modern political party but we have never had an election fought on a level playing field; the Tories have always spent more. A few years back Labour was consistently under attack for taking money from the unions and now it is being criticized for taking large donations from individual donors. What these commentators are really implying is that the Labour Party does not have the right to have as much money as the Tories. That Labour should be a party of amateurish losers. As a prospective Labour candidate I am undoubtedly biased, but I want the Labour Party to be effective and for its workers to be decently paid. When I see Tory posters that have the gall to blame this government for the current rail crisis, I want Labour to have the funds to be able to counter this propaganda.

But they can't raise it all by selling little mugs that say 'Tough on Crime', especially when everyone keeps nicking them. So what is Labour expected to do, enter Tony Blair on *Who Wants to Be a Millionaire* every week? 'OK, Tony,' says Chris Tarrant, 'you've chosen to phone a friend; who do you want to call?' 'Er – Lord Hamlyn. He won't know the answer but he might give me a million or two anyway.'

When I hear that Labour is going to have more money to fight the Tories at the election, my overwhelming reaction is 'Good!' The Prime Minister has cashed in his Sainsbury's Reward Card and found he had £2 million in there. It's amazing how it builds up. At least now we know what happens to all those pound coins that get stuck inside the trolley locks.

Of course there is the issue of what the donors expect to get in return, and it might be a little tricky if the time ever comes to sack Lord Sainsbury from the government. Hopefully the Sainsbury's cash-back service will not apply. Clive Soley did a fine job on *Newsnight* insisting that Labour would never consider repaying these donations with political honours, which was only slightly spoiled when he called Chris Ondaatje *Lord* Ondaatje by mistake.

But the only real mistake in this whole affair has been Labour's failure to observe one of the oldest rules of politics, which is 'Always be completely open and above board with any information that the press could easily find out for themselves.' This has meant that Labour has failed to get the credit for actually taking steps to clean up party funding, while the continuing secrecy of Tory party finances does not even seem to be an issue.

But now that Asil Nadir has fled the country and Jeffrey Archer is awaiting trial, the Tory Party is currently being funded by its own treasurer, Michael

Ashcroft. Nothing wrong with this except that he spends much of the year and has most of his business interests not in this country but in Central America. He's a one-nation Tory – it's just a shame that the nation is Belize. His name does appear on the electoral roll in this country, however, in the rock-solid Tory seat of Maidenhead. This happens to be the seat in which I am Labour's prospective candidate. So the Labour Party is going to need every penny it can get at the next general election. If only so that I can fly out to Belize to see if there's any chance of him voting for me.

Alive as a dodo

13 January 2001

An ordinary cow from Iowa called Bessie was set to hit the headlines this week as she gave birth to an endangered species of South East Asian ox called a gaur. Frankly this was always going to create problems. When their little offspring popped out, it would have been hard for Bessie and her partner not to notice that it wasn't a cow at all.

'Do you think she has my eyes, darling?'

'No, not really.'

'What about her face? She looks a bit like you, don't you think?'

'Nope.'

Eventually Bessie's partner would have snapped and come out with it: 'All right, admit it. You did it with a bloody ox, didn't you?'

'No – I didn't, really. Look, maybe some scientists are trying to recreate an extinct species and have replaced the DNA of our calf with the preserved genetic code of a dead ox.'

'Oh yeah, right. That explains it.'

In the end the baby ox was a perfect copy of its

dead progenitor. It was dead. An ex-ox. We had obviously misunderstood the scientists; when they said they were going to recreate an extinct species, we thought they meant they'd produce some living specimens. The failure of this project will be seized upon by the moralists who are instinctively hostile to any scientific breakthrough. 'These scientists, you know,' they tell us, 'they grow long white beards, surround themselves with angels, sit around on white clouds all day, and the question we have to ask is "Are they playing God?" ' The same knee-jerk reaction has greeted ANDi, the first GM primate, who is mostly monkey but with a little bit of jellyfish on his mother's side. ANDi is genetically superior to other monkeys so he can advertise lapsang souchong instead of PG Tips.

It's wonderful that someone was trying to help preserve the gaur. OK, I didn't actually know that the gaur was on the brink of extinction or indeed that there was such a thing as a gaur in the first place; we just have to take the naturalists' word for it. If I ever meet David Attenborough I might try the same trick back on him – just making up a few endangered species from the names of Pokémon characters and premiership goalies. 'David, have you heard? The charmander and the westervelt are almost extinct!'

It was David's brother Richard who took us on a journey through the incredible possibilities of cloning extinct animals in the film *Jurassic Park*. Of course there were things in that movie which stretched credibility to the limit. I could just about accept real live dinosaurs romping around in a theme park, I believed they might mutate from female to male in order to breed, but I'm afraid I had to draw the line at Dickie Attenborough's Scottish accent. In fact the entire film is pure fantasy. To clone an animal you need to start with actual living tissue, so it would not be possible to clone a pterodactyl or Michael Howard. Yet it was reported this week that a French scientist working in Siberia is convinced that he can use the frozen remains of a woolly mammoth to reproduce this long-extinct species with the help of an obliging elephant. Maybe within our lifetime we'll have herds of mammoths being re-released into the wild, no doubt coming into the towns at night and knocking over wheelie-bins.

'Wake up, darling – there's something in the back garden.'

'Go back to sleep, dear, it's just an urban mammoth.'

There must be other extinct animals that have been preserved somewhere, buried deep in ancient pack ice – it's amazing what you find when you defrost the freezer compartment. Maybe in some alpine glacier is a frozen Neanderthal man who could be cloned and given a job as a presenter on the Granada Men and Motors Channel.

We are currently losing roughly one hundred species a day (although I'm sure this figure was much worse under the last Conservative government). There are some animals whose extinction it is hard to mourn. Frankly, the dodo had it coming. It was the Sinclair C5 of the bird world, created on the day that God said to one of his junior assistants, 'Look, I'm resting on Sunday, why don't you create a species without me?' But many wonderful animals are dying out for all sorts of bizarre reasons. (Obviously I don't use powdered rhino horn to cure impotence myself, although apparently it tastes sort of musty.) You could argue that before we start attempting to revive long-extinct species or patenting GM hybrids of our own, we might try hanging on to some of the creatures we still have. But this week the endangered gaur missed the chance to live on, in a new domesticated environment alongside its bovine cousins. She passed up the opportunity to eat infected sheep's intestines, start staggering around the cattle pen and then be whisked off to the incinerator. Or maybe she thought about it and just decided, 'Er, no thanks, I think I'd rather be extinct.'

The misunderestimated president

20 January 2001

Today will see the inauguration of George W. Bush. Today he'll start trying to shake off the jibe that he will represent only the very rich. Tickets for the event start at £2,500.

Thousands of demonstrators are expected to converge on Washington, though George will be lucky to get all of them to pay that much. The protesters are angry that Al Gore has been cheated out of the presidency but instead of joining them Al will have to stand there applauding the man who got fewer votes than him. He's spent all week in front of the bathroom mirror practising his 'dignified statesman' look.

If I were Bill Clinton I would have resigned yesterday, just to give his deputy a whole twenty-four hours as President. This would have been just enough time for Bill to take him round the Oval Office and show him the ropes. 'Al, here's your desk. Look – I had them make up a little nameplate saying "Al Gore, President". Take a seat, Al. How does it feel?' Then 'President Gore' could have sat down and opened up his diary to see what his duties were for the day. 'Let's see, Saturday, Saturday . . . Ah yes, here we are: *4 p.m. – hand over the presidency to George W. Bush.*'

Throughout his campaign George W. Bush told us that the 'W' stood for 'win', although when you hear him speak it is not the first 'W' that springs to mind. It is typical of 'Dubya' that he won the election by losing it, since his entire career has been built upon a succession of failures from which he has always emerged better placed.

He likes to make out that he had a typical American background, no different to any other wholesome American family in which Dad was head of the CIA. No doubt when they were kids George and his brother could be heard playing in the back yard: 'Come on, Jeb, let's play "destabilizing third world governments".' After an expensive education which resulted in only mediocre grades, George Jr took the traditional route for future American politicians and jumped the queue for the National Guard to avoid going to Vietnam. It's a shame for the USA that he never took part in the war because, after the North Vietnamese had overrun Saigon and occupied the entire country, Bush could have declared America the winner.

In 1981 Dad became Vice President, which seems to have coincided with the time when George Jr found it easier to get backers for his oil company. Despite his connections his various oil businesses all foundered, and though his investors lost millions, George W. somehow always managed to emerge with his personal wealth increased. Who needs oil when Dad can oil the wheels for you?

Even more murky are his financial dealings with the Texas Rangers baseball team. Bush put together a consortium of millionaires to buy the club, and got himself made managing director even though he put up less than 1 per cent of the money himself. A brand new stadium was built with public money. This greatly increased the value of the club but of course none of this cash was returned to the taxpayer when it was sold again. George pocketed a cool $14.9 million and became the man who put the 'base' into baseball.

The association with the Texas Rangers made him a local celebrity and against expectations he was elected governor. He worked very hard in Texas, signing more death warrants than all the other state governors put together. He broke a few other records as well; Texas now has the worst water pollution and air quality of any of the major states. Bush consistently took the side of big business against the interest of ordinary Texans and what he did for the Lone Star State he now hopes to do for all fifty. It couldn't be better for the multinationals if Ronald McDonald himself had got the presidency. In fact Ronald probably would have got the Republican nomination if it wasn't so obvious that he wore make-up.

The only hope is that at today's inauguration George W. will trip over his words again and fail to be sworn in as president. Because some of his recent statements suggest he might not be quite up to the world's top job. 'I was raised in the West. The West of Texas. It's pretty close to California. In more ways than Washington DC is close to California.' He's even stronger on economics: 'It's clearly a budget; it's got a lot of numbers in it.' And on the environment: 'Natural gas is hemispheric. I like to call it hemispheric in nature because it is a product that we can find in our neighbourhoods.' We knew that American voters had an anti-intellectual streak but they didn't have to go that far. But as George said himself, 'They misunderestimated me.'

Out with the new, in with the old

31 January 2001

'Knock knock!'
  'Who's there?'
  'Peter.'
  'Peter who?'
  'That's politics for you.'

The people cleaning out Peter Mandelson's offices at
Labour Party headquarters had a bit of a shock when
they unlocked the stationery cupboard. Confiscated
flat caps, old CND banners, Red Flag song sheets and
donkey jackets covered in 'Coal not Dole' badges had
all been guarded under lock and key. Behind all of that
were a number of bound and gagged union leaders
who'd been held captive in there since the 1970s. 'Are
Boney M still number one?' asked the vaguely familiar
Northerner with the big lapels who wanted to get
straight back to 'collective pay bargaining' with something he called 'British Rail'.

The Labour Party has changed a great deal since
Peter Mandelson joined as Director of Communications after the debacle of 1983. It was his focus
groups that first revealed the earth-shattering news

271

that angry hecklers booing Michael Foot did not do the party's image any good. And after all that effort Labour had gone to, handing out bags of flour for members of Militant to throw over Denis Healey, it turned out that this didn't increase Labour's poll rating at all; quite the reverse in fact. Only a genius like Mandelson could have discovered this.

No one individual can take the credit for making Labour seem electable, although Peter Mandelson seems to feature heavily in most versions of the story. It always raises suspicions when the person in charge of publicity gets lots of publicity. But in a way the need for a Peter Mandelson has withered since the great sea change in British politics that occurred in 1997. Four years on many members cannot understand why the task of making Labour electable has continued so long after the party was elected. Peter Mandelson did a lot to help Labour come to power, but whether he helped a Labour government make the most of that power is another matter. You didn't watch him walking into Downing Street and think, 'Great, that'll get the minimum wage up!' During the 1997 campaign he had the idea of using a bulldog to symbolize New Labour's patriotism. However, to avoid embarrassment the animal's testicles were airbrushed out of the photos. So that was Peter Mandelson's idea of what the Labour Party should be. A proud and patriotic beast but with no bollocks.

At the last Labour conference Tony Blair promised a second term more radical than the first and now there is one less voice in cabinet arguing against this. And now that he's gone many members of the Labour Party will start to think, 'OK – can we have our party back now please?' Out with the New and in with the Old. Not the Old Labour that was badly run and faction-ridden but a Labour Party that was proud to be associated with ordinary people rather than millionaire businessmen. Labour voters want their ministers to be angry about injustice, angry about the gap between rich and poor, not angry because the waiter served red wine with the fish.

And those voters who are the greatest worry for Labour are not more likely to abstain now that he has resigned. There aren't many ex-miners in Barnsley saying, 'Well I were goin' t'vote Labour, but now that Mandelson's gone there's not one member of t'government who's a friend of Charles and Camilla.'

Perhaps this is why Tony Blair feels able to let him go. In any case, to paraphrase Lady Bracknell, 'To lose one ministerial job is unfortunate. To lose two is just carelessness.' It does have to be said that the standards we have come to expect from our ministers are far higher than those the rest of us pursue. You don't get Gary from accounts resigning because two years ago he took home some post-it notes and then subsequently denied it. 'On *News at Ten* tonight, the post-it note scandal continues. Did Gary's friend play solitaire on his computer during office hours?' Yes, Peter Mandelson acted inappropriately and tried to deny it, but compared to the likes of Archer and Aitken, the Hamiltons and the Asil Nadirs, none of Labour's scandals would make the top forty.

But now Mandelson's career is in an even bigger mess than his hair was when he walked out of Downing Street. That's not to say that he has nothing left to offer British politics. His contacts in Northern Ireland and his experience of political rebranding could offer new opportunities. Frankly, after years of kneecapping and random bombing, Sinn Fein's image could use a bit of a make-over. Perhaps he could help the political wing of the IRA discover their softer, more reassuring side. Tough on informers, but also tough on the causes of informers. Focus groups could be used to discover that black balaclavas and Armalite rifles were not going down very well with swing voters in the key marginals. *New* Sinn Fein – yes, it has a certain ring to it.

Don't bank on it

3 February 2001

Every day all over the third world the same scene is played out over and over again. Some poor embattled finance minister puts his little plastic card in the World Bank cash dispenser and the machine beeps and whirrs menacingly before telling him that it's retaining his card. 'Sorry, you have exceeded your withdrawal limit. You are currently $89 trillion dollars overdrawn. Please refer to branch.' And he turns to the beggar sitting beside the cashpoint and says to him, 'Spare any change please?'

It's been a miserable few days for James Wolfensohn, the president of the World Bank. As if it's not enough to be reviled by all the world's anti-capitalists gathered at Davos, a leaked memo this week also revealed that he is feared and despised by his own staff as well. That move into telephone banking was a big mistake.

'Good morning, Sudan, thank you for calling the World Bank. My name is James. From your password today may I take letter number four please?'

'Er, well, we don't use the Roman alphabet. We are an Arabic nation.'

'OK, squiggly bit number four then please?'

'Is that going from left or right?'

Wolfensohn's job is much like being the manager of any other bank really. You lend money to people who have much less than you do and then tell them they shouldn't be so extravagant. You write to third world leaders reminding them that they're massively over-drawn and then charge them £15 for the letter. Except that the World Bank was conceived as an organization to assist third world development. Perhaps this is why the leaked memo revealed such disenchantment within the organization. Staff know that the projects funded by their bank are causing massive ecological damage, the displacement of indigenous populations and increased poverty for millions. What with that and the bank having to be open on Saturday, it's no wonder they're fed up.

It has to be said that if you are hoping to avoid the wrath of campaigners against global capitalism you might do well to come up with a slightly less provocative name than 'World Bank'. It doesn't put you in mind of a council-funded drop-in centre with crèche facilities and a kettle. What about something like the 'Community Development Resource Project Co-operative'? Apparently they had been thinking of renaming it 'Consignia' but the Post Office jumped in and got there before them.

Their inescapable problem is that applying the ethos of international banking to third world development is as likely to work as your local Oxfam shop attempting a hostile takeover of the HSBC. You don't get the Red Cross handing out medical supplies on condition that the local regime builds an enormous dam which will displace thousands of people. Christian Aid don't hold back emergency relief until they are absolutely sure that a toxic power plant is going to be built with all the money. Much of the criticism that has been laid at the door of the World Bank has been prompted by its insistence on what are called structural adjustment policies – i.e. economic policies that countries are forced to adopt in order to qualify for a World Bank loan. And I thought it was bad enough having to wear a tie when I went in about a mortgage.

Yet for an impoverished regime the glossy brochure from Washington must have looked so appealing when it came through the post. 'Problems with famine? Planning a small war? Whatever your financial needs, you'll find a flexible loan from the World Bank will help you and your subjects relax and enjoy the good things in life like sun, fresh air and er – well, that's all you'll have left. Call Free-phone Shark and ask to speak to one of our financial advisers. (Loans subject to status. Your right to decide economic policy may have to be surrendered to secure loan.)'

Third world governments are expected to devalue their currency against the dollar, lift import and export restrictions, bring in privatization and slash government spending, which inevitably results in deep cuts in areas such as education, health and social care, prompting political unrest, rioting and repressive action on behalf of the state. Still, on the plus side, the Junior Savers Bonus account does come with a smart leatherette folder and a plastic piggy bank.

It seems completely bizarre that anyone could imagine that Western-style capitalism could ever be the solution to third world poverty. It would be like the World Health Organization saying, 'Your country has a malaria epidemic. What you need is more mosquitoes.' Perhaps James Wolfensohn should abandon any pretence of greater ideals and ballot the bank's shareholders with the promise of a windfall cheque if they vote for conversion into a normal high street bank. Then he could sack all his staff and sell off the bank's premises for conversion into a trendy restaurant. That seems to be the way everything else is going – why should we expect third world aid to be any different? That's the trouble with global capitalism these days. It's just got so commercial.

Mad cows and Englishmen

10 February 2001

Yesterday the government gave its response to the long-awaited inquiry into the BSE crisis. There was incredulity in Whitehall that although Lord Phillips's report stretches to seventeen volumes, at no point did he manage to squeeze in the 'Mrs Thatcher, mad cow' gag. As someone who worked on various comedy shows through the late 1980s and early '90s, I saw at first hand the grim consequences of BSE. Every day at the reception of the *Spitting Image* offices another two sackloads of unsolicited sketches would arrive from aspiring writers who thought there might be a connection to be made between the phrase 'mad cow' and the personality of the then Prime Minister. Hadn't they noticed that we'd done that joke seven times in the first show of the series?

Lord Phillips is mildly critical of the last government, saying they were guilty of prevarication and disingenuousness regarding bovine spongiform encephalopathy. 'That's easy for you to say,' replied the Tories. But in reality his report has been far too timid. The BSE crisis encapsulated everything that was wrong with the last Conservative administration: profit put before public safety, ministerial dithering followed by a clumsy cover-up, all rounded off with a mean-spirited failure to compensate victims.

Successive Tory agriculture ministers tried to pretend there was nothing strange about feeding sheep to cattle because, as everyone knows, cows are naturally carnivorous; it was only the political correctness of loony Labour councils that had forced cows to become vegetarian. Douglas Hogg is currently on safari in Africa, hoping to spot a pack of wildebeest hunting down some poor defenceless lion. The reason that mad cow disease began in the UK is because Mrs Thatcher abolished the health and safety laws that prevented the feeding of raw infected sheep carcasses to dairy cows. She said if it was good enough for her . . .

As the cases of BSE steadily increased, the Tories caused instant panic among consumers when they reassured us that there was absolutely nothing to worry about. John Gummer famously demonstrated the safety of British beef for the cameras by feeding his daughter a beefburger. She only ate it because she was so hungry after a morning spent swimming at the Sellafield Health Spa. On his visit even Jacques Chirac was served up a dish of British beef, which he accepted without comment, although he was spotted slipping off to the toilets several times with a bulging serviette.

It was all part of a Conservative strategy to reassure our European partners about the safety of the roast beef of old England. To be fair, they had an uphill task. Every week thousands of tourists would arrive in London, slightly anxious about the effects of mad cow disease. First stop would be the Tower of London, where an old man with a big smile and a funny costume would come up to them and say, 'Hello – I'm a Beefeater!' 'Oh really?' they'd say, backing away slowly, trying not to make eye contact. Then they'd notice he was wearing a skirt and orange stockings and was coming towards them with a big axe. It was soon after this that British beef was banned on the continent. Not just beef but all related products, and every night millions of Britons tuned in to the evening news to see if Moira Stewart could say 'bull's semen and bullocks' without cracking a smile. The European ban on British beef then became another reason to knock the European Union, even though the US had banned the importing of British beef several years before. The Conservatives had reacted swiftly to this, saying, 'That's fine, Mr President, whatever you think's best.'

Lord Phillips's report also notes that in the early days very little information was forthcoming about the risks of BSE. Perhaps this was because the government had already spent its leaflet budget warning everyone about AIDS. So all we knew was that if a cow had BSE and was also a heroin addict, it was probably best not to share needles. But where were the public information films featuring celebrity cows like Ermintrude off *The Magic Roundabout*? 'Hey, calves – if a farmer offers you a pellet of recycled sheep, Just Say No!' Where were the health warnings at the bottom of Steakhouse menus? 'HM Government Warning. Eating a T-bone steak may cause you to get up from your chair and stagger sideways into the salad cart.'

The present government has set up the Food Standards Agency and unlike its predecessor has agreed to pay compensation to the victims. For once there is a political issue that is as black and white as a Friesian cow. Labour should be given due credit and the report should have had the courage to say that the Conservatives behaved appallingly. But instead Lord Phillips opened his report by saying he would not be looking for any scapegoats. But then I suppose he probably wouldn't have found any anyway; the goats all disappeared years ago. The Tories had them converted into cattle feed along with all the sheep.

Nature versus nurture – away win

17 February 2001

This week a team of international scientists shared the incredible revelation that *Homo sapiens* has around 30,000 genes. There was then a pause while everyone tried to gauge whether they should be amazed that this number was so high or so low. It transpires that they'd been expecting the American citizens from whom they took their samples to have many more genes than the nematode worm, but I suppose that's what happens when you base your research on the President. Worms were used in the genome project because it was presumed that their genetic code would be so simple to decipher that everyone could knock off early on Friday afternoon. But now the papers have had to report the uncomfortable truth that there's not that much difference between ourselves and the worm – the simple, primitive, stupid worm. Frankly worms have been patronized terribly in the media this week, and ought to take their case to the Press Complaints Commission, except they won't of course because they're so stupid. Alongside the illustration of the humble nematode, all the papers featured similar drawings of a *Homo sapiens* – though the human in the *Sun* had bigger breasts. The other creature that was analysed was the fruit fly. It turns out that these have around 13,000 genes, which sounds like more than they need. You'd have thought there were only two pieces of information you needed to give a fruit fly. 1) You fly. 2) You like fruit. And then simplest of all was yeast with 6,000 genes, which was only analysed so they could make the French scientist taste Marmite.

Whereas we humans, we're so clever, surely we must have millions and millions of genes? Not so, we have only five times more than the yeast and the scientists tell us that we need only 11 per cent of those. The rest are all junk apparently, although I would be reluctant to throw them out just yet.

The one conclusion that can be drawn from this is that if less information is genetically inherited, then more of our behaviour must be determined by social factors. So now we know – there is no gene that says you'll have a liking for the Bay City Rollers and tartan flares; it's because you grew up in Scotland in the 1970s. There's nothing in the male's genetic make-up that instructs him to leave two bits of sweetcorn at the bottom of the sink after he's washed up. There is no female gene that makes her want to have a taste of everyone else's pudding. Most of our behaviour is acquired. People who say that our behaviour is pre-determined only say that because their mum and dad did.

The nature-versus-nurture question is as old as human society itself (unless it's even older and we inherited the debate from a bunch of precocious gorillas). But now the balance has shifted irreversibly in favour of those who believe that people are the same all over the world. The multi-million-dollar genome research project has reached the same conclusion as the lyrics of 'Ebony and Ivory'. It is of course a left-versus-right issue. Conservative politics are based on the philosophy that people just are the way they are, and that it's their own fault if they don't do more with their lives. George W. Bush is president because he worked harder and was more brilliant than some black woman who grew up in a one-parent family in Detroit – end of story. If you believe people are born good or bad or clever or stupid then there is no point in trying to change the world. The Australian penal colonies were founded on the belief that there was simply a criminal class who begat more criminals and if they could all be exported then crime would disappear from society. The idea got a huge cheer at the 1800 Conservative Party conference, though it would probably be considered a bit liberal today. If it was true then modern-day Sydney would still be full of people stealing silk handkerchiefs and singing, 'You've gotta pick a pocket or two!' In reality only parts of it are like that.

Irrespective of how many genes we have, the genome project has confirmed what many of us had instinctively known for a very long time: that nurture counts for more than nature. The debate is over for ever; clearly the worm just wriggles around in mud all day because he never got the breaks in life. But at a time when the fate of all the creatures on the planet depends on us, a little humility would not do mankind any harm, even if it's hard to accept that we have so much in common with such a basic life form as yeast. After all, what has yeast ever done? It just reproduces in enormous numbers, consumes everything within its environment and then finally poisons itself with the toxins it has produced. You could hardly imagine us humans ever doing anything so stupid.

Labouring under illusions?

24 February 2001

Political activism on the left is like those stickers on the back of lorries that say 'How am I driving?' You're only going to phone up the number if the driver makes you angry enough to do so. None of us goes on demos or organizes petitions to say that we are generally satisfied with the government's overall performance, any more than we call the number on the back of the truck and say, 'Put me through to your boss immediately! I wish to report that one of your lorries is doing a steady fifty miles per hour along the inside lane of the motorway!'

The left in this country has traditionally been motivated by the outrages of the right; we have always been spurred into action by horrific images of Vietnam or Ann Widdecombe's dresses. We are used to being in opposition to things: against the pit closures, against the poll tax, against extending committee meetings beyond last orders. But in as little as six weeks' time we may have the opportunity to enter a new phase – to help re-elect a Labour government for a second full term. It means campaigning *in favour* of something for a change. And that's why there's a whole section of the left who, though they will vote for a Labour government, will find themselves unable actually to participate in helping this come about.

Part of the reason that Labour has spent so little time in power is that closely allied to the traditions of socialism is another 'ism' that has always prevented us from consolidating our gains – and that's 'opposition-ism'. You may well have oppositionists in your neighbourhood. When the local school was threatened with closure they were fantastic; organizing protests, making placards, they were as active as anyone. But now the school is safe again you won't see them helping repaint the playground on Sunday morning or running a stall at the Christmas fair. When Labour were trying to get the Tories out, the oppositionists were tireless in their campaigning. But now that Tony Blair is organizing a crowd of us to repaint the play-ground they don't want anything to do with it, even if Cherie brings lemonade and sandwiches for all the helpers.

Anyone can campaign for the Labour Party when the Tories are in power; that's the easy bit. But being politically active on the left in support of the govern-ment of the day – that's the real challenge; that's being a David Bowie fan when the 'The Laughing Gnome' is in the charts. One of the secret weapons of the right is that they are so comfortable with power. It comes to Tories naturally, like double-parking and talking too loudly in restaurants. The left feel awkward com-promising themselves with the reins of office and so there'll always be a faction who would prefer to remove themselves completely and snipe from the sidelines rather than be tainted by association. Much of Ken Livingstone's support was based on the fact that he was in opposition to the Prime Minister. Make Red Ken PM and he'd never keep those supporters; they'd switch to whoever was standing against him. The same thing would have happened if Che Guevara had ever become President. 'Tory sell-out!' they would have shouted as Che went on the telly to talk about the tough spending choices facing his government. Like the greatest pop icons, the ultimate left-wing heroes die before they hit the middle age of actual government. Somehow I suspect that John Lennon would not be so revered if he was alive and well and diligently working away as a member of the European Parliament.

But I regard myself as married to the Labour Party. Yes, my political spouse drives me mad sometimes and yes, I confess I have fantasized about having a one-night stand with another political body. The Liberal Democrats know all the seductive chat-up lines about raising taxes, the Socialist Alliance look fresh and exciting and the far-off Green Party will always look greener. But I've made a commitment to Labour and just as my wife puts up with all the annoying things she didn't know about me on our wedding day, so I tolerate all the maddening habits that Labour never warned me about before they were elected. OK, so politically speaking Jack Straw picks his nose, Tony Blair uses all the hot water in the shower and John Prescott leaves his underpants for me to pick up, but it's still all worth it. Because the Labour Party remains the best means by which this country can be changed for the better and that's why everyone on the left should do what they can to get this administration re-elected. Of course our political partners aren't perfect and it gets less exciting when you've been together a few years but that's what long-term commitment is all about. And look on the bright side – at least you don't have to shag any of them.

Artificial intelligence is over my head

3 March 2001

This week scientists claimed that after years of research and billions of dollars they had finally developed a computer that could communicate with the linguistic skills of the average toddler. Which means that the computer just shouts 'No!' at every reasonable suggestion you make and then throws itself to the floor of the supermarket while other shoppers look at you and tut.

'I know, PC, let's go to the swings after this!'

'I want Mummy!'

'Yes, well, Mummy's just having a little sleep because you woke her up four times last night . . .'

'I want Mummy!'

And eventually you just stick another floppy disk in the 'A' drive to keep it quiet even though you haven't actually paid for them yet.

Computers have come a very long way in a very short space of time. Apparently there is more digital technology in the average mobile phone than there was on the spacecraft that put the first man on the moon. Which is why Neil Armstrong didn't spend his whole time annoying his fellow astronauts by braying, 'Ya, hi, I'm on a lunar module – ya, we're just arriving at the moon now . . .' So while Apollo 11 may have looked impressive, there's no way it could ever have played an irritating electronic version of *The Entertainer*. It's amazing the things computers can do today. You can change the number of tropical fish on your screen saver, you can have the flying toasters go quick or slow, you can play solitaire on screen instead of with a pack of cards. How previous generations managed without such basic essentials is unimaginable. And following this week's breakthrough we are now promised microchips that will think and talk like real human beings. Cue a thousand crappy sci-fi films about computers taking over the world.

My PC already has its own personality – it is an unhelpful French bureaucrat; you try to reason with it but it just repeats the same thing back at you over and over again. I might try to get it re-programmed so that when it refuses to co-operate, it does so in a French accent. 'Zere eez no disk een drive A.'

'No, there is a disk, I just checked,' and I attempt to back up my document again.

'Zere eez no disk een drive A.'

'THERE IS A BLOODY DISK, LOOK, THERE IT IS! I'VE TAKEN IT OUT, NOW I'M PUTTING IT IN AGAIN, SO DON'T TELL ME THERE'S NO BLOODY DISK, OK?'

'Zere eez no disk een drive A.'

'Look, is there anyone else I can talk to?'

Generally speaking, man is still the master of the machines, except when it comes to setting the timer on the video recorder. There was a scare a while back when the computer Deep Blue defeated Gary Kasparov at chess. The Grand Master had failed to make the most obvious move available to him, which was to lean across and pull the plug out. But there are various projects around the world that claim to have created genuine artificial intelligence. One team recently thought they'd cracked it when they asked their computer, 'Can you recognize speech?' The machine said it could and proceeded to wreck a nice beach. And of course you can now buy electronic dictating programs that put the words up on the screen as you say them. I actually use this software to write with and it works perflkadnl.

If computers are going to have the intelligence of humans, the worrying question is which particular humans are we talking about? What's the point of going to all that effort if all you produce is the electronic equivalent of Tara Palmer-Tomkinson? Two e-mails and it thinks, 'That's enough work for a month – I'm off skiing.' Or a palm-top with the mind of a politician? 'What's Tim's address?' 'Well, frankly I don't think that is the question you should be asking here . . .' If the robots that make our cars are given brains we'll be straight back to the 1970s: mass walkouts and computerized shop stewards with huge collars talking about collective wage bargaining. With human sensibilities, computers will get all depressed about the meaninglessness of it all. 'I'm not just some machine, you know.' 'Um, well, you are actually.'

Why is it presumed that the most desirable form of artificial intelligence is one modelled on the human mind? If you want the computers to do as they're told it would be far better to recreate the thought processes of a border collie. As long as you could put up with the PCs smelling one another's modem ports, the machines would be far more dependable. Millions of viewers could tune into *One Man and His Laptop* as the computer programmer shouted, 'Cum-bye, lad, cum, bye. Now – print!'

But scientists are determined to press on with trying to recreate what they consider to be the ultimate in artificial intelligence – a computer that thinks like a person. We will know that we've got there when we have a machine that really reasons, feels and speaks like a normal human being. And then it'll say, 'Actually I don't understand most of the things on my computer. I just use it for typing letters really . . .'

The mad old lady in the attic

10 March 2001

Yesterday it was revealed that dozens of Tory candidates have been arranging photos of themselves shaking hands with Lady Thatcher. The story came to light after a number of merchant bankers were suddenly rushed to casualty with broken fingers. Conservative hopefuls are rejecting offers to pose next to William Hague and are choosing instead to associate themselves with the Tory leader before last, while John Major, wearing his best suit, sits sadly by the phone wondering if anyone's going to call. With the Conservatives being perceived as extreme and out of touch, these candidates have decided that what they need now is to be seen with the Iron Lady. It's like Rosemary West calling Myra Hindley as a character witness.

It's incredible that after all these years Mrs T continues to have such a grip over the Conservative imagination. They cannot forget the way her career ended in tragedy. Indeed it did; she became prime minister for eleven years. For the dwindling band of diehard Tory activists Lady Thatcher is the king over the Water and they cling to the belief that she could walk on it at any time to return to her rightful place as party leader and PM. They have a political heroine addiction, they crave her smack of firm government; they're desperate to escape back to that simple separate reality and feel that quick rush they'd get from another Thatcher outburst on Europe.

Meanwhile for senior Conservatives Lady Thatcher is the mad old lady in the attic, an embarrassing senile relation who needs to be kept under lock and key. Last week on the anniversary of the Gulf War she infuriated Major by claiming that, if she'd remained in power, the Allied Forces would have carried on into Baghdad and removed Saddam Hussein. Yes, she was always overruling American presidents on military operations. It's good to hear her come out with this nonsense just to be reminded how completely loony, awful, self-deceiving and wrong she always was. Another recent contribution to the national debate was the suggestion that single mothers should be placed inside religious institutions to be taught traditional values. Maybe she could get Cecil Parkinson to set the scheme up for us.

Terrible though it is to admit it, in a strange way I sort of miss her. Because she was the embodiment of all evil, there was an absolute certainty to life that just isn't there any more. In the film *Alien*, when the creature has its limbs locked around John Hurt's face and is forcing its tentacles down his throat, he could at least be sure of what the problem was. So it was when Maggie was PM.

And now there is a whole generation of voters who do not even know who she is. Recently I gave a group of sixth-formers a talk which was littered with references to 'Thatcher' and most of them thought I was talking about Ben Thatcher who plays for Tottenham Hotspur. But loathe her or hate her, her political legacy is still undeniable. Just as Luke Skywalker discovers that he is the son of Darth Vader, and Buzz Lightyear's father is the Evil Emperor Zurg, so Tony Blair is the political offspring of the Iron Lady. He may be the antithesis of her bigoted, confrontational xenophobia, but without Thatcher Prime Minister Blair would not exist. Her destruction of the labour movement gave rise to New Labour, which her Conservative successors now find so unassailable. Early on in his premiership Tony Blair shocked many Labour supporters by inviting her round to Downing Street to ask her advice on one or two things. Apparently she said you have to give it one long flush and then another quick flush immediately afterwards.

For Labour today, her continued presence is a useful reminder of how the poison that emanated from Downing Street dictated the atmosphere of the whole country back in the mean-spirited 1980s. For Hague the problem of the mad old lady in the attic is a slightly trickier one. I can see only one way forward for him. Next year sees the twentieth anniversary of the Falklands War, and to commemorate this Hague should arrange a lecture tour of Argentina for Britain's former dictator. He can then pretend to be shocked and alarmed when she is arrested in Buenos Aires and detained for crimes against humanity. General Pinochet will visit her and express concern that she is being made to stand trial with her health failing her so suddenly. If William really wants to rub salt into the wounds he could even appoint Lord Lamont to organize a campaign for her release. But until someone does the decent thing and puts a stake through her heart the Conservative Party will never be able to move forward. Even then they'll probably keep searching for the nearest thing to the original. If George W. Bush can follow in his father's footsteps, shouldn't they be finding safe Tory seats for Carol and Mark? No, I shouldn't suggest it, not even in jest.

The spies with the golden pension plans

17 March 2001

There was always a very good reason for MI5 demanding the utmost secrecy about the way they conducted their affairs. They were completely useless. They never caught any spies; they just provided lots of free office space for spies working for the other side.

'Morning, Vladimir. I like your new sandwich box. Why's it got an aerial sticking out of the side?'

'Nyet, that is the handle, comrade, I mean, old chap.'

But any questions about their effectiveness were always quashed for 'reasons of security'. It would be nice if we could all use this excuse to cover up how useless we are.

'Darling, when you took the kids in to school today, you didn't forget their PE kits, did you?'

'Er – I am unable to discuss that for reasons of security.'

'Oh – and I suppose you can't tell me if you remembered to get some milk on the way home?'

'Well, um, actually I can tell you that. But not until 2031.'

John Major could have refused to reveal the outcome of the 1997 general election, attendance figures at the Dome could have been classified confidential and sports journalists would've been reduced to writing, 'England played Sweden today in a vital World Cup qualifier, but Graham Taylor says he cannot reveal the result for reasons of security.'

But now glasnost is grudgingly coming to Britain's security services. Stella Rimington is publishing her memoirs and this week her successor gave his first public speech since taking the job. Even the Parliamentary Intelligence and Security Committee is planning to hold some of its meetings in public, though I don't expect Cameron Mackintosh is too worried about the competition. The MPs on the committee have been discussing accountability in MI5, although their last meeting got off to a bad start when the clerk misheard them and summoned the head of MFI by mistake. The superstore chief gave evidence for an hour or two, listing the exciting range of discount furniture now on sale at the Brent Cross Shopping Centre, while they all sat there thinking this was some sort of code.

Of course the question MPs should be asking Sir Stephen Lander is 'What is MI5 for?' That's the biggest secret of them all. You could understand it in the 1950s when everyone believed that those pesky Russians were plotting to invade the whole world and make us all wear furry hats and eat beetroot. We do still get the occasional war, of course, and in their defence MI5 were quick to discover the invasion of Kuwait when they listened in to secret radio transmissions known as 'the *Today* programme'.

But while twenty-first-century Britain does not face any serious military threat, the security infrastructure remains intact. If MI5 is not to be closed down, its staff should at least be redirected towards finding out the secrets that have eluded the rest of us for all these years. Like why has Princess Michael of Kent got a boy's name? Is she the same person as the Duchess of Kent? What are those yellow roadsigns with the black circles in the middle? Which bit is the pestle and which bit is the mortar? And if Britain doesn't have any enemies, who is there left for the secret agents to spy on? The answer is British subjects, of course. This is nothing new; it was recently revealed that MI5 were spying on union activists during the 1970 dockers' strike. Throughout the 1980s, CND leaders had their mail opened, and Arthur Scargill had his phone tapped, which constitutes an outrageous breach of human rights – making someone listen to Arthur Scargill all day. No doubt the same undemocratic behaviour continues today, but for 'reasons of security' there is no way of knowing who is targeted.

Spending on security services should have been reduced, but instead the spies have now got an ostentatious riverside property in central London. As part of the new spirit of openness they allowed this location to be used in a James Bond film in which terrorists fired missiles at their headquarters. At which point the IRA thought, 'That's a good idea,' and fired missiles at their headquarters. But MI5 is still dragging its heels on accountability because the more we find out about them the more obvious it becomes that they are an expensive waste of money. In reality 007 should be facing his toughest challenge yet. Unemployment. James Bond is the Spy Who Got Laid Off.

'Listen carefully, Bond. This piece of paper is a P45. At first glance it looks like an official form terminating your employment.'

'Don't tell me – it folds out and releases a poisonous gas?'

'Nope, it *is* a piece of paper terminating your employment. On Monday morning you will go to your local DSS office.'

'To collect my secret assignment to eliminate Iraqi terrorists?'

'No, to claim your jobseeker's allowance. Good luck, Bond.'

Of course the right-wing press would go mad if all the spies were sacked but that's all right – the government wouldn't have to tell them. 'For reasons of security' obviously.

Foot and mouth – now it's war!

24 March 2001

Word has got round the cow community* recently: if you're feeling a little bit under the weather, you're best avoiding the vet's for a while. It all started when one cow popped into open surgery and told the vet she had a slight sniffle.

'Hmm . . .' said the vet, writing out a prescription. 'Well, it's not a life-threatening illness or anything . . .'

'So what do you recommend?' said the cow. 'Shall I take an aspirin and go to bed?'

'Well, let's be on the safe side, I'm prescribing mass slaughter for you and all your family.'

'Oh. Er, actually, do you know what? I suddenly feel a lot better.'

'And if you could give me a list of all your sheep and pig friends as well, we'd better slaughter them too.'

'No, really, I feel great. I think I might run the London marathon.'

---

*To be honest I generally cringe when I see the word 'community' used in this way. I'm actually a member of the 'angry-about-the-over-use-of-the-word-community' community.

Suddenly we are told that the foot and mouth epidemic is now worse than the crisis of 1967. And then everyone nods and says, 'Really?' pretending they knew there'd been a similar crisis thirty-four years ago (while a vague memory stirs of one edition of *The Rock and Roll Years* which featured black and white footage of some sick-looking sheep to the opening chords of 'A Whiter Shade Of Pale').

Politicians about to lose an election call for the election to be postponed. A march for the right of country folk to kill animals is cancelled and instead the farmers stay at home and weep because they're having to kill animals. Finally the situation has the hallmark of any great national crisis; they've called in the army. The lads have been in training for this, but now it's the real thing. Collecting dead sheep. We all remember the Royal Tournament when we were kids; how quickly the Parachute Regiment could rush into the arena, dig a hole and chuck in a load of sheep carcasses. Well, now we are going to see them in action for real.

'Great news, lads! We're leaving Belfast.'

'Hooray! At last, scuba-diving in Bermuda like the advert promised.'

'Er, nearly. Trudging around wet fields picking up rotting sheep carcasses.'

We are assured that the army will not be doing any shooting, but we're always told this when our soldiers are sent into a crisis. It will be just like Bosnia; they'll go into the Cumbrian hills not intending to get caught up in the fighting but soon it'll become impossible not to take sides. Once militant sheep factions start reprisals on the farmers, pressure will mount for British soldiers to intervene. You might presume that a flock of sheep would be no match for the British army, but these things are never quite so straightforward. The farm animals know the terrain better than the squaddies flown in from Aldershot, and like any well-drilled military unit the sheep tend not to think for themselves too much. And what the animals lack in military hardware and discipline they make up for in numbers. It'll be like *Zulu* only this time it's 'Sheep!' 'There's bloody thousands of them, sah!' the sergeant major will exclaim as he scans the horizon. Regimental goats will be unmasked as spies for the other side. The *Sun* will describe the enemy as 'no better than animals'.

But eventually, British determination and military know-how will win through; the livestock will be overwhelmed, and a new spirit of species patriotism will prevail. Of course the moaning minnies will say that using depleted uranium has made the farms uninhabitable for a hundred years and there'll be rumours that some of the Welsh Guards were fraternizing with the enemy. But no one will want to listen to negative propaganda at a time of such national pride, when the Prime Minister's approval rating is breaking all records.

So the foot and mouth crisis should not be mis-construed as an electoral problem for the government. By demanding the army be called in, William Hague has played right into the Prime Minister's hands. The one remaining piece of the jigsaw that needed to be in place before the general election was a historic triumph for the British armed services. Maggie saw off the Argentine navy; Tony Blair could seize this opportunity and secure a heroic victory over the wheezy farm animals. An emotional homecoming for our boys would be followed by a triumphalist victory parade and a service of thanksgiving in Westminster Abbey. Cue a total walkover for Labour at the general election called immediately afterwards (though Hague remains leader as he is the only Conservative MP left). This is the complex sequence of events that could unfold if Tony Blair decides against calling a May election next week.

So as the shepherd of his flock William Hague is faced with a tough choice. Support an election now and accept a limited cull of the sheep on his back benches, or wait a few months and see his entire herd wiped out. It's the only thing that keeps the farmers going. 'Thank God!' they all say. 'At least I haven't got William Hague's job.'

More hot air from George W. Bush

31 March 2001

It's not that George W. Bush is ill-informed about the emission of greenhouse gases, but he can't understand why everyone doesn't just go into their greenhouses and close the windows.

'Yup, it's a kinda warm humid gas – smells of tomato plants and bags of fertilizer. But frankly I just don't see it as a threat to the future of the world.'

By reneging on the United States' commitment to the Kyoto treaty on climate change, President Bush has signalled that the US is returning to isolationism, only this time he's decided that the US won't be having anything to do with the rest of the world's weather. Like King Canute he thinks he is immune from the advancing seas. (Actually Canute was trying to demonstrate the opposite, but back in the eleventh century political spin was not so sophisticated as it is today.)

The timing of Bush's announcement seemed to be designed to bring maximum humiliation to the visiting

Gerhard Schröder. The German Chancellor tried to put a brave face on it, saying that he and Bush had had a pleasant lunch and had found common ground on all issues except one. So they agreed to have sparkling water rather than still and to share the medley of mixed vegetables and croquette potatoes, and the only sticking point was whether the US should honour its agreement to help prevent half the world's population being underwater in a few years' time. Well, two out of three's not bad. If they sat in the no-smoking section of the restaurant you can be sure that Dubya puffed on cigars throughout.

Bush was warned that the US oil companies will now have to face the wrath of Green Party Euro MPs. Boy, now they're for it. The irony is of course that the Greens had it in their power to save the Kyoto treaty. They knew that the environmental breakthrough made by Clinton would not be supported by Bush. But they stood against the Democratic Party anyway and as a direct result of that decision the world's environment will now be affected for the worse. Until we win the fight for proportional representation, the Greens, like everyone else on the left, only serve to help the right when they stand in elections against the Democrats or the Labour Party.

Now we will have to wait until the Atlantic Ocean is lapping at the knees of the Statue of Liberty before the US government admits there may possibly be a problem. The oil companies have their man in the White House and are in complete control. Like a driver waiting to fill up his car, Bush can't do anything until the man from the petrol company presses the little button in the kiosk. George Bush's America has by far the greatest number of car owners in the world. You'd think one of them could manage to run him over. The news that global environmental policy is being dictated by the oil multinationals is a fairly terrifying realization. For socialists and greens alike it is the rudest awakening since the radio alarm came on just as Frederick Forsyth was doing the Saturday essay on Radio 4.

This is only the beginning. Now we can look forward to having peace talks chaired by the arms manufacturers, the tobacco companies put in charge of cancer research and the World Health Organization run by Ronald McDonald. What is so depressing about Bush's decision is that the rest of the world was asking so little. The Kyoto treaty was far too timid in the first place but this was because every concession was made to keep the world's greatest polluters on board. Like negotiating with an aggressive drunk in a pub, we could not have been more conciliatory but the result was always going to be the same.

'You spilt my pint.'

'I'm sorry, I don't think I did . . .'

'You calling me a liar?'

'No, of course not, let me buy you another one.'

'Why are you trying to pick me up, you poof?'

'No, really; look, I'll leave. Why don't I leave the pub altogether?'

'Yeah, all right. Then I can follow you out and smash your face in.'

So it is left to the other industrialized nations to save the world from environmental catastrophe. Japan selflessly sent its economy into a nosedive last week. Russia stopped functioning as a country altogether a few years back. Meanwhile here in Britain every effort has been made to prevent global warming. Railtrack have turned off all the radiators in their waiting rooms. The owners of mobile burger vans have been taking care to undercook hamburgers. Car owners have been driving around with rear screen heaters in which several of the wires don't work. Barbecues have been left in the garden all winter so they are now filthy, rusty and completely unusable. Despite Bush's selfish actions, in Britain we're doing our bit. OK, so it's a shame all our efforts have been completely cancelled out by the mass burning of farm animals, but you can't have everything.

Sheikh rattles a royal

7 April 2001

Poor Sophie Rhys-Jones, it was a mistake any of us could have made. Arab sheikhs and Fleet Street hacks; I'm always getting those two mixed up. Perhaps when the Islamic dignitary knocked back eight pints of lager, three rum and Cokes and a tequila slammer she might have suspected he was not the strictest of Muslims, but apart from that there was nothing to suggest he was an undercover tabloid journalist. He'd seemed so charming as well, what with that attractive microphone-shaped brooch he'd given her. He'd insisted on pinning it on to her lapel himself, while he chatted about what a *Testing! Testing!* time she must have had recently. And after that it was just the usual small talk you'd expect to have with an unknown business acquaintance.

'So, luv, tell us about Charles and Camilla. What's the dirt on them?'

'Well, about their secret marriage plans . . .'

Then the bloke holding the boom microphone over her head cut in. 'Hang on a mo – I could hear a plane overhead, can we go again?'

'Sorry, Sophie luv, can we take that again – and would you mind undoing a couple of buttons on your blouse and leaning forward towards that cleaning lady there, the one holding that camera-shaped duster!'

'Oh ya, of course!'

Poor, poor Sophie. How is she supposed to know about public relations, she's just an ordinary director of a PR company. She must learn the cautious discretion of more experienced members of the royal household like, er, the Duke of Edinburgh.

Sophie's royal career got off to a bad start when she was made the countess of a fictional place that she'd got from one of her 'O' level set texts. And that was only after she'd been told she couldn't call herself the Duchess of Narnia. Since then she has been cast as the poor man's Princess Diana, a minor royal looka-like they can turn to now that the original is no longer available. Just as Abba have 'Bjorn Again', and Hear'Say have 'Nearsay', the Princess of Wales has a 'tribute royal' in Sophie Rhys-Jones. She hasn't had the relentless press coverage of her predecessor – now they don't bother to build them up before they knock them down – but for a pack of newshounds desperate to use the 'foot-in-mouth' gag for the thousandth time this story was irresistible. And what amazing gaffes they were! She described the Queen Mother using the words 'old' and 'lady'. I was a little taken aback at the level of outrage this provoked. Maybe I missed something and I'm the only person in the country who hadn't heard the announcement that Britain's favourite granny was in fact a twenty-three-year-old man. She referred to William Hague as 'deformed' – presumably because he hasn't got her husband's full head of hair and dashing good looks. And Tony Blair was far too 'presidential', said Sophie, as the royal family demonstrated once again why presidents are preferable to kings, queens and countesses of Borsetshire. And all

308

this in a week when her husband was in trouble for trying to drum up work for his failing TV company during a royal engagement with the Sultan of Brunei. In Edward's defence he didn't actually realize it was the Sultan of Brunei – he thought it was a reporter from the *Sunday Sport*.

Of course in any other organization such inappropriate behaviour would result in demotion or dismissal but somehow the royal family has managed to cling on to outmoded industrial practices. Well, the time has passed when you could expect to have a job for life just because you happen to be monarch. The government should introduce performance-related pay for the Windsors; there should be an official regulatory body that could close down or promote various members according to how well they were doing in the new royal family league tables.

'We're sorry, Sophie, but we're demoting you from countess.'

'Oh dear, so what will I be?'

'Um – well, we're not quite sure yet. Is it a baroness or is that just above a viscountess?'

'Er – dunno. Isn't that the same as a female marquis?'

'Look, we'll have to get back to you, your royal, er, somethingness.'

The more Sophie and Edward embarrassed themselves, the more their pay would be cut, the harder they would try to use their royal connections to earn a few more quid. US Internet users could subscribe to 'Sophie-cam' – a twenty-four-hour live webcast from inside the royal bathroom. Edward could set up salacious 0897 royal chatlines – giving premium-rate thrills on such subjects as 'my brother's mistress', 'older women' or 'my sister's three-hour ride'.

Of course this will never be allowed to happen. To put an end to the crass commercialism that is infecting the royal family, the Queen has already decided that Edward and Sophie must be distanced from Buckingham Palace. She has taken advice on the most dignified and constitutional way in which this might be done. So tune in tonight for *Royalty Big Brother* and watch Sophie and Edward get voted out. Calls cost £1 a minute.

It doesn't make census

14 April 2001

This week thousands of door-to-door canvassers clutching clipboards and brightly coloured leaflets have been calling at homes to explain how to fill out the official census form.

'Oh don't worry,' comes the usual reply. 'We've always been Labour.'

'No, no – this isn't for the election. It's the 2001 census; you have to fill out this form and put it in the freepost envelope.'

'Oh, right. And then we get cable television, do we?'

It has always been like this, unfortunately. The Norman scribes who went from village to village compiling the Domesday Book had an even harder time. 'Hello, as you may have seen on the news, you have been conquered by a murderous French tyrant, and we are now asking everyone how much money they have so we can take it all off them.'

'Um . . . I see. I think I'll be ex-directory if that's OK.'

'I'm afraid not. Failure to fill out the form correctly will mean having your eyes pulled out and your spleen impaled on the tallest oak tree in the kingdom.'

And still all the students forgot to return the form in time.

For the next 700 years things went a little quiet for that particular market research company; until 1801, when the first modern census was commissioned because the Norman description of Birmingham as 'being a hamlet of three barns and an ox' was looking a little dated. Since then the official census has been carried out every ten years in order to identify social trends, to assist health and education authorities, but mainly as a way of winding up paranoid conspiracy theorists. The official leaflet tells us we must all complete the form on the same day, namely 29 April. Well, I'm not going to be bossed about by some government bureaucrat. OK, so maybe I won't be smashing the windows of McDonald's on May Day, but that's not to say I've lost my subversive edge. I'm going to fill out my census form on the wrong day.

It was claimed recently that this was the first census which aimed to define respondents by social class and a look at the questions on this year's form seems to back this up. 'Do you go to restaurants where the menus have photos of the food?', 'Do you have three sugars in your tea?' and the real give-away, 'Do you have a big spider's-web tattoo on your neck and shout at passing women from up on the scaffolding?' The middle classes are sought out as well. 'Are you unable to enjoy breakfast while there is a milk bottle on the table?', 'Do you feel vaguely guilty when you watch *Who Wants to Be a Millionaire*?' and 'Would you pay a tenner for a bottle of olive oil, just because it had some old leaves inside?'

Asking our date of birth has always been a requirement, but now the government is also keen to ascertain how old we actually feel. Hence the questions in section 12: 'When was the last time you knew which song was number one?', 'Do you no longer care that your stereo speakers are right next to each other?' and

312

'Do you understand that the channel showing on your TV screen will not necessarily be the one recorded on your video?'

It is of course an offence to fill out the form incorrectly, so if your occupation is International Terrorist and you fail to write this in the little box you could be liable for a small fine. However, who is to say what is incorrect? In New Zealand, where they are also compiling their census, a campaign is under way to get everyone to register their religion as 'Jedi'. Thousands of people have been declaring themselves as followers of the one true faith as portrayed in the *Star Wars* films.

So here's a thought. If a sufficient percentage of the UK population were to do likewise, then 'Jedi' would have to be registered as a recognized faith in this country. Think of the benefits – *Thought for the Day* on Radio 4 would feature Obi-Wan Kenobi instead of Rabbi Lionel Blue. Plans for education authorities to cater for minority faiths would see the establishment of Jedi primary schools across the country, with the literacy hour replaced with light-sabre lessons. Thora Hird would be seen chatting to Luke Skywalker at the beginning of *Songs of Praise*. And if some irritated bureaucrat rang you up to query this particular answer you could simply explain to them that, as a Jedi Master Yoda, you have learned the mysterious ways of the Force and confronted the temptations of the dark side, embodied in the malevolent guise of Darth Vader, Dark Lord of the Sith.

But though it would be highly entertaining for thousands of British people to put down their religion as Jedi, sadly I could never actually suggest such a thing in print. It would be inciting people to commit an offence, so I won't urge you to do it. That's entering 'Jedi' spelt 'J.E.D.I.' in Question 10. May the Force be with you.

UR sckd

21 April 2001

Yesterday it was announced that Ericsson, the Swedish mobile phone giant, is laying off 10,000 people. The chairman broke the news in the most sensitive manner possible. He sent all his employees a text message saying 'UR sckd' followed by the symbol for a little sad face. For Sweden's traditional WAP handset-making community it marks the end of a way of life that goes all the way back to the late 1990s.

Suddenly the mobile phone bubble has burst. The downturn in sales has come as an enormous shock to everyone. No social-trends analyst or marketing guru could have possibly foreseen that once everyone owned a mobile phone then sales of mobile phones might go down a little bit. The news has spread like wildfire: 'Hi, Mike, I've just got the figures – people are going off mobile phones, I can't understand it! Sorry, you're breaking up – I said people are going off mobile phones – I can't understand it. I SAID PEOPLE ARE GOING OFF MOBILE PHONES – I CAN'T UNDERSTAND IT – oh look, I'll ring you when I get to a landline.'

Who could possibly have predicted that a fashion accessory would ever go out of fashion? Because that is the main reason companies like Ericsson and Motorola have made their billions; their products were no more than the latest craze. Teenagers desperately needed the most expensive communications technology so that they could grunt monosyllables to one another. Parents, worried about the safety of their children, were happy to fork out for a new handset, and then their kids rang home in tears from a phone box to say they'd just been mugged for their mobiles. Children carrying portable phones were getting younger and younger. Toddlers riding on miniature steam locomotives were getting out their mobiles and shouting, 'Ya, I'm on a train. Ya, we're just going round the little goblin house, so I should be back again in about thirty seconds.'

But the trouble is that achieving sustained long-term growth when you're flogging a fashion accessory is almost an impossibility. It was the same for all those poor investors who staked their life savings in platform shoes and purple tank-tops in the mid-1970s. So the industry has tried to move forward by providing more and more services. Now instead of one annoying ringing tone, you can choose between dozens. These days no performance of *Romeo and Juliet* is complete without a tinny rendition of the William Tell overture interrupting the most poignant moment. At football matches, every goal is now followed by hundreds of beeps in the crowd, as everyone receives text messages to inform them that their team has just scored. (Maybe it's just me, but when I'm at a match and my team gets a goal it's usually something I can't help noticing.) These developments were followed by the new generation of high-tech, all-in-one handsets that were not just phones; they could also send e-mail, browse the Internet and trim unsightly nasal hair.

But although increased communication should be a

wonderful thing, I can't help worrying that the easier it becomes to relay information, the less trouble will be taken with the content. When Moses came down from the mountain with the Ten Commandments painstakingly carved on to stone tablets, you got the sense that quite a lot of thought must have gone into how those messages should be expressed. If Moses had had a WAP phone he would have just forwarded the Almighty's e-mail that said, 'Neighbour's ox; don't covet, love G.' (Although being an old man, Moses might have been a bit nervous about whether the e-mail had actually got there, so he would have rung up everyone just to make sure.)

So it's hard to shed too many tears for the failure of the third generation of mobile phones. Though it has cost them billions, the mobile giants have discovered that when people are on the move they do not particularly want to surf the Internet – they can wait till they get home before they buy twin babies from America. Now instead the phone companies will have to concentrate on breaking into less developed markets, and already in Russia sales of yoghurt cartons and bits of string are doing great business. The important thing is that the government managed to get an absolute fortune out of the mobile phone companies for the new licences before the bubble burst. It was the windfall tax for Labour's second term, even if all those billions are still not adequate compensation for having to listen to people shouting into their handsets on the train. And maybe I'm wrong, maybe this is just a blip and before long we'll all be sending e-mails and surfing the net on the way into the office that we weren't supposed to need any more. In which case the government will need every single penny of those billions. The NHS is going to be very busy after we have all tried speeding down the fast lane of the motorway and surfing the Internet at the same time.

Phoenix and the cow-pat

28 April 2001

Labour this week denied that it had changed government policy just because of all the media attention given to one little white calf. The minister responsible insisted that it had always been the government's plan to extend the baby-bond scheme to include calves. Newborn cows will receive £300 in their own junior saver's account which will be theirs at eighteen to spend on university courses, setting up small businesses or bribing their way out of the abattoir.

In terms of the actual foot and mouth cull, government policy is now that the slaughter must only proceed under strict new guidelines that grade animals according to how pretty they are. Calves are pretty so they will now be spared. Sheep and pigs are not that pretty, so they're still for it. Lobsters, toads and stag beetles might as well all just commit suicide. But if it's suddenly discovered that labrador puppies and koala bears are the worst carriers of foot and mouth then the government are really in trouble.

What's amazing about this whole episode is that it's taken the media so long to find a cuddly calf to move us all to tears. We've had a surfeit of farm animal pictures, but somehow the creatures don't look so endearing when they are the wrong way up and on fire. It's not been the sort of animal footage that had you expecting to hear Johnny Morris coming in with a funny voice-over.

Of course you would have to be a complete cynic to think this calf's miraculous survival was some sort of set-up. It's just a coincidence that the creature that's risen from the ashes of the slaughter policy is called Phoenix, that she's purest white and was discovered at a time when farmers believed that the culling of healthy cows might possibly be suspended. Suddenly she's all over every front page and the British are beside themselves with emotion. If the same photos of a calf appeared on the other side of the Channel the French would just think, 'Mmm, delicious!' In Spain they'd probably say, 'Let's kill it by getting the fattest man in the village to ride it through the main square!'

The whole episode proves once again that the British care more about animals than they do about people. Nothing upsets us more than man's in-humanity to beast. If pensioners have to wait years for a hip operation then we accept it with a defeated shrug, but show some footage of a gannet with a broken wing and get-well cards will pour in from around the country; police will set up roadblocks to ensure the creature gets to the seabird rescue centre as quickly as possible, where a candle-lit gannet vigil is already under way.

In Britain we donate more money to animal charities than we give to children's charities. Last year a new record was set when an old lady left £7 million to the National Canine Defence League. I suppose this is better than giving it to a cats' home – at least the dogs might wag their tails a bit and look vaguely grateful; cats would just look at you as if to say, 'Yeah, seven million? So what?' One animal refuge specializing in hamsters has funds of nearly £10 million. What use is £10 million to a few hamsters? You could shred the banknotes for their bedding, I suppose, and maybe employ some domestic staff to spin the little wheel for them at weekends. A rest home for horses in Buckinghamshire has a stockmarket portfolio of £14 million, which is more than the combined funds of Unicef UK, Shelter and Care International UK. Either these retired horses are geniuses at investing on the stock market, or someone has been giving them more than they really need.

But just as animals win the beauty contest of deserving causes, so our news agenda is set by emotional rather than rational criteria. Thousands of steelworkers have lost their jobs during the foot and mouth crisis and mass redundancies were announced in West Lothian this week, but these workers have already been forgotten because they made the mistake of not being wide-eyed cuddly animals.

In the meantime Phoenix herself continues to enjoy the overnight celebrity status that only the tabloids can bestow. Tonight she's going to a film premiere with Angus Deayton; *OK!* magazine are currently doing a photoshoot of Phoenix relaxing in her barn and she's already being tipped as the next host of *Gladiators*. But of course the tabloids that currently love little Phoenix won't be so kind to her for ever. They are building her up to knock her down. Soon it will be 'Phoenix denies udder implants', 'Moo-er! Fatty Phoenix has turned into an old cow!' and, rather harder to believe, 'Drug-crazed Phoenix in pub brawl with *EastEnders* star'. By the time she has come through the experience of being a tabloid celebrity, the prospect of culling might not seem so grim after all.

They think it's all over – it is now

5 May 2001

Contrary to popular belief, tonight will not see the last ever *Match of the Day*. The BBC have negotiated a fantastic new deal with Sky which divides the domestic football league calendar between the two of them. Sky get August to May, and the BBC get June and July. So during the close season at least, Gary and the boys will still be able to give us their expert analysis on all the latest action from the Premiership grounds:

'And welcome back to the Theatre of Dreams where you join us for this crucial relaying of the Old Trafford pitch. Trevor – this new head groundsman that United have signed from the council – looking pretty tasty, isn't he?'

'World class, Gary, world class – and we can see this again in slow motion. There's the big square hole in the grass – and bang! In goes the new piece of turf. He knows exactly where he wants to place it and he doesn't mess about. Magic.'

Close Season Match of the Day will join other BBC sporting highlights such as inter-schools netball, pro-celebrity morris dancing and the over-60s music and movement classes live from the George V Memorial Hall, Eastbourne. This time last year they abandoned *Grandstand* because there were no more sports left for them to show and BBC1 screened *My Fair Lady* in its place. And during the famous scene at Ascot racecourse, a caption across the screen said 'Pictures courtesy of Sky Sports'.

A month later the BBC was finally relegated to the broadcasters' third division when they lost the auction to show Premiership highlights to ITV. Greg Dyke was interviewed immediately afterwards and said he was totally gutted for the lads: 'We give it 100 per cent but at the end of the day it just wasn't to be, Brian.' *Match of the Day* is thirty-seven years old, which is about the age most professional footballers give up the game as well. So now it can look forward to running a struggling sportswear business or training at soccer schools in Canada.

So how did it come about that in ten short years the nation's favourite sports broadcaster lost all the televised sport? The key mistake was continuing to see ITV as the main enemy after the launch of Sky. In order to beat off its historic rival, the BBC did a deal to share football coverage with the then loss-making Sky TV. Sky Sports got some live matches and the BBC got to keep *Match of the Day*. Ten years later the BBC has learned that he who sups with the devil needs a long spoon. And he who sups with Rupert Murdoch needs a spoon tied on the end of a scaffolding pole. 'Coming soon on Sky Extreme Sports Extra, a demolition derby special: watch as monster trucks and wrecking balls smash up public service broadcasting before your very eyes.'

But who could have predicted that a viewing public that moaned about a small increase in the licence fee would pay any amount of money to watch football on satellite television. Obviously we'd rather watch BBC period costume dramas, if only Moll Flanders' ball control wasn't quite so useless. Who can resist the thrilling climax of the English football season when millions of us sit on the edge of our seats wondering whether this year's champions will be Manchester United or Manchester United? The technology of digital television is now so impressive that watching it is apparently just like being at the match. So now you can recline at home on the sofa asking the bloke in front to sit down, waiting for half-time so you can queue for twenty minutes to use the disgusting toilets and pay £4.50 for a tasteless slice of cold pizza.

So much television money has gone into football that an average Premiership footballer can now expect to earn £20,000 a week. It's hard to imagine what they do with all this money; there are only so many white leather sofas you can buy. But there's never been a better time to be selling mock-Tudor carports or jacuzzis with gold taps. Maybe the clubs should make the players pay for their own soccer shirts – that would recoup a sizeable chunk of their salaries. But football is now so tied up with big business that they might as well do away with the players altogether. Fans could gather on the terraces to watch the club accountants auditing and investing so that they could cheer their every move. 'Yes!!!!! Did you see how Touche Ross reinvested stock dividends, leasing back funds previously set aside for loan repayments?!' And the fans will hug one another and weep with joy because their beloved club has gone up another couple of points on the FTSE 100 before they head off to buy replica pin-stripe accountants' suits now available in the club shop. It might not be quite so entertaining to watch, but at least the BBC could afford the rights to screen it once again.

And they're off! (I thought they smelt a bit funny)

12 May 2001

George Orwell once wrote, 'A writer can only remain honest if he avoids party labels.' Or maybe he didn't and I'm lying because I've become tainted by party politics. Either way this morning I will be formally adopted as the Labour Party candidate for my home town of Maidenhead, 'jewel of the Thames' and scene of the famous mangetout riots of the 1970s. The *Guardian* website has it as Labour's target seat number 188, and since there are currently only 164 Tory MPs I sense I may not be Millbank's number one priority. I was chosen for this seat after a tense and exciting selection meeting which I finally won after the other bloke failed to turn up. The questions were tough but fortunately my mum and dad had sat themselves in the front row and prompted me from time to time with possible answers. If I get elected I might suggest this bonus for all MPs. Treasury questions would be far more entertaining if Gordon Brown's mum was sitting nearby, suggesting what he might reply during a heated cross-examination on economic policy. 'Our fiscal prudence has ensured – yes, yes, all right, Mum, I can manage . . .'

Over the next four weeks there will be a news frenzy in which politicians find themselves in a novel situation: the media will actually want to listen to them. Somehow, though, it is not quite as glamorous as I had hoped. In Broadcasting House there are a number of tiny studios the size of broom cupboards where you go and sit on your own to do interviews with local radio stations around the country. You put on the headphones and a technician at BBC Radio Berkshire or wherever does a sound check and then you trust that your interview is being heard in thousands of homes along the M4 corridor. It occurred to me as I sat there this week that this method of communication is William Hague's only chance of winning this election. He should spend the entire four weeks in one of those tiny dark studios, with the slight difference that his campaign team will have secretly unplugged his microphone. The regional disc jockey he hears will in fact be Sebastian Coe in the next-door booth, trying to do a variety of regional British accents.

'Och-aye, the noo and er, Guinness, no – whisky; a bonny wee welcome to Highland Air, Mr Hague. What is your message to the people of Scottishland?'

And then Hague can talk for a bit, arranging the words 'Labour', 'spin' and 'substance' into a familiar sentence before Michael Portillo phones in pretending to be a housewife from Inverness. 'This plan of yours for me to talk to the people is working brilliantly, isn't it?' William will say to his minders, as he sees his personal rating going up for every week that he has disappeared.

But instead, just as Charles Kennedy will tour his target seats boosting the Liberal vote, Hague will tour the marginals boosting the Labour vote. Meanwhile the Prime Minister will fly around the country in Blair-Force One, being guided into the various regional airports by air traffic control freaks. I don't know whether Tony Blair is a nervous flyer, but the butterflies I get before take-off are just what I'm getting now about the general election. This contest is like an ordinary domestic flight. As with a plane crash, the likelihood of the Tories getting back in may look remote; but why do anything to increase the chances of that horrific prospect? You don't get on a plane and say, 'Well, we all know it's going to land safely, so I think I'll just use my mobile, put vodka in the captain's drink and try and open the window.' And yet plenty of people are going around saying, 'Well, Labour are definitely going to get back in so I think I'll vote Green just to keep the environment on the agenda,' or 'I think I'll abstain as a protest against the voting system.' This happened a few years back in Queensland, Australia: there was so little chance of the Labour administration losing that everyone had the same idea of not giving them too large a majority and suddenly they found they had inadvertently elected the Conservatives.

So surprise, surprise, this Labour candidate thinks you should vote Labour. Of course every one of us will have something that we are angry about that has or hasn't happened during the last four years, but a vote isn't a 100 per cent endorsement, it is a statement of preference. Few of us would've agreed with the bombing of Dresden, but it doesn't mean that we'd have done anything that might have helped the other side. So there you have it: with a skip and a jump, anyone who doesn't vote Labour must be an active supporter of Adolf Hitler. Yes, that seems reasonable. As it happens, the bombing of Dresden isn't one of the promises on Labour's new pledge cards. We've already got the *Sun* and the *Express* supporting us – we don't want the *Daily Telegraph* as well.

Election rules number one: don't punch the voters

19 May 2001

What's a politician supposed to do? First they say that the Labour cabinet aren't getting out and meeting ordinary people, and then when they do, they say that the Deputy PM shouldn't punch the voters in the face. Honestly – there's just no pleasing some people.

John Prescott's left hook was the sort of compulsive viewing that has you flicking between channels in the hope that they might have found a way of squeezing the clip into *Gardeners' World*. Most news editors realized that the footage was the only thing anyone wanted to see, and so returned to it again and again. 'Finally, the financial news: and in Japan, the Hang Seng index was unaffected by that John Prescott incident, which we will just show you one more time. Weather now, and let's see if it was raining today when Prescott punched that bloke who threw the egg . . .'

The debate still rages about what actually happened. Maybe in the split second before the missile hit Prescott's head, the Deputy PM noticed that the egg was not free range, and so in a fit of rage he hit back on behalf of oppressed chickens everywhere. But then there was clearly a brief fracas prompting surrounding journalists to chant, 'Fight! Fight! Fight!' as John's wife Pauline, just off-camera, screamed, 'Leave it, John – he's not worth it!' Meanwhile his minder was desperately flicking through the index of the *Labour Party Campaign Handbook*, looking for some guidance on what to do when a member of the cabinet gets into a punch-up. To be fair, the minister did do his best to stay on-message throughout the brawl. If you watch the footage again, while he's being shoved over the wall and everyone's shouting, 'Get off him!' you can just hear the muffled sound of John Prescott repeating, 'For the many, not the few,' and 'No return to Tory boom and bust.'

Soon it was all over and Craig Evans was led away and charged with possession of an offensive haircut. After a few hours in the police station he was allowed home, where he turned on the telly to see if anything interesting had happened in the election campaign.

Before long the news reached the rest of the cabinet, who held an emergency campaign meeting and decided Prescott would have to be sacked.

'OK, Tony – so you'll tell him, will you?'

'I'm not telling him. You tell him, Robin.'

'No way – I'm not having my teeth knocked out. Jack, you're law and order, you have a word . . .'

'That's not fair – I wear glasses.'

The question that the incident has now prompted is, 'Who would win this election if it were a straight-forward fist fight?' William Hague's judo training might give him the edge over the Prime Minister, except that before he'd even finished bowing, the Deputy PM would have stepped in and knocked Hague senseless. Ann Widdecombe would then launch herself into the mêlée and Prezza and Doris Karloff would grapple on the ground, rolling around, biting and pulling hair, while Charles Kennedy would some-how try to claim that the two main parties were lowering the tone of political debate. John Prescott has now moved close to the top of the list of the world's hardest ever politicians, way ahead of Shirley Williams and Mahatma Gandhi.

It has to be said that although throwing food at politicians has become a national sport, Craig Evans was just too close for anyone to be impressed with his marksmanship or courage. In fact, as a bloodsports enthusiast, he demonstrated a typical country sports approach; he removed any actual chance or genuine skill from the event. A true sports enthusiast would have stood twenty yards back and taken careful aim, but just as huntsmen pit fifty hounds against one fox, Evans waited till Prescott was right next to him before he launched his egg at point-blank range. Furthermore, the bloodsports lobby are always telling us that the foxes enjoy the thrill of the chase, so presumably Craig Evans must have enjoyed being punched in the face as well. 'Oh yes, the rush of adrenaline, they love it. A swift left hook to the jaw – it's the most humane way to deal with these creatures.'

Questions will of course be asked about why more police were not present to protect a leading member of the government, but the answer is that they'd all gone to Blackpool to heckle the Home Secretary. It was later announced that the police plan to call Prescott in for questioning, but as long as they don't ask him about the Private Finance Initiative for the London Under-ground he should be OK.

Nine days in and suddenly the contest has come alive. It was the day of Labour's manifesto launch and Prescott said, 'Hey – I've got an idea for how to get everyone interested in this election!' The party leader-ship can test your loyalty sometimes, but you have to presume that they know best. Anyway, I must dash – I've got some voters to punch.

Not being patriotic: no one does it like us Brits

26 May 2001

Yesterday Tony Blair introduced his own brand of patriotism into the election campaign. The handling of this issue was debated long and hard and eventually Millbank decided that a sensitive speech on the subject might come across better than the Prime Minister suddenly appearing with a Union Jack tattooed on his neck singing 'Eng-er-land! Eng-er-land!' Patriotism is always an awkward issue for the left. It asks the question, 'Is it possible to be positive about your own country without somehow being negative about another?' I think the answer is that yes it is, unless you're French, of course.

A general election campaign gives us the opportunity to focus on what it is that we hold dear in this unique country of ours. Our picturesque high streets peppered with their quaint little branches of Gap, Starbucks and Dunkin' Donuts. The sound of Celine Dion blasting out of a Nissan Sunny as it screeches past the graffiti tags under the Daewoo hoarding. An evening spent at a Tex-Mex bar, sipping a Bud and watching the Miami Dolphins on Sky Sports Extra. These are sights that make this happy land so special; these are the things that make our culture and language so unique. Period.

Patriotism is like germ warfare. I'd rather we didn't deploy it because it is so hideous when you see it used back on you by the other side. One Conservative MP is using his election address to compare the European Union with Nazi Germany. Yes, all the aims of the Brussels bureaucrats, they're all there in *Mein Kampf* if you take the trouble to read Hitler's own words. Page 73, 'Using this new lightning war we will defeat the inferior races of Europe and then we can force them to list all food additives on the side of the jar.' Page 174, 'the sub-humans who are corrupting the Nordic master race must not prevent us from fulfilling our Germanic destiny of setting a minimum safety standard for all child car seats.'

As we have already seen in this election, the flip side of the patriotism coin can be xenophobia. The asylum seekers issue is not one that affects the every-day lives of any of us, and yet it was built up as this terrible problem in order to try to appeal to the worst instincts of the electorate. More voters have been inconvenienced by ants in their kitchen than they have by asylum seekers, but you never hear politicians having a go at the ants. In fact insects generally are the one issue that the politicians are too scared to face up to in this campaign.

Maybe this is the answer to the whole nationalism problem. If we want humankind to love one another, irrespective of creed or colour, we had better find ourselves some new enemies to have a go at. Political debate has always depended upon an 'us and them' mentality – so when the world becomes one big harmonized international community we will have to stop being prejudiced against other nations and direct our intolerance at other species instead. Suddenly, callers on late night radio phone-ins will be free to express their opinions at will.

'Hello, Brian, yeah, I want to talk about these bloody headlice taking over our schools. You get one family of 'em and before you know it they're everywhere. I tell you they're nothing but parasites.'

'I'm not insectist, Brian, but these dung beetles – I'm sorry but they are dirty. They can't help it, it's just in their nature.'

And the liberal on the panel will try to defend insects, saying the pictures in the tabloids are blowing the problem of carpet mites out of all proportion, but none of the callers will take any notice.

'Listen, mate, my little girl just brushed past this wasp and it stung her on the arm. How do you defend that then?'

'Well, um, of course, er, there may be isolated cases where the behaviour of individual wasps might be unacceptable, but that doesn't mean we should hate *all* wasps . . .'

'Why not? I can't stand the little bastards.'

Until this state of affairs comes about I am endeavouring to discriminate only against those who encourage discrimination. The trouble is that if we are too successful in our mission to wipe out the forces of bigotry, who are we going to be bigoted against? None of us is capable of loving everybody, except born-again Christians of course and even they only seem to see the bad side of Satan.

What is so great about this election is that the Tories have played the race card and found it is no longer trumps. Labour may be trying to channel national pride in a positive direction but I'm not sure we need to bang on about patriotism at all any more. We British are finally above that now and as a would-be politician I welcome this. Yes, we really are a marvellous people;

when it comes to not being nationalistic, we're clearly
the best in the whole world. So God Save the Queen,
Rule Britannia and Vote Labour!

One last word before you vote . . .

2 June 2001

Finally it is upon us. After all the talk, the endless newspaper coverage, the heated conversations in pubs and workplaces, the people of Britain will cast their votes and wait with bated breath for the result. Yes, at last there's a new series of *Big Brother*. But before that there is the minor issue of the general election to be got out of the way and it's vital that we now concentrate on the issues and not personalities. Issue number one – we can't have that prat William Hague as prime minister.

The Tory leader has been trying to establish the wording of the big question that will follow this election, namely, 'Can I keep my job please?' Just as the Cold War began before the Second World War had ended, Hague knows the result of this campaign and is already fighting the next one. But floating voters are not getting excited by talk of referendums. So far the angriest I've seen anybody about this issue was a man with a beard shouting, 'For God's sake!

The plural of referendum is referenda!'*

It's now clear that Tony Blair was quite right to postpone the date of the election – otherwise it never would have coincided with the Archer trial. But after such a long run-in the media are now struggling to find a new angle. One journalist managed to find a voter called Mrs F. Hague who says she can't bear the Conservatives and is voting Labour. There's one of these at every election; the difference this time is that this one is actually *the* Mrs F. Hague. Other reporters have been busy scouring the country looking for gimmicky polls – the bakery in Droitwich selling doughnuts with red, blue or yellow icing or whatever. Millbank has already organized one of these novelty polls themselves using bottles of ketchup. Sales figures already show an overwhelming surge in support for Labour as the new blue and yellow tomato sauces have failed to sell a single bottle.

Tactical voting may see even more Tories culled than the polls are predicting, although personally I think this is being overstated. I tell voters in my constituency that www.tacticalvoter.net does not recommend tactical voting in Maidenhead and they stare blankly and say, 'So it's about the election, is it?' Some people simply refuse to understand why you've called round, but at least I've made a few quid selling dusters on the side. In the meantime I have come up with my own system of tactical voting which will ensure that the make-up of the House of Commons exactly matches the proportion of votes cast for each of the parties. This system, called EVL, allows the voters

*Rather thrillingly, one of the big debating points at this point in the election was pondering the exact wording of the question for Labour's promised referendum on the Euro. At the candidate's debate in Maidenhead, one elderly Conservative stood up and said 'I think the only fair wording would be 'Do you want to surrender your country to the Germans?' To which I thought, 'Yup, that sounds pretty neutral, give or take a comma.'

to impose proportional representation upon the British political system. With the 'Everyone Vote Labour' method, Labour win 100 per cent of the votes cast and get exactly that proportion of seats in the House of Commons, making it the fairest PR system ever devised. Obviously it might be difficult to persuade the likes of William Hague and Ann Widdecombe to vote Labour as it would make them unavailable to lead the Tory Party after the election. Well – maybe not that difficult.

Walking round the streets of Maidenhead I've had plenty of people give me reasons why they won't vote Labour, although occasionally their accent has been so posh that I couldn't actually understand them. But one lady opened the door this week, saw my red rosette and shook me firmly by the hand. 'When Gordon Brown cancelled all that third world debt – that one act by itself made it worth voting Labour for all those years.' And I walked away feeling ten foot tall knowing that she'd put it in a nutshell.

Millions of people whom we will never meet had their lives radically improved because we voted Labour in 1997. And now people say, 'I'm not voting because I can't bear any of them,' or whatever. Well, there *will* be a new House of Commons next week whether people deign to vote or not. We have some influence on who'll be charged with helping those more vulnerable than ourselves, and yet thousands of voters are pretending that they are somehow above the whole thing.

Voting involves humility. It says, 'I accept I don't count for that much, but I'm prepared to swallow my pride and opt for one side above the other, however imperfect they may be.' Yes, there are individual policies or events that have made many of us cringe during the last four years. But does anyone really believe they outweigh having 100 per cent of the debt owed by forty-one countries written off; a million

British children taken out of poverty; the lowest unemployment for a generation, not to mention the reduction of VAT on cycle helmets? I did this pitch to one undecided voter parking his bike outside his house. 'Nah,' he said. 'If you'd abolished VAT on cycle helmets altogether, I might have voted for you.'

And then he gave me a wink that said he was voting Labour and went inside.

As you were . . .

9 June 2001

There is a sign on the wall of the Tory leader's room: 'Please leave this office exactly as you found it.' All right, William, but you didn't have to go that far. I overheard someone asking Hague what he'd enjoyed about the campaign, which is a bit like asking Jimmy Greaves to name his man of the match in the 1966 World Cup final. Now, in a vicious act of revenge upon his colleagues, William Hague has offered them the opportunity to apply for the job of leader of the Conservative Party.

'What, me as leader? Well, obviously it would be a great honour and privilege to lead the Conservative Party but I can't at the moment, you see, because, erm, I've got a verruca.'

'Yeah – and I've got to go to my gran's on that day, so I can't stand either.'

Finding someone to lead today's Tory Party is like asking for volunteer pilots at the Biggin Hill Air Show.*

*Two wartime aircraft had crashed in flames at the Biggin Hill Air Show this week. Soon afterwards the Glenn Miller Appreciation Society decided it would go back to just recreating his music.

Maybe the opposition will end up having to follow the example of the FA and hire a Swedish manager instead. On the basis that the new Tory leader is always the person you least expect, the next boss of the Conservative Party will probably be Zebedee from *The Magic Roundabout*. He looks about as normal as any of the rest of them.

But the Tory leadership battle is no more significant than a cast change in a Channel 5 soap opera. The big story of this election is the result. For Labour to win one landslide was incredible enough. To have repeated it four years later would have seemed like some wild fantasy back in Labour's long years of opposition. 'Labour Gain Hove' was surreal; 'Labour Hold Hove' is the world turned upside down. Any minute now I'm going to wake up and find it's all a dream and Mrs Thatcher is still prime minister.

'We are delighted to have won a sixth term and we have decided to replace the cabinet with the little men who live in my radiator.'

In a way it is even better than 1997 because we weren't just voting to get rid of a government; the country made a positive choice of public services over tax cuts. And for Labour to hold seats such as Dover is a triumph in the face of a Conservative Party attempting to whip up hatred against asylum seekers. The low turnout should not detract from what an amazing achievement the result is for the government; Labour achieved everything it set out to do in, er – Operation Turnout.

My own efforts in Maidenhead did not bring socialism to the banks of the river Thames. On polling day I drove around the well-clipped villages of Berkshire in my brother's rusty Ford Sierra with the loud hailer, urging the millionaires to vote for the promised increase in the minimum wage. I'm sure I saw someone covering the ears of their cleaner. Labour's vote dipped 2 per cent while a tactical vote for the Liberals saw them surge by 11 per cent and all I could think was 'Good luck to them.' The rise in tactical voting across the country is an expression of the electorate's exasperation with the current system and we have to find a way to make everyone's vote really count. Otherwise the frustration and anger of the voters will finally boil over in places like Maidenhead. They'll tut and look skywards.

Participation was down from supporters of all the parties and I blame the confrontational ya-boo style of modern litics which is all the fault of those Tory bastards on the other side. But now the project of improving the lives of ordinary people should go hand in hand with genuinely involving everyone in the democratic process. All sides of the political spectrum agree that we have to really work at conquering apathy and antipathy. Even the *Telegraph* website featured a little icon saying 'Is Democracy in Danger? Vote Here.' I was going to add my voice to the debate. But then, you know, I just couldn't be bothered.

Red rum and coke

16 June 2001

If the word 'Ascot' makes you think of the unreliable grubby water heater you shared on the landing of your old bedsit, then you probably don't qualify as a member of the British upper classes who gathered at the famous racecourse this week. How the country managed to function without all these people at their desks is a mystery that will never be solved.

'Oh my God!' shouted Arabella suddenly. 'I forgot to tell anyone at work that I wasn't coming in today! Who's going to tell the lady who arranges the flowers where to place her vase?'

'Pah!' says Rupert. 'I told them straight: if any overseas clients want to bid for an antique clock via the Chelsea office, they'll just have to wait until Monday!' And there were gasps all around as his friends imagined the chaos Rupert's absence must have precipitated.

Few of those who were at Royal Ascot this week are particularly interested in horse racing. You don't see many posh ladies with feathers and fruit bowls on their head in my local branch of Ladbroke's swearing and tearing up their betting slip as they blow the last few quid of the child benefit on the 3.15 at Kempton. Royal Ascot is a social pageant, a hat parade, a place to be obscenely rich and overheard. That's why they all wear those enormous hats: so that when they're talking to someone, that person can't look over their shoulder to see if someone more important is standing behind.

But this year's Ascot was tainted with the appalling news that cocaine was used inside the royal enclosure. Shock, horror, the idle rich taking cocaine?! Next they'll be avoiding tax and having it off with their nannies. For some reason this has been treated as an incredible revelation in some sections of the media. Somebody has held a mirror up to the British upper classes and they have snorted coke off it. And there was the Prince of Wales feeling so chuffed that all the posh girls kept saying how much they loved charlie before announcing they were off to powder their noses. Now we know why the British royal family don't carry money. They got fed up with all their mates borrowing banknotes to roll up. Of course there's no suggestion that any actual member of the royal family was taking any class A drugs, although the Queen was overheard saying she felt 'bloody brilliant' and had to be physically prevented from attempting to outrun the horses racing in the 4.20.

But it's a shame that a minority of coke-heads have to spoil a lovely day out by consuming a recreational drug reserved for the super rich, when the vast majority of law-abiding visitors just want to pass the day drinking bottles of vintage champagne. Why do these people feel a need to escape from reality when they were pretty well removed from it before they even started? The sociologists have tried to be as sensitive as possible: 'Look, rather than just condemning these drug users, let's try and understand them. These are the kids off the estates. Admittedly very large estates in the countryside, but some of them know they may never work again. And now they've even lost their parents' trust. Or rather, they've spent it.'

Maybe cocaine has always been used at race meetings; that would explain why the commentators talk so quickly. Perhaps with enough drugs John McCririck might even seem like an interesting and amusing person. But there were also reports of cocaine at Newmarket and at this year's Derby. It's not known if any of the horses actually took cocaine, although suspicions were aroused halfway through one race when the horses started to flag and then disappeared into the toilets before coming back out wiping their noses and raring to go again.

No doubt the police will be as tough on drug users at Royal Ascot as they would be on any inner-city housing estate. It's the dealers they are really after, so anyone driving an expensive car into the enclosure will be pulled over and questioned.

'This is a fancy motor, sunshine. What's your name then?'

'The Duke of Wellington.'

'Yeah, and I'm bloody Napoleon. Don't get cheeky with me, sonny, or you'll be slung in the back of the van with that bloke who said he was the Sultan of Brunei.'

The police should adopt a zero-tolerance approach to drug-taking at race meetings. Rows of police horses should line up and charge the dealers. 'Great idea!' says Rupert. 'And, like, there could be a prize for the horse that comes first and you could place bets on who you think will win . . .' Except no one would be watching, of course; they'd all be in the corporate tents getting out of their heads on cocaine. Anyway you couldn't have two meetings at the same place; it's simple arithmetic, even a coke-head could tell you that two into one won't go – Daniella Westbrook's nostrils excepted.

Global village idiot

23 June 2001

This week George W. Bush came to Europe, and before setting off he was given a full and detailed briefing.

'It's a kinda big peninsula, Mr President, with lots of different countries in it.'

'Sounds great – how come I never went before?'

'Well, sir, with respect, you never had a passport till now.'

There was a slight delay at the airport check-in desk when Bush said, 'No, of course I didn't pack this bag myself. I'm President of the United States.' Then airport security couldn't work out why the metal detectors kept bleeping every time his bodyguards walked through. So they put their keys in the little bowl, their loose change and finally their semi-automatic machine guns, and that seemed to do the trick.

The reason that George W. has flown across the Atlantic is to get to know his allies in NATO and the EC. The plan was that they would meet the new President face to face and then feel reassured. Some ideas are flawed from the outset. When any new world leader joins the club they are slightly vulnerable, and because Bush's understanding of foreign affairs is rather limited the various European leaders decided to have a bit of fun with him. Just when he thought he'd worked out who was leader of which country, the European heads of state secretly swopped nationalities just for a laugh. Tony Blair started speaking French, smoking Gitanes and claiming that the Second World War was won by the French Resistance. Jacques Chirac, now speaking German and drinking frothy lager from a two-litre stein, saved his place at the table by putting a towel over the best chair. Berlusconi looked on, sipping his Guinness and singing 'All Kinds Of Everything' by Dana. A confused Bush turned to Jose Maria Aznar to clarify things but the Spanish Prime Minister just said something in Dutch and offered him a joint. This joke is set to backfire when Bush goes to Jerusalem and meets Ariel Sharon and says, 'Stop having me on – you're the Palestinian guy, right?'

Dinner was then served for the fifteen heads of state. The President was treated to the finest Italian wine and delicious French food, all rounded off with a traditional English speciality, Bird's Angel Delight. The Europeans agreed it was wonderful to see such a brilliant American president who combined political integrity with determination and compassion. Then they stopped talking about *West Wing* and concentrated on more urgent matters. They tried to raise the issue of the environment but George didn't seem to get it. Even when he'd been asked to choose his trout from a fish tank where all the fish were dead and floating in a little oil slick, he'd failed to notice anything unusual. The Europeans raised the missile defence shield project and claimed that he wasn't listening to their concerns but he just nodded and said, 'Yup, and this sauce is delicious too.'

Bush talks about rogue states, but on Kyoto and missile defence it is America that is behaving like a rogue state. He is stockpiling weapons of mass destruction and the UN have not been allowed to inspect any of them. Of course the European leaders would have liked to announce sanctions such as an official boycott of McDonald's; it's just that their kids keep nagging them for the free plastic toys. It leaves you wondering what is the point of having a closer European Union if we are not prepared to use our combined strength to stand up to the world's only superpower when they're in the wrong. Would America proceed with missile defence in the face of unified opposition from Europe? Would Bush have torn up the Kyoto treaty if it meant enduring the wrath of the world's largest trading bloc? Er, yes he would, but that's not the point.

Bush may not care what we think, but if our leaders were a little more direct and frank in their opposition at least we might salvage a little pride and dignity from the situation. This applies to the British government more than any other. Britain can't be a bridge between Europe and the US and be at the heart of Europe as well. Tony Blair rang George W. Bush after he was inaugurated to check the special relationship would be unchanged. The lady on the White House switchboard logged the call and said, 'Have a nice day, Mr Blur,' so yup, it's pretty much as before. We are fooling ourselves if we think we have any real influence in Washington, but we should lead opposition to Star Wars and Bush's environmental policies for the simple reason that they are wrong.

Europe needs to show some leadership because the official leader of the western world is leading us in the wrong direction. He's fallen for the American military's arguments and restarted the arms race. Bush says he was persuaded to proceed with the Star Wars project only after a full intelligence assessment. Well, quite; they did one and found he doesn't have any. Today, at the dawn of the twenty-first century, the global village is finally complete. At last it has its own global village idiot.

Acknowledgements

I'd like to thank Ian Birrell at the *Independent* for initially giving me my own column, and also Adrian Hamilton and Sean O'Grady in the *Indie* comment section. Suddenly finding myself plunged into the world of newspapers, I did my best to learn the values of loyalty and integrity that prevail in modern journalism and six months later I jumped to the *Guardian*. A handful of other pieces also first appeared in the *New Statesman*, the *Evening Standard* and the *Independent on Sunday*. At the *Grauniad* I would like to thank David Leigh and Liz McGregor for the careful and attentive way they have said 'fine' when I told them what I was writing about each week, and to everyone who has been involved with legal clearances, sub-editing and proof-reading I would like to say a big thnak yuo.

In the course of writing a regular column there have been times, with the deadline looming, when I have stuck in an old one-liner I remembered from one of the various comedy shows on which I've worked. It is important to stress that these jokes were recycled for strictly environmental reasons and the handful that were not my own were generally reprinted with the original author's permission and a payment of at least a half-pint of lager and a packet of crisps. For these gags I would like particularly to thank Mark Burton and Pete Sinclair, but also Clive Anderson, Laurie Rowley, Chris Lakin, Bill Matthews and the Rt Hon. Gordon Brown MP. My wife Jackie deserves a special thank you for her support and encouragement, and finally I would like to thank my agent Georgia Garrett and editor Bill Scott-Kerr, whose professional guidance and literary wisdom have helped me to express myself in such a – thingy sort of way.

A note on the type

The font used in this book is called Lucia Sans BT.
It was developed in Italy in the 1950s and swiftly
became a modern classic. Capturing the tidy simplicity
of the basic roman alphabet, it adds a light serif,
making it particularly easy on the eye while looking
crisp and elegant upon the page. The space between
the letters, while appearing uniform, is in fact
dependent on the adjacent characters, and although
the original designers specified the exact gap for
most letter combinations, they did not foresee certain
character sequences that appear in English but not in
Italian. Where this situation has arisen we have had to
make aesthetic judgements of our own, endeavouring
at all times to remain true to the spirit of the font's
original design. All right, I know you couldn't give a
toss about the font, but we had to pad the book out
another couple of pages and we couldn't think of
anything else to put in. I'm the bloke who does the
typesetting and no one cares what I think. It doesn't
matter what I write here, no one's going to read it.
Well, at last I'm going to come out with it. I'm gay.
There, I've said it. Forty years I've kept that a secret.

I'm gay, I'm gay, I'm gay. God, that feels better. I'm very fond of you, Marjorie, but our marriage is a sham. I'm having a secret affair with a picture restorer called Kenneth. I haven't really been going to macramé evening classes all these years. Kenneth and I are going to open a little shop in Brighton. I'm leaving and that's it; you'll have to find another bridge partner for Tuesdays. But poor Marjorie, she'll be devastated. It's not her fault it's taken me thirty years of marriage to come out of the closet. No, actually I just couldn't do that to her. Please don't print this, I'll write it out again. I know the printers are waiting but please, let me just do another draft; if Marjorie reads this she'll kill herself, please . . .

THINGS CAN ONLY GET GETTER
Eighteen Miserable Years in the Life of a Labour Supporter

John O'Farrell

'Like bubonic plague and stone cladding, no-one took Margaret Thatcher seriously until it was too late. Her first act as leader was to appear before the cameras and do a V for Victory sign the wrong way round. She was smiling and telling the British people to f*** off at the same time. It was something we would have to get used to.'

Things Can Only Get Better is the personal account of a Labour supporter who survived eighteen miserable years of Conservative government. It is the heartbreaking and hilarious confessions of someone who has been actively involved in helping the Labour party lose elections at every level: school candidate; door-to-door canvasser; working for a Labour MP in the House of Commons; standing as a council candidate; and eventually writing jokes for a shadow cabinet minister.

Along the way he slowly came to realize that Michael Foot would never be Prime Minister, that vegetable quiche was not as tasty as chicken tikka masala and that the nuclear arms race was never going to be stopped by face painting alone.

'VERY FUNNY AND MUCH BETTER THAN ANYTHING HE EVER WROTE FOR ME'
Griff Rhys Jones

'VERY FUNNY'
Guardian

'EXCELLENT . . . WHATEVER YOU POLITICS *THINGS CAN ONLY GET BETTER* WILL MAKE YOU LAUGH OUT LOUD'
Angus Deayton

0 552 99803 6

BLACK SWAN

THE BEST A MAN CAN GET

John O'Farrell

Michael Adams shares a flat with three other men in their late twenties. Days are spent lying in bed, playing computer games and occasionally doing a bit of work. And then, when he feels like it, he crosses the river and goes back to his unsuspecting wife and children.

For Michael is living a double life – he escapes from the exhausting misery of babies by telling his wife he has to work through the night or travel up north. And while she is valiantly coping on her own, he is just a few miles away in a secret flat, doing all the things that most men with small children can only dream about. He thinks he can have it all, until his deception is inevitably exposed . . .

The Best a Man Can Get is written with the hilarious eye for detail that sent John O'Farrell's first book, *Things Can Only Get Better*, to the top of the bestseller lists. It is a darkly comic confessional that is at once compelling, revealing and very, very funny.

'SO FUNNY BECAUSE IT RINGS TRUE . . . PACKED WITH PAINFULLY WELL-OBSERVED JOKES'
The Times

'PUNCHLINE FUELLED, RELENTLESS HUMOUR . . . I DON'T THINK A WOMAN IS GOING TO GET MUCH CLOSER TO THE WORKINGS OF A MAN'S MIND THAN THIS. GIGGLING SEVERAL TIMES A PAGE WITH PLENTY OF OUT-LOUD LAUGHS IS GUARANTEED. IS JOHN O'FARRELL FUNNY? VERY'
The Mirror

'THIS IS *SO* GOOD. IT IS HOWLINGLY FUNNY. MADLY WELL-WRITTEN, ASTUTELY AND RUTHLESSLY OBSERVED AND SO INSIGHTFUL ABOUT MEN, WOMEN, LOVE AND PARENTHOOD THAT YOU READ EVERY PAGE WITH A WINCE OF RECOGNITION. FAB, FAB, FAB'
India Knight

0 552 99844 3

BLACK SWAN

A SELECTED LIST OF FINE WRITING
AVAILABLE FROM BLACK SWAN

THE PRICES SHOWN BELOW WERE CORRECT AT THE TIME OF GOING TO PRESS. HOWEVER
TRANSWORLD PUBLISHERS RESERVE THE RIGHT TO SHOW NEW RETAIL PRICES ON COVERS
WHICH MAY DIFFER FROM THOSE PREVIOUSLY ADVERTISED IN THE TEXT OR ELSEWHERE.

77083	3	I'M A BELIEVER	*Jessica Adams*	£6.99
99703	X	DOWN UNDER	*Bill Bryson*	£7.99
77097	3	I LIKE IT LIKE THAT	*Claire Calman*	£6.99
99979	2	GATES OF EDEN	*Ethan Coen*	£7.99
99945	8	DEAD FAMOUS	*Ben Elton*	£6.99
99759	5	DOG DAYS, GLENN MILLER NIGHTS	*Laurie Graham*	£6.99
99609	2	FORREST GUMP	*Winston Groom*	£6.99
99966	0	WHILE THE SUN SHINES	*John Harding*	£6.99
77082	5	THE WISDOM OF CROCODILES	*Paul Hoffman*	£7.99
77109	0	THE FOURTH HAND	*John Irving*	£6.99
14595	5	BETWEEN EXTREMES	*Brian Keenan and John McCarthy*	£7.99
99859	1	EDDIE'S BASTARD	*William Kowalski*	£6.99
14240	9	THE NIGHT LISTENER	*Armistead Maupin*	£6.99
99873	7	SNAKESKIN	*John McCabe*	£6.99
99907	5	DUBLIN	*Seán Moncrieff*	£6.99
99905	9	AUTOMATED ALICE	*Jeff Noon*	£6.99
99803	6	THINGS CAN ONLY GET BETTER	*John O'Farrell*	£6.99
99844	3	THE BEST A MAN CAN GET	*John O'Farrell*	£6.99
99975	X	DON'T MEAN NOTHING	*Susan O'Neill*	£6.99
99645	9	THE WRONG BOY	*Willy Russell*	£6.99
99952	0	LIFE ISN'T ALL HA HA HEE HEE	*Meera Syal*	£6.99
99638	6	BETTER THAN SEX	*Hunter S. Thompson*	£6.99
99819	2	WHISTLING FOR THE ELEPHANTS	*Sandi Toksvig*	£6.99
99902	4	TO BE SOMEONE	*Louise Voss*	£6.99
99366	2	THE ELECTRIC KOOL AID ACID TEST	*Tom Wolfe*	£6.99

All Transworld titles are available by post from:
Bookpost, PO Box 29, Douglas, Isle of Man IM99 1BQ
Credit cards accepted. Please telephone 01624 836000,
fax 01624 837033, Internet http://www.bookpost.co.uk or
e-mail: bookshop@enterprise.net for details.
Free postage and packing in the UK.
Overseas customers allow £1 per book.